Life on the Death Railway

Life on the Death Railway

The Memoirs of a British Prisoner of War

Stuart Young

Edited by Tony Pollard

Pen & Sword
MILITARY

First published in Great Britain in 2013 by
Pen & Sword Military
an imprint of
Pen & Sword Books Ltd
47 Church Street
Barnsley
South Yorkshire
S70 2AS

ISBN 978 1 84884 820 7

Typeset in Ehrhardt by
Mac Style, Driffield, East Yorkshire
Printed and bound in the UK by CPI Group (UK) Ltd, Croydon,
CRO 4YY

Pen & Sword Books Ltd incorporates the Imprints of Pen &
Sword Aviation, Pen & Sword Maritime, Pen & Sword Military,
Wharncliffe Local History, Pen and Sword Select, Pen and Sword
Military Classics, Leo Cooper, The Praetorian Press, Remember
When, Seaforth Publishing and Frontline Publishing.

For a complete list of Pen & Sword titles please contact
PEN & SWORD BOOKS LIMITED
47 Church Street, Barnsley, South Yorkshire, S70 2AS, England
E-mail: enquiries@pen-and-sword.co.uk
Website: www.pen-and-sword.co.uk

Contents

Author's Dedication

To Wiggy and Allan
Without whose care and friendship these words
could not have been written.

Stuart's wife, Ethel Mary Young (1922–2013), passed
away just before this book went to press. Her strength of
character, fortitude and good humour did much to help
Stuart through the difficult times after the war.

Moon over Malaya

Palm trees are swaying in the moonlight
Casting their shadows on the trees
What, dear, will greet us in the moonlight?
Stay awhile and listen to me.

The moon is shining over Malaya
Stars signal down from up above
Girls in their sarongs and kubayas
In their kampongs, sing their songs of love.
You can hear Tran Bulan and old Sarena
Songs their mothers sang in days gone by.
From Penang to Ipoh and Malacca
You can hear these enchanting lullabies.
Guitars, they are strumming in the moonlight
and the echoes of those keronggjongs never die.
The moon is shining over Malaya
and twas there we met and loved and said goodbye.

(Local song, from Traditional)

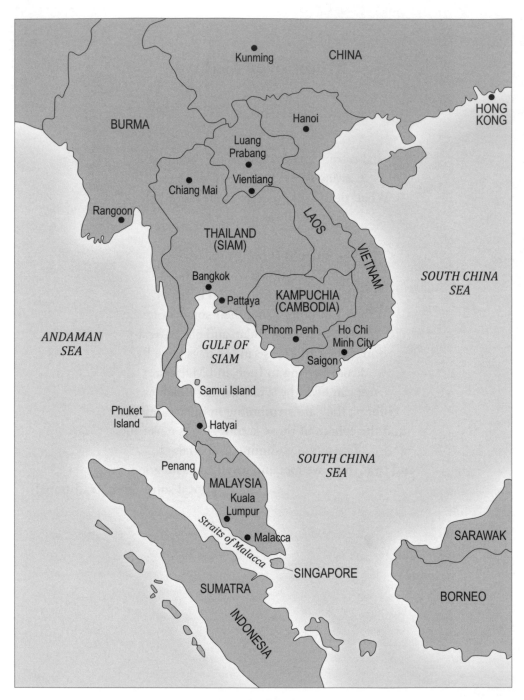

Map 1: SE Asia.

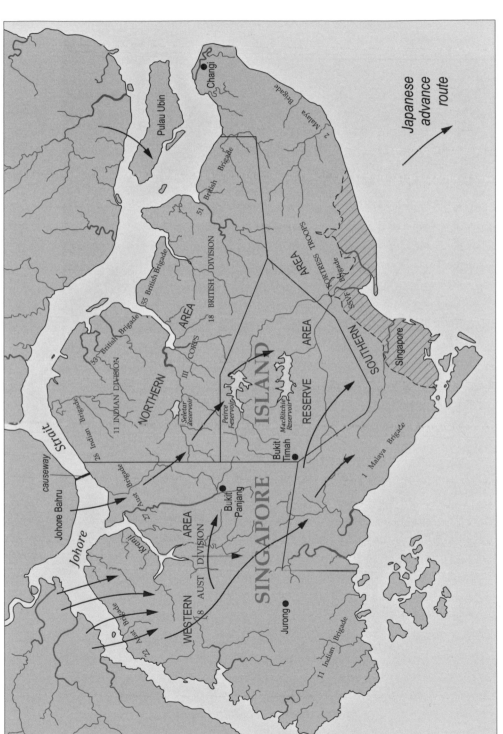

Map 2: Japanese invasion of Singapore Island.

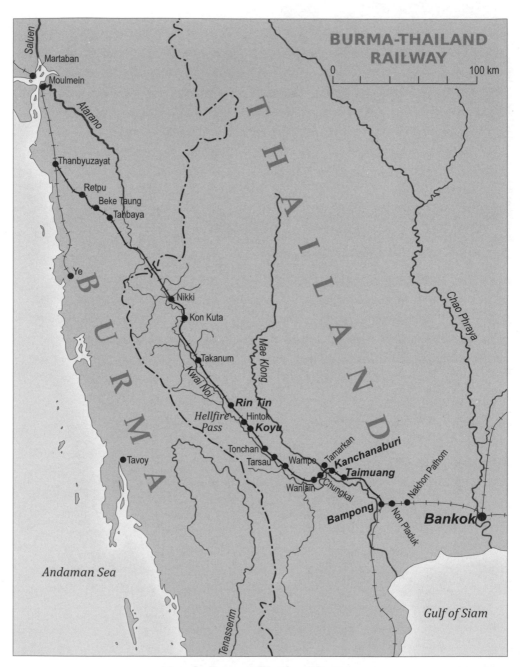

Map 3: Burma–Thailand Railway.

Foreword

by Tony Pollard

A Personal Memoir

The Japanese invasion of Malaya was well on its way to being a complete success by the time Gunner Stuart Young arrived in the port of Singapore on 13 January 1942. But despite the front being only a few miles north of Johore, on the Malay side of the narrow stretch of water separating the small island of Singapore from the peninsula, he noted a distinct lack of urgency among the military personnel and civilians resident in the city. Like many others, Young arrived too late to play much of an active role in the defence, and the reason why these reinforcements were not put to good use is just one of the many questions that have been asked about the British failure to hold Singapore, a bastion of empire which many regarded as an impregnable fortress. The controversies surrounding the Fall of Singapore are not, however, the subject of this book, though there is a growing library of relevant volumes for anyone who cares to find out more. This is not a military history, or an essay on the end of empire; it is a personal memoir, a closely observed and incredibly honest account of one man's experiences of capture and imprisonment by the Japanese. As such it also takes its place among an expanding sub-genre of Second World War memoirs.[1]

Nor is what follows a narrative based on a journal left behind by Young or a memoir based on interviews given in the later years of his life. It is all his own work, a well-crafted and polished account, which he intended to have published. Like others he was fully aware of the historical importance of the times through which he was living and so kept a diary. Writing may also have served as a survival mechanism, giving some sense of privacy while also forcing him to confront and overcome his dreadful circumstances rather than burying them in his head where they would fester like one of the many dreadful tropical diseases to which he and thousands of others fell victim. As the end of the war approached, however, and it was clear that Japan was on the losing side, the risk of being caught with an account of the horrors served up by his captors was not one that he or others was prepared to take. And so, after years of pilfering or recycling whatever scraps of paper he could, he ditched his precious writings. It may have been his regret at this which in part motivated him to recreate his journals after the war, though it would be a long number of years before the manuscript contained here was produced.[2]

As I write this it seems hard to believe that any publisher with an ounce of sense would turn down the manuscript, which Young titled *Blood, Sweat and Dysentery*, but that's what happened in the 1970s, when there was limited interest in this type of material. Since then, however, our appetite for books based on the personal experiences of those who lived through the Second World War, and who are now a dying breed, continues to grow on a daily basis. Pen and Sword have already demonstrated a commitment to PoW memoirs and I am delighted that they agreed to my proposal to add Young's to their catalogue.

His original title was a good one, but even now, in these more enlightened times, it was not felt to be commercial enough to attract sales. So it is that I chose *Life on the Death Railway*, a title which counterpoints the two main themes of Young's memoir and name drops the dreadful engineering project which most people bring to mind when they think of British PoWs under the Japanese – it should be stressed though that many other PoWs suffered just as badly elsewhere under Japanese custody.

Stuart Young's manuscript first came to my attention during a visit to my aunt's house in Derby, where my ailing grandfather was fast approaching the end of his own life (I had some years previously talked him into writing his own memoirs, though his wartime experience as a conscientious objector obviously had little in common with Young's). It was typed on A4 sheets in a blue ring–binder and included photocopies of a few photographs, also included here along with others that have come to light since. My aunt said a neighbour had lent it to her and that I might be interested. It was not the first time I had been handed a wartime diary, but this was something else entirely. It was well written, full of detail, and even managed to make me laugh in places, something which virtually no other Japanese PoW memoir has managed to do – and I read a lot of them while working on the manuscript. He has a particularly good eye for the ridiculous, and on several occasions draws attention to the questionable nature of the rules and regulations still insisted upon by command while all around them went to hell in a handcart. Even before I was a third of the way through reading it for the first time, it was clear that it deserved publication.

There might be dozens of PoW memoirs out there, but to my mind they all deserve their place on bookshelves. These men may have shared similar experiences but, as a historian, I firmly believe that we cannot have too many of these individual accounts. Each one of them offers a different perspective on the suffering and fortitude of the many thousands of British and other PoWs held by the Japanese. Young also brings important new light to our understanding of the PoW experience; his is, for instance, the only first-hand account I have encountered which makes explicit reference to homosexuality among PoWs – a subject that is really an elephant in the room as far as published PoW memoirs are concerned.[3] He does so with a characteristic pinch of humour, but he also places the issue within the context of the day-to-day reality of life on what became known as the Death Railway.

Young also paints a vivid picture of Britain, particularly the Midlands, in the immediate pre-war period, where as a lad he took his first job in a shop and entertained himself as lads do. There are gems of observation there, as elsewhere, and his comments on Mosley's Blackshirts are particularly evocative.

I spoke to Young's widow and son during the process of editing this volume and they were very helpful in sketching in some further background to his character and his life after the war. Back in 'civvy street' he returned to Woolworth's in Long Eaton, where he had volunteered for military service back in 1938, and worked in the stockroom before his promotion to the floor brought about a move to the Listergate branch in Nottingham. There he met Ethel, who was working in the office and, after a covert courtship, they got engaged and then married in 1947 (there were restrictions on behaviour even after he gained his freedom – staff members of the opposite sex were not permitted to fraternize). According to Ethel, Stuart's wartime experiences did not cause him much in the way of mental trauma, or what is today referred to as Post Traumatic Stress Disorder (PTSD). Whatever his feelings were in those post-war years, it is clear that the same strength of character which got him through three and a half years of captivity also stood him in good stead for the rest of his life. Unlike many others he did not hold a grudge against the Japanese, who had treated him and his comrades so atrociously. Ethel explained that, to his way of thinking, the camp guards were just soldiers following orders; if he had disobeyed orders from his own officers he would have been punished, but he was in no doubt that if a Japanese soldier did the same thing he would be summarily executed. The only time he did express a negative reaction was in 1971, when the Japanese emperor, Hirohito, visited the UK and planted a tree, presumably as a peace offering, at BBC Television Centre (former PoWs also turned their backs to the Emperor at public engagements). It wasn't long before someone dug up the tree and sprayed the roots with acid. Stuart thought this was a hilarious and, more importantly, a valid protest against the figurehead of a system responsible for the wartime atrocities committed by the Japanese military.

Young was also quick to give credit to acts of humanity shown by his captors – and in his memoir he cites the case of the Korean guard who allowed him to rest in the shade all day after being sent out to work with a malarial temperature of 103. What he does not include in his memoir is a story told by his son, Andrew, of a guard who took a great risk to get medication that was to save his life when, later on, he was struck down with blackwater fever. According to Ethel, however, this lifesaving action would not have been taken without the selfless intervention of his two friends, 'Wiggy' Marsh and Allan Pratt (who sold his prized signet ring to buy fresh fruit and treats to aid convalescence), and to whom Stuart has dedicated this book.

Stuart Young may have returned home mentally strong but his wartime experiences left him with a lifelong legacy of serious health complaints. Although he went for periodical check-ups at Queen Mary's Hospital in Roehampton, which specialized in tropical diseases and treated many returned Far East PoWs, little seems to have been done to cure his various long-term ailments. First off, there was the malaria which would return every spring, when his response was to take paracetamol and go to bed for a couple of days until the fever passed. He also carried a tapeworm which, like the malaria, showed itself every spring as a disturbing lump on his stomach. Most serious of all though was the parasite that his son described as a small worm that entered his blood stream through the soles of his feet and, after proliferating, ended up damaging his lungs.

There seems little doubt that he was suffering from chronic schistosomiasis, also known as bilharzia, which is not uncommon in South-East Asia. Given that many of the PoWs spent time with little or nothing on their feet and, in areas of contaminated water, it seems highly likely that many of them contracted this very unpleasant parasite, which today affects around twenty million people. There was an attempt to treat him for this condition at Roehampton when doctors tried to extract the worms on a cord taken in through his mouth. Unfortunately, he was by then diabetic and went hypo after swallowing the cord, as he'd been on a starvation regime for twenty-four hours in advance. The only way to bring him round was to feed him a well-known energy drink, but as a result of this any worms attached to the cord were washed off as it was removed. The parasites continued to wreak havoc with his internal organs and over time his lungs deteriorated to the point that he required an oxygen mask.

Stuart eventually succumbed to his symptoms in 1995 and, sadly, his medical conditions were only officially recognized after his death, and even then it took a fight. Like many servicemen in 1945–46 Stuart signed away his right to a full war pension in return for a one off payment of £75, which seemed quite a sum back then. What pension there was ceased immediately on his death and Ethel found it hard to make ends meet. Eventually, after taking advice from the Far East PoW (FEPOW) Association, she attended a tribunal in Birmingham. As a result, Ethel was awarded a war widow's pension but, as Andrew pointed out, it is a shame the government wasn't prepared to do anything about the situation while he was alive and really needed the assistance. But Stuart was never one to complain, because, as he was fond of saying, he was one of the lucky ones.

For days after his arrival in Singapore Stuart Young enjoyed the normal existence of a soldier in a new and exotic posting during peacetime – albeit at the height of the Japanese invasion of neighbouring Malaya. Like thousands of others he settled into the barracks at Changi before going on to sample the delights of the city, though a rigid class system was very much in place and, as another rank, he was denied access to that epitome of planter opulence, the Raffles Hotel. Instead, he relaxed in the far more modest surroundings of the NAAFI, went to the cinema, ate in the Union Jack Club, inspected 'Change Alley', a bustling shopping district and 'sampled the delights of the Great World', which was an amusement park with cinemas and restaurants on the site of an old Chinese cemetery. One reason for the lack of action were delays in the unloading of equipment, caused by the ship having to anchor half a mile offshore, thanks to the massive quantities of ammunition on board. It must have been a surreal experience, knowing that fierce fighting was taking place not far away, while the population of Singapore carried on regardless, seemingly without a care in the world.

Young was in an anti-tank regiment, in which he served as an orderly. After what must have been well over a week, perhaps two, guns and equipment were finally landed ashore and some units from his regiment were sent across the causeway into the jungle on the southern tip of Malaya. Stuart Young was not called upon to leave the island, but for those who had it was a short expedition, as no sooner had they arrived than they were forced to retreat, after destroying their guns and equipment and, along with what remained of the British, Indian and Australian force which had been fought from one end of Malaya to the other, find a way back to Singapore (when not specifically referring to one contingent or another 'British' will be used to describe the overall force). Even after the Japanese had arrived on the north side of the straits and men returned with terrible tales to tell, life seemed to go on as normal for the general population.

It is perhaps here that a brief introduction to the background to the Japanese invasion, the Battle of Singapore and the treatment of PoWs by the Japanese might help to place Young's account into its wider historical context.

A Collision of Empires

Stuart Young was just one of 80,000 servicemen (and women) captured by the Japanese after the fall of Singapore, a small island dominated by a city sharing the same name and connected to the southern tip of the Malay peninsula by a narrow causeway (Map 1). Anyone who wishes to understand the events which resulted in him spending three and a half years in captivity, and the treatment to which he was subject during that time, has first to negotiate the historical complexities of British involvement in Singapore and the rise of Japanese militarism. It is hoped that the following summary may help to illuminate the way.

The first British toehold in the region came in the late seventeenth century when the East India Company set up a trading post at Bencoolen in south-west Sumatra, on the opposite (southern) side of the Straits of Malacca to Malaya. The first leap across the Straits, which served as a vital shipping lane between India and China, was made in 1786, when the island of Penang, off the west coast of Malaya, was leased to the company under the auspices of Captain Francis Light by the Sultan of Kedah. Singapore, an even more advantageously situated island, sitting off the southern tip of the peninsula, was acquired by treaty for the East India Company in 1819 by Sir Thomas Stamford Raffles, the Governor of Bencoolen. The island's position at the eastern entrance to the Straits made it an ideal staging post for British ships trading between India and China, but also offered a strategically important naval base.

The security of the island was strengthened by the procurement of a strip of land on the neighbouring southern tip of mainland Malaya, which became known as Province Wellesley. Further consolidation came in 1824 when a treaty between the British and the Dutch, the other major colonial power in the region, saw the exchange of holdings, with the Dutch taking Bencoolen and the British Malacca, on the west coast of Malaya. The result for the British was what became known as the British Straits Settlements of Penang, Malacca, Province Wellesley and Singapore. The settlements were governed from India until 1867 when they became a crown colony and fell under the responsibility of the Colonial Office.

If there was any doubt that the British had set their sights on the entire Malay peninsula these were quashed in the 1870s when various independent but volatile sultanates making up Malaya fell under British protection – like many other places coloured pink on Victorian maps they were controlled as much by civil servants as they were by the soldiers of the Queen.

Thus it was that by the last quarter of the nineteenth century Malaya had become a vital outpost of the British Empire, along with Sarawak to the east and Burma to the north-west (the latter securing a continuous land bridge between Malaya and British India to the west). Other European states also had serious colonial interests in south-east Asia: the French had made Indochina (Vietnam and Laos) their own, while the Dutch, whose rivalry with the British stretched back to the origins of the spice trade in the 1500s, had settled for Sumatra, Java and most of Borneo (North Borneo on the border with Sarawak was British).

It was not just Malaya's geographic location, in relation to maritime trade routes, which ensured its importance. The peninsula was also rich in mineral wealth, initially in the form of major tin deposits, which were worked from the 1820s onwards by Chinese labourers imported by the tens of thousands to serve British interests (by 1939 Malaya had a population of five and a half million, of these 43 per cent were Chinese and 41 per cent Malay, the majority of the rest being Indian, with the British representing a distinct minority).[4] In the early twentieth century another local resource came into its own, and brought with it a fresh influx of immigrant workers, this time from India.

Although the rubber industry had been in existence for decades it was only with the revolution in motor transport, especially in the USA, that it became the second lynchpin of the Malayan economy. To give some idea of how important these two resources were to the economy one only needs to look at their standing on the global market by 1939, when 38 per cent of the world's tin and 58 per cent of the world's rubber originated from the peninsula. Other lesser important industries included the production of palm oil and the farming of bananas.

Singapore continued to grow throughout this period of Imperial economic expansion, with the population of the settlement growing from 10,000 in 1822 to 311,303 in 1911. From the outset of British involvement in the region it was naval power, rather than the army, which was expected to play the dominant role in the protection of her interests. It was, however, the British inability to deploy sufficient naval assets (as well as aircraft) in 1942 that was in part responsible for the rapid success of the Japanese invasion of Malaya. Nor was it expected that when conflict came it would be with the Japanese. In 1905 the Anglo-Japanese treaty established an alliance that was to hold fast until it was abandoned in 1923. The Japanese fought on the allied side during the First World War, with British troops standing alongside their Japanese comrades in China, while Japanese troops assisted the British in putting down a revolt by Indian Sepoys in Singapore in 1915. Japan's navy also played a role and, with capital ships seeing service as far away as the Mediterranean, it was clear that the nation had entered onto the world stage, a position that could only add fuel to the expansionist fire which had been burning for decades.

The lapse of the Anglo-Japanese Alliance in 1923 did not cause sleepless nights for British administrators, because if Japan was going to go to war with anyone, so the military planners thought, then it would be with the USA. Indeed, it was this eventuality that prompted Britain to move away from the alliance as, given the changing political map, she would be unable to support Japan in any future conflict with the USA (it was not, however, a condition of the 1905 treaty that one country had to go the aid of the other if it went to war with a third party).

Japan underwent a dramatic period of transformation in the nineteenth century, going from an isolationist, inward-looking archipelago, where the presence of foreigners was not welcome, to a nation state which underwent an industrial revolution and enthusiastically adopted aspects of European government along with western style imperial ambitions.

This process of change was, at least in part, initiated by outside forces, most obviously in 1853, when an American naval squadron under Commodore Perry threatened punitive action if Japan did not follow the path of China, and open herself up to trade and diplomatic ties with foreign nations. Up until this time the Emperor had been little more than a puppet of the Shogun, a self-imposed ruler who presided over a feudal-style clan system policed by the samurai. However, foreign influence, coupled with ill feeling directed toward the Shogun for allowing it, brought about the end of this regime in 1868, when power was transferred to Emperor Meiji and administration channelled through a system of government partly based on European parliamentary models. Reinforcing this social change was Shintoism, an ancient form of worship that accepted the emperor as a divine being, which was adopted as the state religion.

The military also underwent a series of dramatic reforms, with training, organization and technologies again borrowed from the west. As a result of this military revolution, the samurai, the warrior class which had enjoyed high social status for centuries, lost standing and influence. Bushido, the honour code by which the samurai lived was, however, to live on, and not just among the officer class, as its basic tenets were drummed into Japanese servicemen at every level.

Industrialization, anathema to the sword- and bow-armed samurai, depended on the importation of raw materials such as iron, coal and, later, oil, and allowed for the building of iron ships, with the overhauled navy looking to the British Royal Navy as a model. Next on the shopping list was overseas military influence, initially to secure the nation's borders, but it did not take long for this to develop into imperial ambition. China, Japan's much bigger neighbour to the west, was the first obvious target, for it was through her, if not from her directly, that the most obvious threat was likely to come. Like Japan, China was experiencing increased outside influence and in 1860 she ceded the port of Vladivostok to the Russians. In the 1890s the Russians began work on the Trans-Siberian railway, which would connect Vladivostok to the mother country. Keen to create a secure buffer zone, Japan went on the offensive in 1894–95 and took territory in and around Korea. Her gains were, however, limited thanks to the diplomatic intercession of European nations, in which France, Germany and Russia acted for China's interests. Japan retained Formosa but was forced to relinquish other conquests, including strategically important Port Arthur on the Manchurian coast. Following settlement of the issue, the Chinese proceeded to lease the port to the Russians and in so doing so seeded a deep-rooted animosity, which was to find terrible expression during Japan's occupation of Manchuria (North-east China) in 1931. The Russians immediately commenced work on the construction of a branch line from the Trans-Siberian railway to link up Port Arthur with Vladivostok and Russia.

Despite fighting alongside the Russians as part of the multinational force that liberated the European legation in Peking during the Boxer Rebellion of 1900, war between the two nations seemed inevitable. In 1902 the Anglo-Japanese alliance was largely geared to keeping a check on Russian activities in the region and, with her confidence boosted by the treaty, Japan went to war in 1904. A surprise attack on the Russian fleet at Port Arthur, an action that was to presage Pearl Harbor in 1941, was soon followed by the arrival of Japanese troops from Korea to lock the port into a siege, which lasted almost a year before it fell to the Japanese. In response, Russia threw her Baltic Fleet into the conflict, only to have it smashed by the Japanese fleet in the Battle of Tsushima on 27 May 1905. If nothing else, Russia's defeat highlighted the difficulty of maintaining a strong fleet in the east, while retaining a viable force in western seas. It was a quandary that was to tax the minds of British naval strategists in the lead up to the Second World War and the failure to resolve it, in part due to a combination of limitation treaties and strategic misjudgements during the inter-war years, was to leave Singapore exposed in 1942. In making repeated fanatical charges on fortified Russian positions the Japanese army also demonstrated its willingness to give all for the emperor, no matter the cost. This total disregard for personal safety and human life in general, born out of the heady brew of Bushido, Shintoism and blind devotion to the emperor, was to serve Allied prisoners of war badly after the fall of Singapore.

On 27 September 1940 Japan signed the Tripartite Pact and joined the Axis with Germany and Italy. The benefits for Japan were not long in coming as the fall of France in May 1940 freed up those territories formerly held by the French in the Far East, notably Indochina, and these were quickly occupied by Japan with her allies' consent. This expansion gave her a vital operating base in the region and provided the jumping-off point for the invasion of Malaya, and airfields within range of Singapore. Hoping to gain indigenous support under the banner of the 'Greater Eastern Asian Co-Prosperity Sphere' Japan disguised her own ambitions for an empire by promising liberation from European colonialism, which most notably included the British Empire.

Japan's latest war with China, which had never ceased to figure in her territorial ambitions, nor to be regarded with anything but malevolence by the Japanese, began in 1937 but had its roots in the 1931 invasion of Manchuria. It was turning into an extremely bitter and drawn out affair but with massive reserves of coal and iron at stake, along with a mountain of national pride, it was not a fight Japan was going to give up. However, in order to prosecute this colonial war Japan needed oil and, as of July 1941 this was in very short supply. This date marked the imposition of a US-led embargo on the sale of oil, which also included the British and the Dutch in the Far East. As reported in newspapers at the time[5] this embargo was a way of ameliorating a shortage of oil in the USA. However, when viewed alongside acts such as the closure of the Panama Canal to Japanese shipping it can be argued that this was a deliberate act of provocation on the part of Roosevelt, who was keen for an excuse to enter the war on the side of Britain, and latterly also Russia.[6]

As a result Japan turned her attention to the archipelago of islands to the south where, in what the Japanese termed the *Southern Resources Area*, the Dutch and the British controlled valuable oil resources while, as previously noted, Malaya was also a key provider of other commodities which could assist the war effort, such as rubber and tin.[7] The Japanese assumed that when they made a grab for British territory the Americans would immediately enter the war against them but this would not necessarily have been the case. It did, however, become inevitable when Japan attacked the US base at Pearl Harbor in Hawaii in order to prevent the US Navy from coming to Britain's aid when British Malaya was invaded – the two attacks being separated by just seventy minutes on 8 December 1941 (Malaya coming first). Japanese attacks on the American-held territories in the Philippines and Manila would soon follow.

The Japanese Invasion of Malaya

When Japan went on the offensive in late 1941 she did so with a ruthless efficiency that was take all of her enemies off-guard. That's not the same as taking them by surprise though, as a Japanese attack on British interests had been long expected – naval signals related to the build-up of an invasion force had been intercepted for two months in advance and the fleet was spotted in transit by an aircraft two days prior to the landings. In response, but somewhat belatedly due to indecision by the high command in Singapore, British, Indian and Australian troops in Malaya stood to, including those manning an unfinished stop line at Jitra which, in any case, was of limited extent as the jungle was believed wrongly to be impenetrable. Operation Matador – a plan to make a pre-emptive strike into Thailand – was left too late, for fear of antagonizing the Thais, and so abandoned.

The amphibious landings in north-east Malaya by the Japanese Twenty-fifth Army (consisting of the 5th and 18th Divisions and Imperial Guards) began at 12.25am on 8 December, on the sandy beaches of Kota Bahru, 400 miles north of Singapore, and at Singora and Pattani in southern Thailand. The Kota Bahru landings did not go uncontested and men of the 56th Infantry Regiment hastily dug into the beach in the face of a fierce onslaught of fire delivered by Indian troops from the 3/17th Dogra Regiment. The defenders were, however, stretched too thin and, by 1am, after vicious hand-to-hand fighting, the beachhead was established. In the following days British aircraft from bases in Malaya, such as the one at Kota Bahru, put up a stiff defence against their Japanese counterparts but in the face of greater numbers and more up-to-date aircraft, including accurate high-level bombers that did great damage to the airfields, British air defence quickly shrank away to almost nothing.

The first most Singaporeans knew of the outbreak of war was when, at around 3.30am on 8 December, Japanese long-range bombers flew 700 miles from Indochina to drop their bombs on a city with no blackout. The Royal Navy capital ships, HMS *Repulse* and HMS *Prince of Wales*, were in dock during that raid, and fired on the aircraft without attracting any bombs themselves. The Japanese did not make the same mistake twice, and on 10 December both ships were attacked and sunk by Japanese aircraft while on their way to intercept the invasion fleet, in no small part thanks to an absence of effective British air cover. These events should have served as a stark warning that 'Fortress Singapore', which had been built around an out-dated over-confidence in sea power, was far from impregnable. But, as Stuart Young was himself to remark, even as the Japanese were knocking on Singapore's door, nearly two months later, much of the population seemed to be in a state of denial, with life pretty much carrying on as normal.

Life was, however, very far from normal for the troops who through December 1941 and January 1942 were engaged in fierce fighting in Malaya. The total British force numbered around 85,000 men under Lieutenant General Percival (General Officer Commanding Malaya), while there has been considerable debate about the size of the Japanese force under General Yamashita, with figures between 36,000 and 125,000 variously quoted (e.g. Wikipedia – 36,000; Thompson 2005 – 30,000 frontline troops and 35,000 support; Farrell 2005 – 125,400 [based on Japanese figures]).[8] Recent assessments favour the larger figure and Arnold (2011), who agrees with Percival's estimate of around 150,000, has argued that it was in Churchill's interests to downplay the number of invaders in order to distance himself from any fault over the disaster (the low number allowed him to heap blame on Percival, who became a scapegoat).

Whatever the numbers, the Japanese spearhead units made good progress from their beachheads in Malaya and Thailand. Yamashita focused his attacks and repeatedly outflanked the enemy, moving through a jungle that the Allies expected to serve as a barrier. They also used boats to insert men along the west coast when a flanking attack was required. This combination of directed force and fluidity of movement worked well against the defender's more rigid strategy of deploying units along discontinuous stop lines, which then failed to support one another when part of the line was assaulted. A good example of this comes from fighting near Gemas on 18 January, where a line straddling the road and rail corridor had the 2/26th Battalion AIF (Australian Imperial Force) on the left flank, the 1/3rd Frontier Force (Indian) in the centre and the 2/30th AIF on the right. The war diary of the 2/26th AIF reported heavy fighting on their right flank, where the 1/3rd was posted. With telling aloofness, the entry relates how the assault against the 1/3rd developed from artillery bombardment and Japanese infantry attack (5th Division) to a breakthrough, followed by an order to retire – with no attempt to intervene while the situation deteriorated.[9]

The Japanese also had tanks (230 light and medium models) and, despite various incidences of delays caused by lead tanks being knocked out on narrow roads, these played a key role in driving forward the Japanese advance. A more effective defence could have been put up with more anti-tank guns, but the arrival of Young's regiment late in the campaign and the further delay in unloading the guns meant that by the time they were deployed it was too late. The invaders also had effective air cover (534 aircraft, including the latest mark of the Zero – which at the time was one of the best fighters flying), whereas the British had no tanks and very few aircraft (158 largely out of date machines). But it wasn't just mechanized superiority that helped to secure Japanese victory; they deployed bicycles to great effect, using them to move troops at speed along the narrowest of tracks through the jungle (a tactic also successfully adopted by the Viet Cong during the Vietnam War). The Japanese were so well prepared that they even provided units to carry out the specific tasks of repairing bicycles and mending punctures.

More fundamentally though, the Japanese were good soldiers. Whereas the Allies, thanks to propaganda with a racist underpinning, had expected an army of myopic midgets, lacking even the capability to shoot straight, what they got were troops who were highly motivated, battle-hardened and ideally suited to jungle warfare. The Japanese had put considerable effort into training for the operation, carrying out landings on Japanese islands and blowing up bridges and repairing them under combat conditions. The Twenty-fifth Army was chosen for the task because its men had seen action in China, and, as discussed below, came away from that campaign with a particularly hardened attitude towards the enemy.

The experience and training of the Japanese invaders stood in stark contrast to the very mixed bag of combat troops making up the British and Commonwealth force, which included around 19,000 British, 15,000 Australian, 37,000 Indian and 7,000 Malay troops (prior to the arrival of several thousand reinforcements – including Young's unit – following the invasion). Many of the units had been recently raised and too many, including elements of the Indian brigades and some of the Australians, were poorly or only partially trained. Most had no combat experience and many new arrivals had little or no experience in jungle conditions (there were battalions from thirteen British regiments but among these only three – the Argylls Leicesters and Manchesters – had seen active service before). Additionally, there was the enormity of the task at hand when geography is taken into account. Around 20,000 of these men were left to defend Singapore, while a force of somewhere in the region of 68,000 were up country in Malaya, defending an area of 51,000 square miles, with a coastline stretching for over 900 miles.

The defenders were constantly on the back foot, retreating and regrouping, rushing to plug gaps and turning to fight the enemy as he appeared unexpectedly on the flank or to the rear. The brunt of the initial attack in the north was taken by the men of the not-long-formed Indian III Corps, which fought valiantly until sizeable elements were overrun and had little option but to surrender.

Despite heavily contested actions through mid to late December the Japanese pushed their way down the west coast of the peninsula, while elements also progressed along the less well defended eastern coast – the defenders finding it near impossible to give both fronts equal weighting.

There were occasions when the defender's artillery was used to great effect – a prime example being the action by the Australian 2/10th Field Regiment at Mersing, on the east front. The gunners had pre-prepared the position, staking out the target area into quadrants and, laying their guns accordingly, were able to deliver incredibly effective artillery, mortar and machine-gun fire directed by observers. But, not for the last time, the defenders were pulled in too many directions – with elements transferred to the 'hotter' western sector – and also overestimated the strength of the attackers, a combination of factors which resulted in another withdrawal.

The weather also wreaked havoc, and on one occasion monsoon floodwater from the burst banks of the Endau river flooded minefields which had been carefully laid alongside the road, disabling the fuses – the idea had been to prevent passage along the road by cratering it, thus forcing the Japanese into the minefields.

The Japanese tanks were to prove their worth during the Battle of Slim River, fought between 6 and 8 January. Despite sticking to the roads and at times being held up by disabled vehicles at the head of the column they spearheaded a Blitzkrieg-style attack, which penetrated around sixteen miles. Indian and British troops (including 4/19th Hyderabad Regiment, 5/2nd and 5/14th Punjabis, the 2/1st, 2/2nd and 2/9th Gurkhas and the 2nd Argyll & Sutherland Highlanders) put up a stiff fight but, in the absence of effective artillery support, due to poor communications, and the weak anti-tank capability, one position after another fell. As a result, the bridges across the Slim River were captured intact (the wires for the demolition charges on the road bridge were cut by the sword of Lieutenant S. Watanabe, whose tanks had led the lightning assault). British and Indian troops who didn't make it back across the river escaped into the jungle, where some of them managed to stay at large until the end of the war but, in addition to around 500 killed, over 3,000 men were captured (the Japanese killed surrendered men too badly wounded to walk).

Despite their capture of Kuala Lumpur on 11 January it still wasn't all plain sailing for the Japanese, and an entire battalion was wiped out in an ambush put up by the Australian 2/30th Battalion, part of the 8th Division, at the Gemencheh Bridge on 14 January. But such successes were few and far between and when Australian troops bolstered the hard-pressed Indian 24 Brigade at the Muar River, two mixed battalions were encircled and overrun on 22 January. It was in the aftermath of this action that the Japanese massacred around 161 Australian troops at Parit Sulang, further proof if it was needed that this was not an army that stood by the recognized rules of war.

The action at Gemencheh also highlighted a fundamental problem with communications which, thanks to a shortage of wireless sets, relied largely on field telephones. This technological shortcoming particularly impacted on the effectiveness of long-range artillery support – the intention at Gemencheh had been to blow the bridge and, then using artillery, to decimate the trapped Japanese. The ambush didn't go off as planned as the enemy cut the telephone cables connecting the advance force to the artillery and, as it was set so far back, it was impossible to hear the explosion of the bridge which could otherwise signal the bombardment.[10]

As January dragged on so the Japanese got closer to their goal – Singapore. It was while the last British positions around Johore, on the southern tip of the Malay peninsula, were being taken up in mid-January that Stuart Young arrived in Singapore, with little idea of the fate that was about to befall him. Following the delayed landing of his unit's equipment, the Anti-tank unit, which did not include Young's mortar team, crossed the causeway to Johore but, almost as soon as they had arrived, the order was given for all Allied units to retire back into Singapore. There had previously been requests to dig in at Johore, to create field fortifications which would slow the Japanese advance, but Percival believed that the very presence of the defences would only serve to encourage forward British elements to retire on them – which does not say much about his confidence in his men. It was yet another display of bad judgement by the commander at a time when good judgement could mean the difference between life and death, if not victory and defeat. With nothing left to slow Japanese momentum the defenders had little option but to cross back over into Singapore and pull the drawbridge up behind them.

With the causeway blown on the morning of 31 January, last to cross being the 2nd Argylls with pipes playing, the 80,000-strong garrison regrouped, while on the other side of the water the Japanese, having conquered Malaya, planned a second amphibious operation. They had the ideal location from which to do it in the form of the palace of the Sultan of Johore on the high ground of Bukit Serene, which provided a grandstand view of the enemy positions across the water. The British were aware of this but left the palace untouched for fear of upsetting relations with the sultan. Japanese scouts also swam across the straights on 3 February and returned with sketch maps of the Australian artillery dispositions.[11]

British preparations for the Japanese assault on Singapore Island took place between 1 and 8 February, with troops digging in on the north shore and guns targeted so they could fire on any part of the shore when called upon. Percival was convinced that the Japanese would assault the beaches on the north-eastern side of the island, which was closest to the naval base. Thus it was that he concentrated his strongest force, the 3rd and 11th Indian Divisions and the 18th British Division in that sector, to the east of the causeway. The shore to the north-west, where the straits were narrowest, were assigned to the weaker Australian division under the command of Major General Gordon Bennett, which included over 1,900 newly-arrived recruits, some of whom did not even know how to operate a rifle. These dispositions were made despite contrary suggestions from General Wavell, recently appointed Supreme British Commander in the South-west Pacific, who visited Malaya during the invasion. It was on his advice that the British withdrew as far south as northern Johore, following defeat at Slim River, a controversial move that left Kuala Lumpur to the Japanese.[12] To Wavell and others it seemed obvious that the Japanese would cross where the straits were narrowest, a location which also coincided with the largest concentration of Japanese troops following the main thrust down the western side of the peninsula. But Percival was convinced that the naval base was the main target and was not to be persuaded otherwise. The Japanese also did their best to deceive the defenders into believing the landings would take place in the east. During the evening of 7 February a force of 400 Imperial Guards landed on Pulau Ubin, a small island in the eastern part of the straits in front of the 3rd Indian and 18th British Division positions. The artillery bombardment which preceded the main landings the following night were also targeted across the entire north coast and not limited to the west.

It was this historical reliance on naval defence that led to a total absence of fixed defences along the north shore of Singapore and the efforts of that first week of February were just too little, too late. The defenders were stretched out along vast expanses of a shoreline broken up by creeks and mangrove swamps, which would work as much against them as they would the Japanese invaders. It is, however, a myth that the big naval guns in fixed positions along the south coast could only fire out to sea, to the south. They were traversed and fired into Japanese positions in Malaya but their effectiveness was greatly reduced by a lack of high explosive shells. The guns were intended to protect against attack from the sea and so were equipped with armour piercing shells, which were very effective at sinking ships but totally inappropriate for work against enemy positions on land, where they merely drove themselves into the ground with little destructive effect.

Percival's unwillingness to construct defences – be they in Johore, on the north shore, or air-raid shelters in the city – was due to more than his concern over the negative impact these would have on morale. Yes, he didn't want to panic the mixed white colonial, Chinese, Malay and Indian population, but, more importantly, he was under great pressure not to give the impression that the British Empire was in trouble. The fear was that if weakness was shown then the Asian population would rise up against their white overlords and perhaps even go over to the Japanese. He clearly understood that the impression of stability imparted by Empire was veneer thin, and he was to be proved right when around 25,000 Indian troops went over to the Japanese after the surrender.[13]

The final breakdown was still to come though, and while last-minute preparations were underway along the north coast the impression of normality was maintained in the city, just twenty-four miles to the south. Dances were still hosted by the Raffles hotel, and the cinemas and restaurants were not short of patrons, despite regular air raids. It wasn't all business as usual though, and a steady stream of civilians, many of them families packed off by husbands well enough connected to know how bad the situation was, began to leave the island by plane, but mostly by ship.

The Fall of Singapore

The expected Japanese assault came after dark on 8 February 1942, commencing at around 8.30pm in the wake of a heavy artillery bombardment. As Wavell predicted, the attack fell on the Australians to the west, leaving the greater part of the defence force entirely redundant in the east (Map 2). Hundreds of landing craft and other boats took less than ten minutes to reach their destinations, but were subjected to a hail of small arms and machine-gun fire from the Australian troops from about the halfway point. Many Japanese were killed on the boats or in the water as they struggled ashore but their determination drove them onto the Australian positions and a bloody battle raged along the shore. Despite the defensive preparations of the week before, artillery support was noticeable by its absence, due in part to the guns being too far away to see the flare signals and the severing of telephone cables – another instance where an absence of wireless sets was to cost dear.

The Japanese made their strongest gains in the gaps between the thinly spread Australian positions, edging inland along creeks and attacking the defenders from the flank and the rear, just as they had in Malaya. By first light around 13,000 Japanese troops had come ashore, and a further 10,000 were to follow during 9 February.

Over the next couple of days the Japanese repeated their successes of the preceding campaign, pushing their way south by over-running one defensive position after another. Reinforcements continued to pour in from the peninsula, including tanks equipped with flotation devices, which were towed across even before the causeway was repaired. With the defenders and a civilian population of around one million people squeezed into the south-east of the island and the city the outlook was bleak. It was about to get bleaker, as late on the 9th when, just as the main airfield at Tengah was about to fall into enemy hands, the order was given to fly the surviving eight Hurricanes to Sumatra. That was the last of the British air cover.

The situation back on the ground was not helped when some units fell back precipitously, not because they were broken but because they were ordered to do so by senior officers who lacked a full grasp of the situation. This happened to the 2/26th Battalion of the AIF, which had been engaged in fierce fighting against Imperial Guards coming ashore at Kranji pier but were pushed off the beaches around midnight on 9 February and retired about 300 yards to a strong position at the neck of the Kranji peninsula. On learning of this setback Brigadier Duncan Maxwell, Commander of the Australian 27 Brigade, ordered them to retire along with the 2/30th to a new position in the vicinity of Bukit Mandai, a good 2,000 yards further south. This move allowed the Japanese to consolidate their position at the beachhead, exploit a hill dominating the causeway – which allowed engineers to move and repair it on 11 February – while also exposing the left flank of the 11th Indian Division. It didn't help that Maxwell's command post was positioned far behind the line (he was six miles south of the causeway), and so it was impossible for him to keep fully appraised of the situation, especially with telephone lines getting cut (though he had been told not to go forward, and check whether his orders had been carried out by his divisional commander, Major General Bennett). It seemed that none of the lessons of the preceding two months in Malaya had been learned.

A new defence line was formed between Kranji and Jurong, which ran from the north between the two rivers bearing those names and formed a thin shield against the Japanese advance from the north-west. But this too was infiltrated by the Japanese, whom a frustrated Percival referred to as 'clever gangsters'. The situation worsened further when he issued plans for a last ditch defence of the city, along a tight perimeter taking in the Kallang airfield and two of the city's reservoirs and the supply depots at Bukit Timah, to his senior commanders. The message had been marked 'Secret and Personal' but the orders were distributed further down the chain of command by the likes of Bennett. Brigadier Taylor believed they referred to an immediate withdrawal to the new line and so pulled back a number of units. To make matters worse, General Paris pulled his 27 Brigade back off the Jurong Line to the road junction at Bukit Panjang. Percival began to re-deploy some of the British and Indian troops on the north-east shore but again it was too little too late. The Japanese were building up their strength to the north and west of the city, but they too were badly stretched, having taken great risks with their long lines of communication through Malaya, which meant that by now they were getting perilously low on ammunition.

The final blows before the end game came quickly. On 11 February, a day which saw counter-attacks by the defenders on the Jurong Line fail to stop the Japanese advance, a last ditch attempt was made to defend the vital high ground at Bukit Timah, where food stores and the city's precious water reservoirs were located. Japanese tanks smashed their way through hastily erected roadblocks, having had a straight run down the Bukit Timah Road. By midnight the objective was in Japanese hands with the day ending on a very dark note, when twelve men from the Argylls, who had been captured in the action, were bayoneted and shot, though one survived to tell the tale. The 11th was also *Kigenestsu*, Japan's national day, and although Yamashita would have liked to have marked it by delivering up the city to his emperor, he had to be satisfied with raising his flag over Bukit Timah. Although they had made good progress the Japanese could not afford a protracted siege and, so hoping to coax the British into surrendering, messages were dropped from an aircraft over Percival's HQ. Even if he had wanted to surrender, which at this stage he did not, Percival had no means of responding to the letter.

The last of the ships carrying civilian and military refugees left on 13 February, with HMS *Vyner Brooke* sailing with 300 passengers, including sixty-five Australian nurses. The ship was sunk by Japanese bombers the next day, off nearby Banka Island. Twenty-two of the nurses, along with other survivors, made it to the shore, only to be shot on 16 February by Japanese troops after being herded back into the surf – one nurse survived to tell of one of the most infamous acts of cruelty committed by the Japanese army during the Second World War.

Horrific as it was, this massacre of nurses was not an isolated incident, as on the 14th and 15th it had been preceded by the slaughter of medical staff and patients at the Alexandra Hospital, on the south-western outskirts of the city, in the wake of forty-eight hours of hard fighting between the 1st and 3rd Battalions of the Malay Regiment and the Japanese 18th Division on the Pasir Panjang Ridge. With the ridge finally taken Japanese troops found release by bayoneting patients in their beds and slaughtering surgeons and nurses even while they were carrying out an operation (Young muses that one his comrades, Gunner Bird, taken to the hospital for treatment of a wound, was a victim of this massacre). Prisoners taken during this frenzied attack were locked up overnight only to be shot in a coldblooded fashion the next day. The perpetrators of these atrocities were veterans of the Nanking Massacre and the message was clear – surrender, or see the events of 1937 repeated.

As the last British perimeter around the city, which was twenty-eight miles long, was pressed to breaking point, so fierce fighting turned previously sleepy planter suburbs into bloody battlegrounds, among them the opulent Adam Park Estate, to the north of the city. Dug in here was the 1st Battalion Cambridgeshire Regiment, which had been moved from its position in the 18th Division's eastern sector, around Seletar airfield, as the Japanese advance progressed from the north and west. The positions were assaulted by the Japanese 41st Regiment and close-quarter combat took place among the colonial houses for three days, between 12 February and the British surrender on 15 February. It is here, in the now peaceful gardens of Adam Park, that archaeological investigations have recently located slit trenches dug into lawns and all manner of debris related to that desperate fight buried not far below the surface.[14]

Capitulation on 15 February came on the same day as the shootings at the Alexander Hospital. Letters were exchanged between Percival and Yamashita and then, in the late afternoon, Percival was driven to the Japanese headquarters at the Ford Motor Factory. Although Percival had wanted to put in a last counter-attack he finally acquiesced to the majority opinion among his senior officers, including that of Bennett, to surrender. The priority now was to minimize civilian casualties – there was a fear in

Singapore and in London that fighting on with disregard to the city's Asian population would cause unrest across the Empire. This pragmatic long view did not however square with Churchill's thoughts on the matter:

> There must at this stage be no thought of saving the troops or sparing the population. The battle must be fought to the bitter end at all costs. Commanders and senior officers should die with their troops. The honour of the British Empire is at stake.[15]

Had these instructions, which were relayed to the Malaya Command by General Wavell on 10 February, been carried out there can be little doubt that a massacre would have ensued – as it is unlikely that by then the hard-pressed Japanese would have had any truck with quarter (pretty much in the same way that in the sixteenth and seventeenth centuries in Europe the right to mercy was forfeit if a besieged force insisted on defending the indefensible). In line with the orders, as much matérial as possible had been destroyed, including fuel depots and facilities at the naval base – but there were still incredibly rich pickings left for the Japanese. After some rather one-sided negotiations the surrender document was signed and the ceasefire came into play at 8.30pm.

With the end there was confusion and a sense of disbelief among the defenders as the realities of their situation sank in. The last shots fired might have come from men of 2nd Loyals (North Lancashire) on a group of Japanese troops celebrating by yelling their famous 'Banzai' war cry.[16] With the breakdown of military authority, looting was rife and many of the men, Young among them, sought what solace they could from liberated bottles of spirits. There were also riots among the civilian population fuelled by shortages and the panic brought on by Japanese victory. During the surrender negotiation Percival asked to retain a company of his own men under arms so that some form of martial law could be maintained. General Yamashita declined his request but sent in his own military police units – the Kempeitai, who were themselves to earn a fearsome reputation for brutality.[17] He was careful, however, to keep the bulk of his army out of the city, as he knew another Nanking would probably be the result (rather confusingly Young mentions large numbers of Japanese troops in the city after the surrender – and then goes on to say that he didn't see one until two days after the surrender).

The surrender of 80,000 British troops was the biggest military disaster ever to befall the Empire. It had taken the Japanese seventy days from landing on the beaches of north Malaya and south Thailand to the British surrender – exactly the period of time which Singapore had been expected to hold out before relief as set down in an strategy document drawn up in 1937 (this period had increased over the years but not in keeping with the size of garrison).

In Japanese Hands

The vast number of British, Indian and Australian prisoners falling into their hands with the surrender of Singapore came as a surprise to the Japanese, and over the first few months they didn't know what to do with them. At first PoWs were concentrated around Changi, in the camp and even in villages in the vicinity. The European civilians were housed in Changi prison. As the weeks passed, however, and the prisoner population grew, men were dispersed to other makeshift PoW camps across the island, including former military camps, refugee camps such as the one at River Valley Road (built but not used as such) where Young spent six months, and even the Adam Park estate where each of the battle-scarred houses was used to accommodate hundreds of PoWs. During this period they were left largely to their own devices. This relatively relaxed period, remembered by some as the 'phoney captivity'[18] was to last for months, during which time the PoWs entertained themselves with concert parties, cricket matches and lectures, with the latter giving birth to the 'Changi University'. It was during this period that camp life in Singapore probably bore its closest relationship to that experienced by allied PoWs in European camps run by the Germans and Italians. This is not to say that life was easy – far from it.

Things began to take a more ominous turn when, in August 1942, the Japanese herded around 15,000 PoWs into the parade square at Selarang Barracks because they refused to sign a no-escape declaration (Young was spared this as only the men still in the Changi camp were concentrated at Selarang.) The men suffered horrendous conditions with no sanitation and, as a further incentive to sign, four men who had previously tried to escape were executed by Indian National Army (INA) firing squad. After three days the Japanese ordered the men to sign the no-escape document – rather than requesting them to do so. This they did, but as it had been signed under duress it was regarded as invalid. This notorious incident was no mere show of strength on the part of the Japanese, quite the opposite in fact. What lay behind it was a lack of manpower to do the job of guarding 80,000 PoWs.

The theory was that a camp full of prisoners who had agreed not to escape would require fewer guards than one where the inmates were liable to breakout (as was their right according to the 3rd Geneva Convention, which the Japanese had not signed up to). Despite a draft of Koreans and the secondment of the Indian National Army in Singapore (much to the latter's chagrin) this lack of manpower was to prove a headache throughout the war. For example, in May 1943 the commander of PoW Group 3, Lieutenant Colonel Nagatomo, had charge of around 10,000 PoWs of mixed nationality and only eight officers, twenty NCOs and 325 Korean guards to oversee them in around ten camps scattered over sixty miles of railway.[19]

PoWs were used for labour in Singapore during 1942 and 1943, either clearing up the mess of battle and aerial bombardment, including burying the dead, repairing the harbour facilities or building a shrine dedicated to the Japanese dead at Bukit Timah. By and large, these excuses to leave the camps were welcomed as it gave the PoWs the opportunity to procure food from the locals – access to the godowns (warehouses) on the docks also provided plentiful opportunities to pilfer from the stockpiles of supplies left over after the surrender.

For many though, what in retrospect would seem like halcyon days came to an end in October 1943 when the Japanese began to move contingents of PoWs up through Malaya and into Thailand and Burma, where they would be put to work on a new railway construction project.

Given the high risks involved in moving troops and supplies by sea, where American submarines hunted with seeming impunity, the Japanese opted to build a railway linking Bangkok in Thailand to Rangoon in Burma, a distance of nearly 260 miles (Map 3). Although not commenced until October 1943, the original Burma railway plan had been hatched in 1939 when it was envisaged some 250,000 native labourers would do the work. Once again, however, the Japanese were only emulating western Imperial ambitions, as the British had twice carried out surveys for the line back in the late nineteenth and early twentieth centuries – on both occasions they decided the project wasn't feasible due to unsuitable terrain and the extreme environment. Rivers, mountains and dense jungles were not however going to dissuade the Japanese from attempting this daunting feat of engineering. Now, with a large captive workforce, the operation was put into action, and over the next twelve months some 60,000 PoWs joined between 200,000 and 300,000 Asian labourers on this massive construction project.

The PoWs were spread across numerous camps built from nothing more than bamboo and rattan in jungle clearings, and were moved to new sites once their designated length of line was completed. When the work fell behind schedule the infamous regime of 'speedo' was introduced, during which men were literally worked to death. Incredibly, the project was completed in just over the allotted twelve months and the surviving PoWs, by now reduced to little more than skin and bone, were returned to Singapore, where conditions were not quite so extreme – though many PoWs who had remained in Singapore had suffered and died during the construction of the new airfield. Many men were also to die on their return to Singapore as diseases contracted up country by men who were now at their lowest ebb took their toll, and indeed Stuart Young was almost carried away by blackwater fever at this point late in his captivity (though at Tamuan in June 1944 rather than Singapore).

Captivity continued into 1945, but as the year progressed it was clear to both PoWs, thanks to clandestine radios, and the Japanese which way the wind was blowing. Although there does appear to have been some easing off by the Japanese, no doubt to curry favour, this was a time of great uncertainty for the PoWs as they had no way of telling how their captors were going to react to defeat (an anxiety shared by PoWs under the Germans in Europe at this time). It was during these final months and weeks that many of the diaries kept, Stuart Young's among them, were disposed of, a lot of them in latrine pits, as the Japanese began to seek out any documentation which might incriminate them.

The end when it came, in the wake of mushroom clouds over Hiroshima and Nagasaki in August 1945, must once more have been a surreal experience, with guards in many cases just vanishing overnight. On liberation, all of the PoWs were to spend time recuperating in hospitals, many of them in Australia. For many though the scars of imprisonment, both mental and physical would remain with them for the rest of their lives, and it is sad to say that it was the latter which eventually killed Stuart Young.

Not Honoured Guests – Japanese Treatment of PoWs

Any attempt to rationalize the motivations behind the numerous war crimes committed by the Japanese army during the Second World War is doomed to failure, not least because, unlike the twin ogres of Facism and Nazism, they did not appear to be driven by a semi-coherent, albeit warped, philosophy (anti-Semitism being an obvious core underpinning of these closely-related European manifestations of totalitarianism). It is, however, possible to identify a number of factors which combined to create a military mindset which condoned and indeed promoted a way of making war which ran counter to both the written laws of war and the unwritten rules of common decency, manifest through the absence of compassion, an inability or unwillingness to empathize with fellow human beings and a general disregard for what in the western world was and is regarded as civilized behaviour.

The historical legacy of the Japanese in the Second World War, at least as far as the non-historian is concerned, can probably be reduced to two striking aspects of their behaviour, their willingness to die for their cause, or at least their emperor, most obviously as Kamikaze pilots crashing their planes into Allied ships, and the dreadful crimes they committed against Allied prisoners of war, a legacy reinforced by Hollywood movies such as 'Bridge Over the River Kwai.[20] Although the true picture is, as ever, far more complicated than these examples of cultural shorthand would suggest they do together serve to emphasize the importance of the Japanese military credo of Bushido, an honour code identified with the samurai warrior caste, which bears some resemblance to the medieval European concept of chivalry.[21] Famously, a follower of Bushido would rather take his own life than live under the shadow of dishonour, and ritual suicide was integral to the code. Bushido fell by the wayside during a period of Europeanization in the late nineteenth century but enjoyed a resurgence during the inter-war period as the military became the dominant force in Japanese politics, via a series of purges and coups that saw some parallel with the rise of the Nazi party and its military wing in Germany during the 1930s.

A sure way of courting dishonour was to show weakness in battle, and surrender under almost any terms was not regarded as an option. These beliefs appear to have been widely held, and were exemplified in the story of Major Kuga, who was captured while unconscious in Shanghai in 1932.[22] On his release the major did not go home where shame would greet him but returned to the place of his capture and there committed suicide. Major Kuga's story became a press sensation in Japan and he was feted as a national hero. No surrender became a military regulation in the Field Service Code issued by the Minister of the Army in 1941, which told every soldier: 'You will not undergo the shame of being taken alive, You shall not bequeath a sullied name.' Thus it was that during the Second World War the Japanese ratio of captured to dead was 1:40 compared to 4:1 for the Allied powers (the ratio for the Japanese during the Burma campaign was 1:120).[23] It would appear then that the Field Service Code was largely adhered to, and even when Japanese soldiers did fall into enemy hands it was often because they had been wounded. Many Japanese PoWs also took the 'sullied name' clause seriously as they often gave false names to their captors, having shamed their own.

An unintended side effect of this identity crisis was that Japanese prisoners did not have the same compunction as Allied PoWs about handing over information to their captors. Under the Hague Convention this would go no further than stating name, rank and serial number but, between 1942 and 1945, many Japanese PoWs gave up useful information about their own side, as in effect they had mentally removed themselves from it.

Unfortunately for the thousands of prisoners of war to fall into Japanese hands during the Second World War their captors regarded Bushido as a universal code and, therefore, held a surrendered enemy in very low esteem; Lieutenant Tanaka, commander of the camp at Tarsao until March 1943, was not alone in believing that there was no place in a war for humane feelings.[24]

This belief was in part responsible for the Japanese refusal to ratify the Geneva Convention as it applied to PoWs (see below) as adherence would mean that prisoners were treated in a more humane fashion than the troops guarding them (the Japanese soldier was subject to tough discipline and the sight of an officer striking a man of lower rank was regarded as commonplace). How would it look to the average Japanese soldier if the PoWs he was guarding were treated decently, while he had been indoctrinated with the idea that there was no greater shame than being taken prisoner? As Lieutenant General Uemura Mikio, Director of the PoW Panel of Information put it: 'Prisoners of war are not honoured guests'.

There was also a sense of equality enshrined within the Convention – the living conditions of prisoners and guards was to be of an equal standard. There is, however, plentiful evidence, including Young's account, that prisoners were kept in far worse conditions than their captors, with men living in structures mired in filth and incapable of keeping out the elements while malnutrition and death due to dietary imbalance and inadequate rations were rife.

Throughout the war inspectors from the protecting power (Switzerland) were constantly making complaints about the conditions in which PoWs were kept in Europe. However, one only need look at the statistics on PoW fatality rates to see that there was a world of difference between the experience of the PoW in Europe under the Germans or Italians and in the Far East under the Japanese. In Europe just four per cent of the PoWs in German or Italian hands perished (this does not include Soviet prisoners who died in much greater numbers at the hands of the Germans), whereas the proportion of PoWs to die in Japanese hands is far greater – on the Burma Railway between 46,000 and 56,000 PoWs were put to work and around 16,000 died (35 per cent or 28 per cent).[25]

In many cases the PoW's worst nightmare was a hardened Japanese NCO, who had served in Manchuria, and due to his experience was probably allowed a freer hand than he should have been by his commanding officer. One such example, encountered by Young and others who have written of their experiences,[26] was Staff Sergeant Hiramatsu Aitarō, known to the PoWs as 'Tiger', a man proud of his record in Manchuria and capable of random acts of cruelty, especially after he had been drinking (a possible legacy of his time in China). He was executed for war crimes after the war, but despite this Young feels some sympathy for him, musing that he probably did the best he could in circumstances not of his making

This attitude is markedly different to the Japanese treatment of Russian PoWs during the 1905 war, which was entirely in accordance with the first Hague Convention of 1899,[27] while her treatment of PoWs during the First World War took its cue from the second Hague Convention of 1907. Although Japan had been happy to adopt the Brussels Declaration and both Hague Conventions, the same did not hold true of the Geneva Convention in 1929, and accordingly the PoW status of Chinese and Korean captives was not recognized. At the time of the earlier Conventions Japan had been keen to be taken seriously on the world stage by adopting western ways, but as Lieutenant General Uemura Mikio wrote in 1942, 'In the war with Russia we gave them excellent treatment in order to gain recognition as a civilized country. Today such need no longer applies.'[28]

Japanese attitudes to PoWs have understandably met with incomprehension and horror in the west, where there has been a long-lived tendency to regard the oriental mind-set as unfathomable or 'inscrutable'. In 1946, Ruth Benedict, cultural anthropologist in the US Office of War Information, wrote that the Japanese 'were the most alien enemy the United States ever fought'[29] and there can be little doubt that the war between the Americans and Japanese had a strong racial element to it. However, the truth is that these crimes were in part born out of an admiration for the western way of war, although this is perhaps not quite the impression one would get from Mikio's quote above.

Since the 1880s, up to which time the French had provided advisers, the Japanese had modelled their army on the German military, which was greatly admired even if relations between the two nations were strained during the first decades of the twentieth century. Germany began to take a very hard line with civilian fighters (partisans) during the Franco-Prussian War of 1870,[30] and their lack of respect for human life and property was again demonstrated in France and Belgium in the early part of the First World War. While the Russians had fought an entirely conventional war in 1905, the Koreans and particularly the Chinese communists under Mao Tse-tung preferred guerrilla tactics with conscripted peasants making up a large proportion of the fighting force. The Japanese, therefore, came to regard anyone as a potential enemy combatant and, with the rules of war thus disregarded, the way was open for atrocities such as the 'Rape of Nanking' of December 1937, in which Japanese troops massacred between 200,000 and 300,000 men, women and children.

The horror of Nanking came immediately after the Chinese National Revolutionary Army, which was itself at war with the communists, had given the Japanese Imperial Army a bloody nose at Shanghai. Though after three months of heavy fighting the Japanese eventually won the battle for Shanghai, the resistance put up by the Chinese damaged Japanese self-esteem, and did little to dampen animosity against the Chinese people as a whole. Also within Shanghai was the International Settlement, which included a Japanese cantonment, and French Concession, and this had always been immune to interference, though the Japanese illegally increased the size of their own protection force in preparation for the attack on the city. It was from here that a strong cadre of British and American pressmen had long been strongly critical of Japan's war in China. Again, this served to deepen resentment and, by 1938, British citizens in other parts of China were under constant threat of harassment and worse from the Japanese military.

Links between the Japanese Imperial Army and its German counterpart grew through the latter half of the 1930s. The Anti-Comintern Pact, signed in November 1936, for the first time allied Imperial Japan with Nazi Germany, both of which were totalitarian states anchored on the military, in the fight against communism – and in doing so helped heal the rift between them over China. Despite the temporary hiccup brought about by the 1939 Molotov-Ribbentrop non-aggression pact between Russia and Nazi Germany, which was reneged upon by Germany in 1941, the two nations, along with Italy, entered into the fateful Tri-partite pact, which created the Axis powers, in September 1940.

The treatment of Allied PoWs by the Japanese in the Second World War bore some similarity, at least in its basic brutality, with the German treatment of Soviet PoWs, who were literally regarded as sub-human by the Nazis (an attitude with which the Japanese had sympathy). It is not too outrageous to suggest that the Japanese, who continued to look to the German military for guidance and had entered into treaties with them against the Soviets, might have taken a leaf from their book and dealt with their own prisoners in a similar fashion. Though we need to be careful here as there is no documentary evidence known to the author and there is testimony enough to show that they had set their own precedents in China where people were compared to pigs.[31] However, the Russians were kept in terrible conditions, fed starvation rations and worked to death on forced labour schemes in a way that, aside from differing climatic conditions, would seem entirely familiar to a British PoW working on the Burma railway. Where Japanese treatment of PoWs diverged from that meted out by the Germans to Soviet PoWs was in the absence of a policy of deliberate extermination, which was responsible for a sizeable but unknown proportion of the around 3.3 million Soviet PoWs who died in captivity (this figure equates to around 57 per cent of the total number captured, which compares with 27 per cent of the Allied PoW population dying in Japanese custody).

Germany did not, however, treat PoWs from the western Allies in the same way. By and large, the Geneva Convention was adhered to and Göring in particular felt that if prisoners were kept in reasonable comfort then they would be less inclined to try escape, though in this he was to be proved wrong. The Germans were also concerned that maltreatment of western Allied PoWs would have repercussions for their own men in Allied hands (until 1942 there were no German PoWs in the Soviet Union but ultimately nearly 400,000 would die in captivity there).

Taking the opposite stance to Göring, the Japanese believed that by instigating a harsh regime against western Allied PoWs, which included brutal punishment and even execution for minor offences, discipline would be maintained and escape minimized. Making an example of prisoners would also deter locals from assisting in escapes or taking up arms against the Japanese. In both of these objectives the policy was largely successful, with very few escape attempts made and the Malayan locals regarded by the PoWs, not always fairly, as untrustworthy. Again, one very basic reason for this harsh approach was that the Japanese had a huge number of PoWs in their custody but, due to their extended commitments on the various war fronts, could spare very few men to guard them.

The harsh environment also played a part here, as the unwelcoming jungles of the Malayan peninsula and in Burma and Thailand, along the route of the railway, almost stood in as a second guard, alongside the troops assigned to the task.

Other motivations for cruelty did, however, exist. Where the Nazis regarded the Soviets as sub-human, being communist and, according to them, racially inferior, the Japanese viewed the British especially as arrogant imperialists, who needed to be taught a lesson after too long ruling the roost in the Far East. In propagating this view, regardless of the hypocrisy inherent in her own colonial ambitions, Japan also hoped to attract the various peoples of the region to her cause, one which would at last bring the hated British Empire to its knees. Some degree of assimilation is evidenced by the recruitment of Korean troops into the Imperial Japanese Army, where they proved reliable men – being among the first troops ashore during the invasion of Malaya. Also, in June 1942, following the decision to build the railway, a further 3,000 Koreans, with some Taiwanese among them, were recruited to serve as guards. They were drafted as civilian auxiliaries and given just two months' training, which instilled in them the need to be tough on PoWs.[32] Thus it was that the Korean guards had a reputation for being particularly brutal but, training notwithstanding, it is now well known that abused children can grow up to be abusers – a situation which may have some parallel in Japan's treatment of Korea.

The Japanese had some success, via the puppet INA, in recruiting Indians, and also in dissuading the general Malay population from assisting the PoWs, though many individual acts of humanity and bravery will have gone unrecorded. Ethnic Malays, as well as Indian Malays, did operate militarily against the Japanese, but the wellspring of resistance came from the largely communist Chinese Malay population. Prior to the Battle of Singapore, the British recruited many Chinese into Dalforce, an irregular unit that fought alongside the British during the final defence of the island. Following the fall of Singapore the survivors fought on as the People's Anti-Japanese Army, which carried out guerrilla operations against the Japanese for the duration of the occupation (they would go on to cause the British much difficulty during the Malayan 'emergency' of the 1950s).

There can be no doubt that the Chinese in particular were treated incredibly harshly by the Japanese in Malaya and Singapore, in part as a continuation of the cruelties directed towards them in their own country. A programme of ethnic cleansing, the *Sook Ching*, which is usually translated as 'purge through cleansing' or 'purification by elimination' (both of which sound eerily like the Nazi 'final solution'), was initially instigated by Yamashita as a means of punishing Asian Malays who supported the British and were likely to continue as a thorn in the occupier's side. Prime candidates were members of Dalforce but the remit was extended, if not by Yamashita then his senior officers, into a much wider programme which for the most part targeted the Chinese population. Suspects, essentially any Chinese male between the ages of eighteen and fifty, were herded into processing centres such as the Jalan Besar Stadium where decisions over who lived and who died were made by Japanese officers, almost on a whim. Young provides some indication of the resulting executions when he notes reports from Australian ambulance crews of heads on posts in the street, placed as a warning against sedition but mostly just to petrify the Chinese residents. They also told of the machine gunning of suspected Chinese insurgents on beaches. As ever, there is debate as to the actual number of civilians killed during *Sook Ching*, but they range from the official Japanese figure of 6,000 up to local estimates of 25,000 to 50,000.[33] These figures smack more of Chinese genocide than a purge of insurgents, especially so when they are viewed in the context of the war in China, which by the time it came to an end in 1945 had cost the lives of around fifteen million people (figures cited for civilian deaths of all nations at the hands of the Japanese during the Second World War range between 5 million and 20 million).

The Japanese behaved abominably to both PoWs and civilians in occupied territories before and during the Second World War, but as the Nazi and Soviet regimes demonstrated, as have others since, they were not alone in their ability to commit barbarous acts.

Stuart Young clearly had the strength of character not to hold a grudge against the guards who treated him so badly, but that does not mean that those acts of cruelty should be forgotten. If anything, Young's memoir and the others like it should stand forever as testament to man's inhumanity to man but, on the other hand, they should also endure because they serve up wonderful examples of the indomitable nature of the human spirit. It has been said that if we do not learn from the lessons of the past then we are doomed to repeat them, and, though it may seem at times that we never learn, it is good to know that books like this one are there if we should wish to make the effort.

Notes

1. At the time of writing, the cinema adaptation of probably the best known of these books, *The Railway Man* by Eric Lomax (1996), is in post-production.
2. Young's widow, Ethel (who sadly passed away before this book could be published), told me that some of these scraps of paper were retained by Stuart, and they included a list of his comrades who died during captivity (the list appears here as a Roll of Honour at the end of his account). After the war he tried to write to the families of as many as he could. He also had an incredible memory and his abilities at recall must also have proved valuable while he wrote the book. According to his son, Andrew, he would go to bridge matches after the war, having learned the game as a PoW, and on his return home would be able to recall every hand and individual card played throughout the game.
3. The subject of homosexuality in Japanese PoW camps has been touched upon in *The Barbed Wire University: The Real Lives of Prisoners of War in the Second World War* by Midge Gillies (2011: Aurum, Kindle edition), in which testimonies from a very small number of PoW veterans make mention of homosexual practices among others, with none of them claiming it as personal experience (loc 1093). The author also refers (loc 3220) to sexual assaults committed against PoWs by Sikh guards, and this is something that Young also alludes to in his own memoir (the editor of the present volume is at pains to point out that it is a minority referred to here and drawing attention to the issue in this note is in no way intended as a slur against Sikh units in general).
4. Warren, M., 2002. *Singapore 1942: Britain's Greatest Defeat*. Hambledon and London, London. 8.
5. As Tasmanian newspaper *The Examiner* reported on Wed 18 June 1941: 'Washington – Tuesday – Mr H. L. Ickes Petroleum Co-ordinator for National Defence has prevented the shipment of 252,000 gallons of lubricating oil from Philadelphia to Japan. He stated that this was not because of international policy, but was due to a shortage of oil on the east coast.'
6. Arnold, M., 2011. *The Sacrifice of Singapore: Churchill's Biggest Blunder*. Marshall Cavendish Editions, Singapore.
7. Other factors also lay behind Japan turning her interests to the south-east and these included her defeat at the hands of Soviet troops in part under Zhukov at the Battles of Khalkhyn Gol (Nomonham), on the Mongolian side of the Chinese border fought between May and September 1939.
8. Thompson, P., 2005. *The Battle for Singapore: The True Story of the Greatest Catastrophe of World War II*. Portrait Books, London.
9. Farrell, B.P, 2005. *The Defence and Fall of Singapore 1940-1942*. Tempus, Stroud. 244.

10. Farrell, *ibid*: 245–6.
11. Yong, Y.S., Bose, R., Pang, A., Singh, K., Lim, S. and Foo, G., 2004. *Fortress Singapore: The Battlefield Guide*. Marshall Cavendish International (Asia).
12. Farrell, *ibid*: 276.
13. On 16 February 1942, following capitulation in Singapore, around 45,000 Indian PoWs gathered at Farrer Park, where Major Iwaichi Fujiwara (of the Fujiwara Kikan, a Japanese unit tasked with recruiting foreigners, and particularly Indian nationals) expounded the benefits of an independent India joining the Japanese as friends and allies in the Asian Co-Prosperity Sphere. Then Captain Monah Singh, formerly of the 1/14th Punjab Regiment and captured on 10 December in north Malaya, gave a rousing anti-British and anti-Imperialist speech, in which he also implored the men to join the Japanese, fellow Asians who were determined to rid the region of the scourge of European imperialism. The prize was an independent India, but this would require desertion from the British Indian Army, betrayal of the oath to the crown and fighting against their former comrades-in-arms. For some this was no sacrifice, and around 25,000 men accepted the proposition, seemingly without a second thought. For many though there was initial doubt and the anguish caused by this decision has perhaps been overlooked in most histories of the campaign.
14. Cooper, J. 2010. 'Park Life: Revealing a Hidden Battlefield from the Fall of Singapore.' *Britain at War Magazine*. Issue 43, November 2010: 75–7.
15. A cable sent to Wavell on 10 January, quoted in Thompson, ibid 446. While nearly all the senior officers, including Percival, went into captivity with their men, Major General Gordon Bennett left the island in a small boat with two of his officers the day after the surrender, leaving his men to their fate. Young also mentions an officer of his own regiment escaping in a small boat immediately after the surrender.
16. Farrell *ibid:* 381.
17. In reality they arrived with this reputation for brutality already well earned, as their activities in China had done much to destroy any chances the Japanese may once have had in winning hearts and minds. Yamaguchi, N. 2012. 'An Unexpected Experience in Hybrid War: The Japanese Experience in North China, 1937-1945' in Williamson, M. and Mansoor, P. R. (eds.) *Hybrid Warfare: Fighting Complex Opponents from the Ancient World to the Present.* Cambridge University Press: 247.
18. Best, B. 2004. *Secret Letters from the railway: The Remarkable record of Charles Steel – A Japanese PoW*. Pen and Sword, Barnsley: 26
19. Flower, S. J. 1996. 'Captors and Captives on the Burma-Thailand Railway' in Moore, B. and Fedorowich, K. (eds.) *Prisoners of War and their Captors in World War II*. Berg, Oxford: 236.
20. The movie, 'Bridge Over The River Kwai,' was held in very low esteem by Young and most other ex-Japanese PoWs for bearing little similarity to the truth. Indeed, his widow Ethel and his son, Andrew, told me that he went to see the film at the cinema sometime after its release in 1957, while on a business trip to London. So disgusted was he with the inaccuracy of the portrayal of life as a PoW of the Japanese that he walked out of the cinema before it was halfway through – this response to the film seems to have been shared by many ex-PoWs (the overly healthy appearance of the actors was one complaint). Young had nothing to do with the bridge while he was a PoW, but he did spend a short time in the camp occupied by those who built the bridge, and longer

periods in the vicinity of the river itself which, for much of its length, followed the course of the railway.

21. It was in fact a modified form of the older Samurai code introduced at the time of the war with Russia in 1904 in order to try and make up in commitment, turning soldiers into 'human bullets', what Japan lacked in technology and numbers. Citino, M.C., 2013. 'Japan's First Big Surprise.' *Military History*. Vol. 25, No. 5: Weider History Group, Leesburg VA: 48–56.

22. Young, L. 1998. *Japan's Total Empire: Manchuria and the Culture of Wartime Imperialism*. University of California Press, Berkley and Los Angeles: 75.

23. Hata, I., 1996. 'From Consideration to Contempt: The Changing Nature of Japanese Military and Popular Perceptions of Prisoners of War Through the Ages' in Moore, B. and Fedorowich, K. (eds.) *Prisoners of War and their Captors in World War II*. Berg, Oxford: 269.

24. Flower, S.J., 1996. 'Captors and Captives on the Burma-Thailand Railway.' In *Prisoners of War and Their Captors in World War II*, edited by Bob Moore and Kent Fedorowich, 227 - 252. Oxford: Berg: 245.

25. Lord Russell of Liverpool cites 47,000 while Sibylla Jane Flower cites 57,000 – her total seems the most reliable as it's based on figures typed up by an American PoW under orders from the Japanese. A number of authors agree on 16,000 dead, though Rummell cites 13,000. Referring to 16,000, Russell states that each mile of railway cost the lives of sixty-four Allied PoWs and around 240 Asian labourers. Around 11,000 Indians and 8,000 Australians also died in Japanese captivity.

26. Flower *ibid:* 237.

27. Towle, P., 1999. *Japanese Prisoners of War*. Continuum, Hambledon: 3.

28. Quoted in Hata, *ibid*: 266.

29. Benedict, R., 1947. *The Chrysanthemum and the Sword: Patterns of Japanese Culture*. Houghton Mifflin Co. Boston.

30. Jones, M., 2012. 'Fighting this nation of liars to the very end': The German Army in the Franco Prussian War, 1870-1871 in Williamson, M. and Mansoor, P. R. (eds.), *Hybrid Warfare: Fighting Complex Opponents from the Ancient World to the Present*. Cambridge University Press.

31. Slim, H., 2007. *Killing Civilians: Method, Madness and Morality in War*. Hurst & Company, London.

32. Flower, *ibid*: 238.

33. Farrell, *ibid*: 385.

Chapter 1

The End and the Beginning

S
uddenly I was awake, feeling cold and cramped. It was broad daylight, and the silence hung clammily over the stricken city.

Singapore was licking its wounds. The night had been long and hot. Spasmodic bursts of gunfire, punctuated with staccato small-arms fire, had filled the hours of darkness. The sound of screams and hoarse shouts in various tongues were evidence of the grim struggle. The sky had been made bright with the flames of burning buildings, the moans of the bereaved mingling with the crackle of blazing homes. Now all was still, but a hundred palls of smoke pinpointed where someone's life had fallen into ruins.

I put my hand down to steady myself, and my fingers closed over a bottle, Cherry Brandy, filched from Shaw Brothers' studio in the city, a few days previously. It was empty and I slung it carelessly into the hedge, where it joined others that had gone the same way.

It was eight o'clock on the morning of 15 February 1942, and still the expected Japanese final assault had not materialized. We lived another day. As we left the slit trench and walked down the hill for breakfast, I thought of the newspaper I had held in my hands a couple of days previously. For the past couple of years I had read newspaper reports of battles in France and on the Eastern front with a curious sense of detachment. The happenings were all taking place in another world and concerned me not at all. Now the same feeling was there as I read the final issue of the *Singapore Times*, with its report of the Japanese advance within four miles of Singapore city, till, with a curious sense of shock, realization broke that this time, it was real, and that this front line was not only four miles from Singapore, it was four miles from me. After two and a half years of playing at soldiers the war had finally caught up with me.

The cookhouse was a makeshift affair in the garden of one of those sprawling Chinese houses, and was crowded with members of RHQ (Regimental Headquarters), snatching a hasty meal while the going was good, for the lull surely wouldn't last much longer. Half-cooked tinned bacon and beans and a cup of lukewarm tea swallowed, I picked up my rifle and made my way down to the Regimental Orderly Room, which was in the grounds of another Chinese house nearby. Who the Chinese owners were, we neither knew nor cared. This time tomorrow we would all probably be past caring.

The little house slept in the morning sun, green shutters closed tight over its sightless eyes. Of the family, there was no sign, Donald was seated at a table, tapping away at a portable typewriter, Dickie, the Transport Sergeant, head in a bucket, was sluicing away the dust of the previous night's guard duty.

The 15-cwt truck, which served as mobile Orderly Room, was parked rear on to the house, beside the ugly bulk of an air-raid shelter,

I loosened the buckles of my equipment, and dropped my steel helmet on the table. Four soft thuds from over the hill were followed rapidly by the sound of four mortar shells landing nearby, and palls of smoke rose from the cookhouse area. Unthinkingly I stepped between the truck and the house wall. Like the proverbial ostrich, I imagined that what I couldn't see, couldn't see me – I was safe.

Donald cast a wary eye over the hill as more explosions followed, this time appreciably nearer.

'Quick, the shelter,' cried an unidentifiable voice, and I saw Dickie, ablutions abandoned, streaking for the entrance. I followed, and a blast of warm air picked me up and helped me inside, as someone landed on top of me. We heard no sound. I struggled to my feet and gazed outside.

It was nine thirty in the morning, and I had just seen my first – and my last – action in Singapore.

Cautiously we emerged to survey the damage. The last shell had scored a direct hit on the upper part of the house, bursting inside, and the green shutters hung drunkenly awry. The blast had blown back and ripped through the 15-cwt, which dripped petrol, oil and water from the shattered engine. Somewhere in a locker had been a few tins of baked beans, and a slow drip of reddish fluid made me shudder as I thought that a few seconds earlier, I had taken refuge behind the shattered wreck of a truck.

Of the family, there was neither sight nor sound, and I went in search of them. At the rear of the house was another shelter, twin to the one we had just left. I shouted at the door.

'Hello. Anyone there?'

'Hullo,' came faintly from inside.

'You all right?'

'Yes, we all light.'

'I'm afraid there isn't much house left.'

'Never mind. We all light.'

Thus I had my first introduction to the ubiquitous philosophy of 'never mind' that was to stay with us for the next four years, the non-committal shrug of the shoulders, the casual *Tid apa* that took care of everything. *Tid apa*, what does it matter? *Tid apa*, the adopted motto that followed us everywhere through Malaya and Siam.

I rejoined the others at the front of the house. They were just examining Gunner Bird, whose body it was that had landed so heavily on mine in the shelter. As he walked away, someone noticed that the seat of his shorts was missing, and further examination had shown that wherever it had gone, a hefty slice of his personal seat had gone with it. Persuaded, much against his will, to lie on his stomach, he was patched up to await evacuation to hospital where the hard-pressed medical orderlies could attend to him. When he finally departed, grinning and waving to us, neither he nor we knew that it would be the last we should see of him. We imagined later that he had been caught up in the infamous massacre of Alexandra Hospital.

'Can't stop,' puffed the orderly as they picked him up. 'They've copped one at the cookhouse, and another on the officers' mess. They're in a hell of a state up there.'

I doubled up the hill. Half an hour earlier this had been a pleasant garden where some fifty or so troops had been eating breakfast in the shade of a house built on piles in traditional native fashion. Now one house was in ruins, and a second half-demolished. Between the two, a figure in KD (khaki drill uniform) lay, arm pillowing his head as if asleep. Another, legs shattered, lay nearby convulsively moaning. In a waiting truck, screaming and wailing, a Chinese woman was taking the body of a child from the red-haired medical orderly. A white cloth covered its head, pinned securely all round.

'Had to pin its head on,' he said, 'otherwise it would have bloody well dropped off.'

A loud wail broke out behind me. A fat man in the dress of an upper-class Chinese was pulling at his hair and crying aloud as he knelt down. In front of him, two figures, barely recognizable as women, lay feebly moaning, incapable of coherent sound.

* * *

'Half an hour ago, a car bearing our envoys under cover of a white flag left Singapore to meet the Japanese Commander in Chief. It is expected that the ceasefire will operate from 20.30hrs. The HQ will be returning to Shaw Bros studio immediately.'

The Intelligence Officer finished speaking and we looked at each other in silence. Once again we had been 'put in the picture' as army parlance has it, and we didn't much care for the picture that was painted. We completed the move back to our previous position, and I borrowed a truck to see if I could salvage any last items from the shattered MT 15-cwt. A listless, brooding silence covered the city. Even the low-flying spotter plane that had circled the area for the last few days, was absent. One of these planes had been continuously in the air during daylight hours, flying at fifty feet and shooting up anything that moved. One had been brought down by small-arms fire but, within ten minutes, another had taken its place, and we were once again taking to the monsoon drains at the sound of its approach. Now nothing disturbed the hot sultry afternoon heat.

The old Chinese was standing by the wreckage of his house when I arrived. Most of the dust and rubble and been swept up, and he indicated the wrecked truck.

'You move,' he enquired, 'want to clear up.'

'Plenty of time,' I replied, 'War all over. Clear up tomorrow.'

He stared blankly. 'War no over.'

'I'm afraid it is. All over, and the Japanese have won.'

As I left, bearing all that was worth saving, the Chinese was already fixing flags to the front of his house. Plain white flags with a red disc in the centre. I had never seen them before, but they soon became very familiar under the affectionate nickname of 'fried eggs'. The news had spread fast, and the roads were filled with groups of impassive-faced natives, silently watching the end of an era, the last hours of European rule. On many of the buildings, the Japanese flag already hung limply in the still air, and many more were appearing by the minute. The 'wily orientals' had evidently backed the winner both ways, and the Union Jacks, no doubt, were at that moment being burnt, or carefully hidden away for some theoretical future use.

We slept that night in an abandoned house, near the studio. Sleep was not easy to woo, and we turned to a large HMV radiogram that stood in the corner of the room. It was in working order, and we played the comprehensive store of records for some time. One that fitted our mood was a 'pop' called 'Wonders of the Wasteland', but our concert was interrupted by the arrival of the RSM.

'Turn the bloody thing off,' he yelled. 'This isn't a bloody party. We're prisoners of war now, and we haven't anything to celebrate.'

We lay in the darkness talking in hushed tones.

Waves of tiredness swept over me. The sound of conversation ebbed and flowed. It sounded like waves surging up on some sandy beach. No, it was the sound of shells rushing by overhead. I drifted into uneasy slumber.

We awoke early on our first day of captivity. Breakfast was meagre, for we didn't know how long our small stock of rations would have to last. We waited in the house for instructions. Despatch riders were still operating normally, and from them we heard of the scene in the city centre. In the past day or so, there had been a wholesale move to the dock area, by thousands of troops whose one thought was to get off the accursed island at all costs. Any craft that was seaworthy, and many that were not, had been pressed into service. This had been foreseen by the Japanese, who had ringed the approaches with naval craft to prevent any such attempts. Many were not heard of again, but a few lucky souls got through, and one such, an officer of our own Regiment, later wrote to his friends from Ceylon, the letter being received some eighteen months later when we began to receive mail. Others arrived back with us some days, or even weeks later, and one group of officers, after having reached Sumatra and struggling frantically over to the west coast a mile or so ahead of the advancing Japanese, obtained a boat and provisions and set sail for India. Weeks later they were within a few hundred miles of Ceylon, when they were sighted and picked up by a patrol boat. It was Japanese, and they were returned to Singapore, about two months after escaping.

For the majority, however, it was impossible. There was no longer any way of escape, and they drifted back into town in aimless groups. Military policemen were posted to discourage would-be escapees and, on Sunday and Monday, the streets were filled with mobs of frustrated would-be deserters, wandering aimlessly, looting sporadically here and there, totally unable to come to terms with reality. Or was it, rather, the rest of us who genuinely had never encompassed the idea of escape, who were out of touch with life?

The victorious Japanese were now all over the city, on cycles, on 'borrowed' motorbikes, in cars, or on foot. The majority of them had never before seen white men at close quarters and in bulk, and they, as much as we, were a little unsure. The atmosphere was one of watchful amiability. Any British soldier was likely to be peremptorily stopped and his watches, rings, fountain pens and other little trinkets removed for souvenirs or spoils of war, quite often the Jap being ready to leave his own in exchange. Our despatch rider on his Norton motorcycle, was stopped by a Jap, who rode triumphantly away, leaving his own rather decrepit sidecar machine in payment.

Conflicting reports of our immediate prospects were circulating. It was considered most likely the Japanese would concentrate us in Changi, but how and when was still in doubt. Whether we would be allowed to take our kit and whether equipment for cooking etc. would be transported, was also anyone's guess.

In direct contravention of the terms of the capitulation, which stated that all arms and equipment would be handed over to the Japanese unharmed, the LAD (Light Aid Detachment) were busy putting as much of the transport as was not needed, out of action and there was much tyre slitting and wielding of hammers inside the engines, to while away the time. In a similar way, we all attended to our personal arms, burying the bolts, and scattering ammunition to the four winds. I came across the CO, the eternal cigarette drooping from his lips, and a glint of satisfaction in his eyes, as he tried to wrap a Bren gun round the trunk of a tree.

'You know, these things are damn well made,' he said, having done far more damage to the unoffending tree than to the gun. RSM Barr amused himself for hours. A shed in the studio grounds was literally stacked to the roof with cases of drink; grosses of bottles of Sandeman's port, cherry brandy, gin, whisky, sherry, and all imaginable wines and spirits. It was more like a bonded warehouse. He personally smashed every bottle, and the yard was high with discarded crates and cartons, and smelling like a boozer's delight,

'There'll be enough trouble as it is without those little yellow bastards getting hold of this and getting fighting drunk,' quoth he as he did his little bit for the anti-war effort.

That night we got Radio Delhi on the radiogram. Among the news items we heard that Mr Churchill had 'announced to a stunned and sorrowing nation' the news of the fall of Singapore. We also heard of the escape of the *Scharnhorst* and *Gneisenau* from Brest. This latter cleared up a misapprehension, as in the absence of official news in the last few days, we had heard garbled accounts of a German invasion of the south coast of England, evidently started by the Channel incident.

Day two passed much as the previous one, except that in the afternoon, a Japanese NCO cycled into the compound, all smiles and brass teeth glinting in the sun. He dismounted and beamed expansively, showing more gold than Fort Knox. 'Gasolino,' he intoned pleasantly. We gazed at the RSM.

'Give it to him,' he said disinterestedly, 'it's his now, anyway.' We handed over a four-gallon can and, bowing gallantly, he withdrew. After two days as a prisoner of the Japanese, I had at least seen one and now knew for certain that they existed.

So for day three, when we all assembled for the grand march to Changi, for this was indeed to be our place of concentration. As we stood in the boiling sun, a long straggle stretching into the distance, we were surrounded by smiling Chinese, who showed their apprehension for the future in their attempts to be helpful. We had an endless supply of hot sweet tea and little sticky cakes, which were produced from all the neighbouring, Rising Sun decorated, houses. We shifted from foot to foot, sat on our packs, and still the order to march was not given. After all our fears, adequate transport for the heavy equipment had been allowed by the authorities, and the heavily laden trucks had already left, including, in our case, a 15-cwt water truck which we thought would be invaluable.

At last, after about an hour, we began to move, the convoy, four in line, shunting and extending, like rookies on their first march. As we shuffled along we saw few people in the streets, and there wasn't a Japanese in sight. Surely we must have been the strangest body of prisoners ever, unescorted, marching alone into our 'cage' there to literally shut ourselves in, and still unsupervised by the enemy, to draw our lines of demarcation in an as yet, unguarded and unwired camp. Every yard of the way bore some grim reminder of the carnage of the past few days; buildings in ruins, power cables sagging drunkenly till they brushed the roads. Everywhere wrecked and burnt-out cars and army vehicles, many still containing the charred and blackened bodies of their former occupants. On the air hung the sickly sweet smell of burnt flesh. At one spot, we passed what had been a complete kampong at the side of the road, only a few charred posts in the blackened ground showing where, a few days before, a smiling community had dwelt in peace. Here, too, the smell was overpowering.

At Paya Lebar we passed a small group of Japanese armoured vehicles, drawn up at the side of the road, the almond-eyed soldiers leaning on their vehicles, and studying us impassively. No word was spoken. No sign of emotion. Our lives touched for a moment, and once again contact was broken, and we marched on. Here and there we had a quick glimpse of a white face, peeping furtively from behind the drawn curtains of a darkened room or caught sight of a waving hand. These were some of the people destined to spend the rest of the war in the infamous Changi jail. We did not stop, we shuffled on, mostly in silence, each coming to terms with himself in his own way.

We were startled once by an apparition at the side of the road. At the top of a bank was a soldier, black of face, on one knee, rifle held loosely at the trail. His bush hat was still on his head, and he was frozen forever in the act of dropping to the road below. For him the war was over, for he had obviously been dead for several days, his colour dark, the colour of rotting flesh, his face puffy and swollen. Apart from this, he looked uncannily alive, as though, once we had passed, he would drop lithely into the road and continue the battle he had left so abruptly.

Halfway along the Tampines Road, our transport, having dropped its load in Changi, met us and collected our kit and as many men as could scramble aboard. From then on they operated a shuttle service between Changi and the diminishing column until eventually we all reached Roberts Barracks, where we settled in for the start of our PoW days. The barrack block, apart from a huge sagging piece of reinforced concrete hanging from the roof, was undamaged, only the toilets being out of action due to the lack of mains water. Some of us were lucky enough to obtain beds and mosquito nets. Life did not look too bad. So we thought.

Chapter 2

The Wasted Years

Every year, whilst I was at school, we had the esoteric ritual of Remembrance Day. We all filed into the great hall at five to eleven, and faced the stage, on which were assembled, silent and grim, the entire teaching staff, fronted by the august figure of the Headmaster in board and gown. The radio was switched on for the sound of Big Ben and, for two minutes, we stood in silence, thinking about the dead of the First World War.

At least, that was the theory of the thing, but in practice, as far as I was concerned, it never worked out that way. My mind was usually a complete blank. The war had finished before I was born, and the world as I knew it bore no resemblance to that of pre-1918. Those pathetic, mud-engulfed figures ranked in my imagination with Henry VIII, Joan of Arc and the Romans, as cardboard dry-as-dust puppets of the historical stage and, try as I might, I could not identify myself with them. So must we now seem to the post-war generation. It is hard to realize that nigh on fifty years now separate us from the events that in retrospect seem only like yesterday, and that most of the present day population have only films and TV programmes to rely on for having any idea at all of what went on in those hectic years.

I lived in a typical Midlands town of some 25,000 people, a cocky, brash and hustling urban sprawl. It boasted three cinemas, converted in the early thirties to those new-fangled talkies, and a small dance hall, which at times had doubled as a roller-skating rink. The leader of the 'broadcasting' band which played each Saturday night was, like me, a product of the local grammar school.

The big event of the year was the local hospital carnival each September, an eight-day affair during which the whole town went *en fête*. The streets were filled continuously with groups in fancy dress, and with carnival bands which, starting in 1930 grew to elaborate concourses of up to 150 members in brilliant costumes and, after dark, masses of perambulating coloured light bulbs. Something was afoot every night, and on the final Saturday sports and gala held sway on the local park.

For the rest of the year, entertainment was less riotous. The cinemas did not, by law, open on Sundays, and the forbidding nineteenth-century nonconformist chapels were filled to overflowing with the faithful. Every Sunday school had its own banner, which was paraded through the streets on May Day and, as a reward, the regular attenders were taken all of three miles by lorry once a year for the annual picnic, or 'Sunday school treat'. In our teens, most Sunday afternoons we frequented the park, where a concert would be given by one of the many brass bands of the area. In the evening, that peculiar mating phenomenon of the thirties, known to one and all, as the 'monkey run' would take place in the precincts of the town's High Street. Within strict bounds and during strict hours we would parade the High Street from end to end, a distance of some half a mile. At five to eight in the evening, the street presented its usual dull, deserted look to the world, then, on the stroke of the hour, it became alive with teenagers, in groups of two or three of one sex, strolling from the market place to the corner of Station Road, then turning on their heels, and returning to the market once more. Liaisons were formed with groups of the opposite sex, and the parade would be depleted by some four or so bodies, the remainder continuing to walk up and down, till, on the stroke of ten, they all vanished like wisps of mist before the rising sun, and the street returned once more to its Sunday somnolence. Those who had struck 'gold' were out of town trying to lodge a claim, the rest returned home.

'Where have you been tonight dear?'

'Only out for a walk mum.'

As a shop assistant I can hardly say that I consciously took up retailing as a career, rather that I drifted into it from lack of any pre-conceived idea of what I wanted to do with my life. Hours were long and pay was not of the best. Work started at eight forty-five, and the first three days of the week lasted until after seven in the evening. Thursday, being half day, finished at 1 pm, Friday around half past eight, and Saturday somewhere between nine thirty and ten at night. This left little time to get into mischief, especially as, in those days, it was incumbent on most teenagers to be home by about ten thirty. In the week before Christmas, the Shops Act, which governed the hours shops were allowed to be open for business, was suspended. This meant that shops could stay open as long as there was any business to be had. In effect, shops opened to around midnight each night, as no manager worth his salt was going to close his door before then and risk losing a sale to that fellow Bill Jones in the same line of business down the road, or missing that last inevitable customer who always seemed to knock the door just as you had given a sigh of relief and pulled down the blind. My wages in 1930 started at ten shillings per week (50p), and I was over the moon that I was getting exactly double the amount my brother had received on starting work some four years earlier.

A fair average wage for a married man bringing up a family was about three pounds a week, and this had to cover all eventualities. Few married women went out to work; indeed in many firms female employees were compelled to leave on getting married. There were none of the state maternity benefits that there are by right today, and no family allowances. Still, a house to rent, and there were many, cost some five shillings (25p) a week, while a well-built semi was about £350 to £450 to buy, a smart three-piece suit to measure thirty shillings (£1.50), while my usual Thursday treat, a trip to Nottingham on the bus, a seat at the Empire to see a top variety bill featuring maybe Max Miller, Gracie Fields, a magician, dancers, and one of the top dance bands of the time with fish and chips, bread and butter and tea afterwards before returning home would knock quite a sizeable hole in five shillings.

In the summer of 1939 a strange unease descended on the country. We had, the previous autumn, as requested, dug our air raid shelter in the back garden but, of course, it was all a bit of a giggle. It would never be needed, would it? Of course not! Meanwhile, strange young men, hard faced, earnest, and glib of tongue, invaded our market place on Sunday nights, talking of their creed. Some from the monkey run deserted their usual haunts and listened to the strange gospel they preached. They could be seen on the late bus from similar meetings in Derby, and they spread all over the Midlands from their London Headquarters, knee-booted and black-shirted, telling of the saviour, Mosley, whilst a circle of uniformed heavies surrounded the speaker and heavy thugs roamed the scanty audiences, ready to deal with any brave soul who dared to question the new creed. Glib and persuasive, they came near to carrying the day, and only a tough line by the authorities following the London marches, seemed to have prevented the Blackshirts from becoming a real menace. I wonder if the British public as it was at that time could have been swayed sufficiently by the mob oratory? What happened to the rank and file after war broke out, and the leaders were interned? Did they, like the Oxford Union, join up enthusiastically and fight for King and Country? Did they have any option? Are there still uniforms neatly folded, mouldering away in the attics at the home of many a beloved grandpa? Did they, like old soldiers, just fade away?

There were, in those pre-war streets, uniforms of a different type. Thick, heavy shoes, black flannel blazers, blanket-thick grey flannel trousers, and a jaunty (at least, that was the original idea) black beret, formed the courting plumage of the militiaman who burst forward on to the streets of Britain, determined to sweep all eligible females off their feet. For, in 1939, all males who had reached the age of twenty by 30 June were required to register for military service. Those not in vital occupations were weeded out and called up for six months service in the Regular Army, followed by three and a half years TA and reserve service. I was in the net by a few days, and expected to be called up in early 1940. I was quite looking forward to it. I would enjoy the army as it was only six months. Six months of freedom from tight parental discipline, and a chance to see something of the outside world.

For some reason which now escapes me the entire staff were in work on 3 September 1939, and we gathered in the dining room to hear the Prime Minister's speech. I was staggered. I had seen men hurrying to join their units during the past few weeks, had listened, awed, to the nightly rantings on German radio, the speeches, followed by the frightening response of 'Sieg Heil', repeated ad-infinitum by the throats of the thousands of assembled faithful. Such was my immaturity that I had never for one moment admitted the possibility of imminent war. Had not Chamberlain stated 'Peace for our time?' Hitler, of course, was only bluffing. He would never dare to take on the might of Britain with only his cardboard tanks. But he had.

So it was that, on 19 October, I was on a train bound for Sheffield, with the ultimate aim of honouring the Edmund Street Drill Hall with my presence. I had a little case with soap, towel, toothbrush, and pyjamas and I thought that, after a leisurely look round the shops in the city, I would make my way to the hall, and give the army the pleasure of my company. I needn't buy much, for in my little case reposed most of the items likely to be needed by a well brought-up young man, leaving his mama for the first time.

The train drew into the station, completely deserted except for a little turkey cock of a man, dripping with gold braid and red sashes, strutting to and fro. It is a peculiar characteristic of this type of NCO that they never ever stand still, but strut interminably up and down, up and down. As the train drew in, he ceased his ritual war dance and, facing the train, drew himself to his full height, chest expanded to twice its erstwhile circumference.

'Right you lot, get fell in, look sharp, you're in the army now. Right turn quick march, Left ri' left ri',' and we were at Edmund Street Drill Hall in less time than it takes to tell.

'Any of you that's mates and want to stay together stand over here.'

Wc huddled. He approached.

'You over here, you over there, you that way.'

I have never seen any of my travelling companions to this day.

'You join the mob for Halifax over there. Anti-tank, the suicide mob.'

'Halifax – where the hell is that? Scotland I think. Fancy going right up there?'

'Dinncr up, come and get it.'

'Baked beans? Ugh, can't eat them, I don't like 'em.'

'Now lads on this truck, look sharp.'

We were off, clinging like limpets to the framework of an ex-builder's lorry, whipping canvas, tearing wind, smarting eyes, until we arrived at Elland, the nearest we learned we were to get to Halifax until we were trained.

Attestation papers, tea (baked beans) allocation of numbers, thirty of thcm in a block, starting with 1511201 and ascending. Down to the Harold Savage Memorial Hall (I ncver did find out who Harold* was) and we laid our brand new blankets on the almost brand new parquet floor. At lights out I dithered like a blushing bride. I wanted to see what the others did. The others apparently wanted to see what I did. Someone had to make the first move. There was no rush but, next day, thirty little cases complete with unworn pyjamas were posted home to thirty doting mothers. Way back in the family tree of our Regiment loomed the figure of that grand old man, the Duke of Wellington. The 2/4th Duke of Wellington's were turned into Royal Artillery and became the 58th Anti-Tank Regiment with headquarters at the Drill Hall, Prescott Street, Halifax. At the doubling up of the TA, the 2/58th were formed at Elland, with batteries from Cleckheaton, Elland, Todmorden and Halifax, and when the 58th, on the outbreak of war, moved out, the renumbered 68th took over the Halifax stamping ground. Elland became the training cadre, which was us.

For weeks we formed threes, and drilled in the shadow of huge mills, with appreciative audiences of giggling millgirls. The route marches took us over the towering hill to Halifax. There was the well-remembered day when a young second lieutenant gave the entire cadre right turn into a pub when a heavy downpour began as we were miles from any other shelter. Then came

---

* He was the captain of the local Boys' Brigade who in 1931 agreed to build a new hall to mark his twenty-one years as company captain.

the introduction to that nasty rough game, rugby. A great exponent of the game was Sergeant Sharp, a hulking brute of a man, with shoulders like a barn door and a snarl that would have put a shark to shame. After the first time I saw him pick up one of the opposing forwards and spin him round his head before releasing him with the impetus of a 2-pounder shell I took great care to be selected for Sergeant Sharp's side when the usual auction for players went on.

Came the day when, on camp duties, I saw the cadre swing into the road at the end of the day's march, and realized that the untidy gaggle of a few weeks before had at last turned into something approaching a body of soldiers. This was due to no small measure to the advice of the local fish and chip shop proprietor, a brawny ex-matelot, who, when we complained of blistered feet, replied, 'Piss in tha boits. We alias did, en it werked.'

Had Hitler ever realized what was cooking for him in that village, he would never have slept easily in his bed again. We knew what was cooking for us; baked beans, morning, noon and night. If Mr Heinz did half as well from his other fifty-six varieties, he doubled his millions in the first weeks of the war. I came to love them. There was not much option.

In December the cadre split up and I joined the Regimental Orderly Room, piqued that I hadn't been one of the half dozen awarded lance-jack's stripes. I experienced my first taste of Yorkshire snowfalls – outsize, like most things in that great county. Used to a heavy snowfall being when the pavements were lightly sprinkled, I was amazed to find, one morning, the depth almost to my knees, and when the streets were cleared, piles nine or ten feet high at the side of the road.

As a second-line unit, we were woefully short of equipment, four guns from a complement of forty-eight, and as many 15-cwt trucks. Larger trucks had we none at all, and when the guns were sent out to each battery in turn for training, the regiment's motive power went with them. To enable mobility to be improved, the MT staff were sent off to purchase fifty secondhand cars from a scrap dealer some few miles away, at a cost of five pounds each. About ten of them didn't survive the journey back, and were abandoned where they coughed their last. The CO commandeered a Humber, the best of the bunch (it even had a cigar lighter), and the rest were divided out. They did yeoman service for the next two years or so.

In the early spring we moved to Kedleston Hall, and spent the whole of that glorious summer encamped in Nissen huts on the lawns in front of that imposing edifice. We heard on the radio of the fall of France and of the incredible miracle of Dunkirk. We became a rifle brigade for the defence of Derby, and spent hours boiling the grease out of rifles that had not seen the light of day for many years, Lee Enfields and old Canadian Ross rifles. Fortunately for Derby we were not put to the test and our two rounds per man remained in the pristine condition we received them.

The abiding memories remain of the lovely lake. One night an officer, who had wined and dined a trifle too well, misjudged the width of the drive and the following morning, the LAD had a little unforeseen exercise. They had to retrieve a large black staff car from the water where it rested after sliding down the steep side of the moat in front of the house. The other incident involved the artificer, who being 'attached' was not subject to the discipline endured by the rest of us. While we paraded, washed, shaved and correctly dressed for breakfast at seven, he still snored blissfully in his bed. At the end of the summer, patience gave way, and one autumn morning, the grass thick with hoar frost, four stalwart gunners carefully lifted his bed, complete with 'Tiffy', and carefully took it into the middle of the lake, where they lowered it until the water lapped round the springs. With one flourish they swept off the blankets and departed. Tiffy always slept the way nature intended, and all his charms were exposed to the morning frost.

From then on we infested various stately homes around the north of England. At Hutton Rudby we slept, the drone of hundreds of bombers setting out on their mission in our ears each night. We sent parties to guard vulnerable points – piers, formerly thronged with holidaymakers, aerodromes, and aerodromes under construction. At one, the guard commander coming off duty was stopped by a party of Pioneer Corps who asked him how his Bren worked. He obliged with a demonstration, dropped flat and pulled the trigger. He had a full magazine, and the safety catch was off. Some distance away, an impressed bus was parked, the 'impressed' driver sleeping the sleep of the just on the rear seat. Suddenly a row of holes was stitched from side to side, bare inches above his nose, and an immediate vacancy arose for sergeant.

In Middleham we took the place of ousted racehorses and used their stables as sleeping quarters. One day in a convoy outside Divisional HQ in Bedale, a low-flying aircraft swooped towards the earthbound troops. Enviously they cheered and waved, then dived over the sides of the vehicle when the plane opened up with all guns. A bored Luftwaffe pilot had made a solo sweep in search of a little excitement. Fortunately no one was hurt except the German when an interceptor was sent up from Leeming.

In Wolsingham, where we arrived in time to be completely snowed up for a week, an orderly officer, horrified to find the entire guard asleep in the village market place, removed the breech-blocks of the guns they were supposed to be guarding, in order to teach them a lesson. He was even more horrified the next day to find himself charged with endangering the safety of the regiment, and rendering it unable to fulfil its duties in case of need.

By this time, still short of the authorized 2-pounders, we had been equipped with French 75s and naval 6-pounders, which guns were used in various camps at Larkhill and Redesdale. Transport was also coming through and we were nearly up to strength in 15-cwts, 30-cwts and 3-tonners. We were feeling more like a regiment, and wondering when and where we might at last see action. To our horror, 270 Battery was detached complete, and sent as part of a fresh regiment, which then went out to Malaya. The deficiency was filled with a draft of 110 recruits, straight from civilian life. They were a cross section of Midlanders, aged thirty to thirty-five. To help decide how to use them, they were given a test known as Army Test FH3. Seven were unable to take the test, as they could neither read nor write.

In autumn 1941, mobilization arrived, again in part. HQ and one battery were despatched to Clacton on Sea, there to join with one regular, and two more TA battalions to form 85th Anti-Tank Regiment. We inhabited John Groom's Orphanage and Flower Girls' Home, and a prettier bunch of flowers would be hard to imagine. Hurriedly we took our embarkation leave, rushed to Colchester Barracks, where we fired the requisite number of rounds to certify us proficient in the use of rifles and light automatics. At midday on 10 November we boarded the train at Clacton Station.

Previously, on the rumour of a move to fresh pastures, it was only necessary to visit the local hostelry. There the barmaid could tell us exactly where and when we were going. This time security was complete. At every halt armed guards were posted front and rear at both sides of the train to deter anyone who might have suddenly discovered a pressing appointment elsewhere.

'York,' said one well-travelled gunner, late at night.

'Edinburgh Castle,' said another, as it loomed grey through the early morning gloom.

At ten o'clock we detrained, and formed three lines, facing a blank steel wall at the end of the huge shed in which we found ourselves.

Chapter 3

City of the Lion

'Pick up your kits. Quick march.' Good God. This is no steel wall. It's the side of a bloody great ship, and what a ship. To those of us who had spent the bulk of their lives in comfortable landlocked security, and that was most of us, it looked like the biggest ship in the whole world. We filed on board, and were detailed to the deck which was to be our home for the next nine weeks. It was 11 November, a Remembrance Day I am hardly likely to forget.

'E Deck. Where's that?'

Next day, we found out. We upped anchor shortly before midnight. They don't like to start the voyage on the 13th, was the general opinion. The ship began to creep slowly downstream in the murk, and came the thump, thump of the great propellers just below our right ear as we tried to sleep in those infernal hammocks. I grew dizzy as the bed swung gently to and fro, and eventually I deserted the sailor's friend, and bedded down on the solid deck, never to return to my hammock. Thump, thump went the propellers. We were on the lowest and farthest aft deck, just the one bulkhead between us and the interminable thump, thump, thump, thump.

'Isn't it rough,' I said. 'I think I'm going to be sick.'

'Rough be buggered,' came the reply from an old hand at this sort of thing. 'We aren't out of the bloody river yet.'

I was seconded to the ship's orderly room, and bade the E deck mob a thankful farewell. As I moved, with three others, into what had in pre-war days been a second-class cabin, it was luxury beyond compare. Our home, SS *Narkunda* was an ex-P&O liner, designed to take 300 passengers on the India and Far East run. Converted for 800 troops, she now carried 1,300 assorted troops, army and RAF, and all luxuries had been stripped out for accommodation space. The swimming pool had been removed, the ceiling-mounted fans didn't work, the iced water gave up the unequal struggle, and even the saltwater showers ran lukewarm. We heard and believed that she was only rescued from the breakers' yard by the outbreak of hostilities when every available ton was needed.

We edged into Freetown, where we swung at anchor with the tide for two days, savouring the unaccustomed sight of buildings, lights atwinkle after darkness had fallen, threw 'glasgow tanners' for the divers, Charlie and his minions, and dodged the picquets to trade with the chattering bumboat men for oranges, bananas and more revolting items piled in their unsavoury craft.

We crept on South. Crossing the line would be fun. We had all heard of the frolics of the crew when faced with poor souls who were crossing the equator for the first time. A notice appeared on the board.

THE CAPTAIN GIVES NOTICE THAT HE WILL LOOK MOST SEVERELY ON ANY UNSEEMLY BEHAVIOUR OR DEPARTURE FROM NORMAL ROUTINE ON THE OCCASION OF CROSSING NOUGHT DEGREES LATITUDE.

Oh well, it was a thought.

We knew that we were bound for the Middle East. Somewhere on board were some 300 RAF personnel, although we never saw them, as they had to be kept well away from those nasty rough army types. Someone knew someone, who knew someone, who had seen crates being swung into the hold, and those crates were marked RAF Habbaniyah (Iraq). What we didn't know, until it suddenly appeared on the information board one day, was that certain oriental gentlemen in the Pacific Ocean were playing games that were to have a decided effect on our future destination. We docked on 20 December at Durban, and stayed for three days, while the cargo was unloaded to allow segregation of our effects and those of the RAF. For three days, we were entertained right royally by the people of Durban, and we were all invited out for Christmas dinner. We set sail on 24 December, while the RAF, transferred to another vessel and went on their way – to Habbaniyah. Out of port, we dropped anchor to await the formation of the convoy, and immediately had it carried away. We spent the whole of Christmas day tied up in Durban harbour while a new anchor was fitted, unable to go ashore, and dreaming of those piled plates of rich fare that we had been invited to share.

With *Exeter* and *Emerald*, we sailed east and, on 1 January, lay at anchor in the Maldives. Joined by units of the Netherlands Indies Navy we had now more escorts than escorted. We inched up the Sundra Straits towards Singapore, the famed island of Krakatoa sliding past on the port side. The officers made our flesh creep with briefings of murder on the beaches and mayhem in the jungle as we would have to fight our way ashore. I wasn't at that time frightened of the Nips. What worried me was the thought of the ship sinking in an air raid. I had always had a pathological horror of being eaten by sharks. Then, quietly and without incident, we sailed majestically into Singapore roads. All hell broke loose.

'Everyone below decks. Air raid.' We had a reception party. For fifteen minutes we were cooped up below decks, while the sound of engines, and the spasmodic crump of anti-aircraft fire could be heard faintly from outside. After a period of silence the all clear was given, and we were marshalled on the deck by our boat stations as we approached the quay. Fleets of the soon familiar little minibuses met us and we were transported to Birdwood Camp, a palm-thatched, wood-built encampment in the Changi area. Smiling Malay cooks dished out cups of hot sweet tea made with condensed milk. It was nectar and the taste can be remembered yet.

Contrary to expectation, the war still seemed far away on that 13th day of January, and there was no sense of urgency, no panic, no feeling that the end of an epoch was at hand, or that only a few miles beyond Johore, the bloodiest battles were being fought, with men dying in thousands before their lives had properly begun. In the next few days we were issued our little bits of paper, and made our little telephone calls. Each evening we relaxed in the NAAFI at Roberts Barracks, or revelled in the peaceful air-conditioned luxury of the little Changi Cinema. On days off, a custom which was immediately introduced, we visited Singapore, inspected Change Alley, sampled the delights of the Great World, or the culinary excellence of the Union Jack Club. Raffles Hotel was out of bounds to other ranks.

After one such trip I was introduced to the 'proper way to treat 'em'. After we had had our fill of Singapore, we went to catch the bus back to Changi. It arrived, and a swarm of Malays, Indians and Chinese descended and filled the vehicle to overflowing. We stood dismayed. A little sergeant walked by, and enquired what we wanted. We told him we couldn't get a seat, and he turned to face the packed vehicle. His chest expanded and his face turned red. Two or three words in a foreign tongue exploded out, and the effect was electrifying. Bodies poured out of the bus in every direction and, before his bosom had completely subsided, the chariot was empty.

'Get in,' he said, and we meekly complied. He spoke again, and the motley throng re-entered, clung to the step, and crowded the driver in his cab. The babble all the way back was incessant, but fortunately we couldn't speak a word of Malay.

Days passed, but still the purpose for which we had come to Singapore remained unfulfilled. We had hit a snag. When the equipment had been reloaded in Durban, it had been packed in the bottom hold, and thousands of tons of other stores had been loaded on top. Included with these was a tremendous amount of ammunition and explosives, and these the authorities flatly refused to have in the docks. The consequence was that the vessel was forced to lay some half a mile or so offshore, and the cargo was off-loaded by lighter, a slow and laborious process. Meanwhile we fretted for action that would not come, and kicked our heels in Birdwood Camp. Our greatest crime was to be caught at night with our hideous knickerbockers still buttoned up into shorts, Instead of tucked into our hose tops. The sand-fly and mosquito were far more dangerous than the little yellow man rapidly approaching from the north.

I slept on an Indian *charpoy*, my first acquaintance with one of those instruments of torture.

'Heat lumps,' said the MO when I reported sick with strange red blotches over my entire body, and I obediently applied the calomine lotion he supplied. The rash persisted. Then one morning I awoke early to find little brown beetles commuting home from work to the top corners of the mosquito net. I investigated. There were dozens of them, and catching one between finger and thumb, I pressed hard. There was a soft 'plop', leaving blood on my fingers, and an overpowering musty smell vaguely reminiscent of almonds. It was my first brush with bed bugs, which I found in every nook and cranny of the strings of the bed. I never slept on it again and my heat lumps were cured.

The front line was nearing Johore when sufficient guns and equipment were at last brought ashore to equip one troop of four guns and send them into action. They set up their positions, and prepared for battle, only to find that they were completely surrounded and cut off. Nothing for it but to destroy the guns and transport and to take to the jungle to find a way round. Eventually, dirty, tired, and ragged, they reached the coast, where they were picked up by a naval patrol and returned to Singapore.

The regiment had by this time moved south from Birdwood camp to positions in the rubber, already occupied by the Manchesters. They had not yet been in action, but were held in reserve for the defence of Singapore. Our own scruffy, bedraggled men arrived, were debriefed, and went off to the canteen in search of a much needed beer. The following day a signal was received from the CO of the Manchesters:

> IT HAS COME TO MY NOTICE THAT MEN OF YOUR UNIT
> HAVE BEEN USING THE CANTEEN WHILST IMPROPERLY
> DRESSED. IF THIS IS REPEATED IT WILL BE NECESSARY TO
> PLACE THE CANTEEN OUT OF BOUNDS TO ALL RANKS.

We withdrew south to Payer Lebar where we took up positions in the centre of the village. We had sufficient equipment to send several more troops up country, but in Singapore, life was still peaceful. We sent our KDs (khaki drill uniforms) to the local Chinese laundry, and Raffles Hotel was still out of bounds to all other ranks. A constant stream of Malays and Chinese flitted through the camp in all directions, and the interpreter gave up the unequal struggle of attempting to check who and what they were.

One day, I saw a figure from a bygone age, straight from the pages of history, when, from one of the houses, an old woman emerged, tottering as if on stilts, on high platform shoes. Her feet were only a few inches long, the result of infant binding, a Chinese practice that I thought had died out years before. She turned and went back into the house, and I was suddenly back in the twentieth century. I never saw her again.

At regular intervals, the bombers came over, usually flights of twenty-seven in 'vics' of three. We knew they were coming even before the air-raid warning, for it was usual to see the Buffalo fighters take off and head south before the enemy came in sight. Then the twenty-seven came over, a flash was seen from the leading plane, and all the planes then dropped their bombs together.

'Why the hell don't they ever bomb Fort Canning?' 'Don't be daft. Their best hope of winning the war is to leave that intact. Fort Canning was the pre-war headquarters of Singapore Base District but had been taken over as General Percival's Command Post.

Wavell flew in. Wavell flew out. The impact of his visit was not noticed at all, save for the order of the day he left behind him. It concluded 'It will be a lasting disgrace if we yield this, our boasted island fortress'.

We were exhorted to fight to the last man and the last round. The message from Fort Canning took a different view.

> IT HAS BEEN BROUGHT TO MY NOTICE THAT PERSONNEL
> HAVE BEEN SEEN IN MILITARY VEHICLES WITHOUT
> HATS. THIS PRACTICE WILL CEASE FORTHWITH. ALL
> PERSONNEL WILL BE PROPERLY DRESSED AT ALL TIMES.

Raffles Hotel was still out of bounds to all other ranks. Meanwhile the bloody fight in Johore continued without respite. Losses piled up as weary troops, many raw or half-trained, struggled to contain an enemy with the scent of victory in his nostrils. Famous units were decimated, reformed, amalgamated, and decimated again. The Indians, untrained and unfit in many cases to take the field, fought gallantly, and the Australians, when they knew what their objective was, were lacking neither in valour nor application.

'Hurricanes come to save Singapore,' trumpeted the *Singapore Times* in banner headlines. It was a bid to raise morale, but too late. A few got into the air, but had not been adapted or tuned to local conditions. They proved unequal to the Japanese, and failed to make any significant impression on the war. After the capitulation, it was said that some were still crated up on the dockside where they had been unloaded, and still intact. By the end of January, there was no air force left in Malaya, planes and personnel having been withdrawn to carry on the fight from further back.

The tattered remnants of the retreating Allied forces were scrambling back into Fortress Singapore and, then on 31 January, the rearguard, flag flying and pipes skirling, marched over the causeway, and figuratively pulled up the drawbridge. A dull explosion was heard, when a gap was blown in the causeway, and, the land link with Malaya having been destroyed, we felt, like a host of little pigs, we were safe in our house of straw. Poor little pigs. If only we had known.

The garrison prepared to defend this last stronghold. Sectors facing the sea and the enemy were allocated to British, Australian and Indian divisions, and a grim waiting game began. Even the imperturbable elite of Singapore realized that, at last, this was the real thing, but Raffles Hotel was still out of bounds to other ranks. Except perhaps to one, the regimental mystery man.

We first crossed paths in November, the previous year. The regiment was in Clacton on Sea, fully mobilized and ready to leave for a destination reputed to be in the Middle East. Preparations were complete, all embarkation leave had been taken, when, suddenly, a last-minute posting, Private Maurice Williams, as I may perhaps call him, a name sufficiently like his own to make no difference.

He was re-mustered as gunner, and hurriedly despatched on leave. He returned only days before we moved out to Glasgow, and to the boat. He himself professed to have no idea why he had been sent so hurriedly to a unit moving immediately abroad, and we had no inkling of why he had been sent. If the Colonel knew, he didn't divulge it.

Maurice had previously been in one of the new radio location units, and the general opinion among the cognoscenti was that he had had pre-war business contacts in Germany among the Nazis, was suspected of being a security risk, and had been moved from the highly secret unit as a security measure. There were no vacancies in the batteries, or for that matter in RHQ, so he was attached to BHQ as a supernumerary.

We went abroad with Gunner Williams virtually unemployed. He was a tall, slim, languid young man, obviously expensively educated, and professing an address just off Park Lane with directorship in some of the country's larger companies. Unlike the majority of his companions in the other ranks he had no photographs, or if he had he never showed them to others. The nearest I ever came to seeing his private life was half a photograph cut from a magazine, which showed a restaurant table or night club, and seated was a striking dark-haired woman. All other people had been carefully cut away. This, he informed me, was his wife.

No battledress of rough khaki decorated his slim frame, instead he wore uniform of well-cut material similar to that sported by officers, though perhaps better fitting. We shared a cabin on the *Narkunda* by dint of a little wire pulling and palm greasing but at night, though the other three occupants often lay on their bunks, reading or chatting, Maurice was never there. He would return after lights out, and to a query of 'Where have you been all night?' would rejoin, 'Oh, up on C Deck,' which was a deck out of bounds to the hoi polloi, and reserved for officers.

'It's a wonder they haven't told you to come back down to your proper level,' I remarked once when he returned late one night. 'I wouldn't consider them to be gentlemen if they did,' was his only reply,

In Singapore, similarly, he spent all his free time in Raffles, possibly the only gunner to have done so in the history of the place, and never once was he asked to leave.

In Singapore, he was at last allocated duties, as CO's bodyguard, and whenever the Colonel went out in his armoured car Maurice was there, head poking through the turret, Bren at the ready. Before he left, he turned over to me his valuables for safe keeping: gold pen, gold rings, gold lighter and gold cigarette case, in addition to other sundry knick-knacks. I used to look at this small fortune and hope, but no, he always returned at night.

In the last days the regiment withdrew from Payer Lebar, and set up battle headquarters in Shaw Brothers' studio on the outskirts of the city. We had been on the island a little over three weeks and, even at this late date, reinforcements were still arriving for the beleaguered garrison.

It is futile to discuss the rights and wrongs of the night of 8 February when Nips gained a foothold on the island. Many excellent accounts have been written by men much more capable than I to discuss what actually went wrong. Suffice to say that the landing was made in force on the Australian sector and we withdrew to 'prepared positions'.

'To put you in the picture,' said Lawrence Turner, the Intelligence Officer. 'The Japs have gained a foothold, and we are retiring to positions as planned.'

'We are holding a line – '

'Retiring as planned – '

'Holding – '

'Fierce fighting – '

'Retiring as planned – '

And with his 'picture' completed in his clipped, pedantic voice, he would tuck his swagger stick under his arm, and march briskly back to his office, unflappable, and looking as if he had just stepped out of a bandbox.

There were bloody battles at Payer Lebar, the Racecourse, Bukit Timah and the tide of battle ebbed and flowed, but inexorably we were squeezed back to the city limits. Two of our men, who for reasons best known to themselves, went to Changi behind the Jap lines, reported on their return that the whole area was completely deserted, and that they had not heard or seen a living soul. Piles of food and ammunition were lying around intact. All the action was in the south and the west.

We moved half a mile from the Studio, and set up our mobile Orderly Room in the grounds of a Chinese house. The racket of the holocaust drew nearer. Every second was filled with the sound of big guns, the rattle of small arms, the boom of mortars, the perpetual spotter planes, and the lazy rushing noise of shells passing overhead. We took refuge in the monsoon drain as the spotter approached, machine guns kicking up puffs of dust from the unmetalled roads. The horizon was filled with the smoke of burning buildings.

The reservoirs passed into Jap hands, and the taps, already depleted by previous damage, gave up the struggle to yield precious water at all.

As dusk fell, we motley collection of cooks, clerks and batmen, wended our way to the top of a small hill overlooking the area. We had previously dug slit trenches in the position, and we settled down for the night for a twelve-hour guard. The crunch was at hand, and we wondered idly if we would still be alive to see the dawn.

Hundreds died that night, but the expected attack on our position never materialized, and, cold and stiff, we went down the hill to breakfast.

Chapter 4

Changi

Our first job in Changi was to sort out what was left of the unit, and to prepare nominal rolls showing those in captivity, those missing or killed in battle, and to send the completed lists to Divisional HQ. We had still the full echelon operating, and it appeared that we were to be allowed to operate as before. We began to settle into our new surroundings. Cooking was done on army field kitchens, for a day or so fired by petrol. They were soon converted to wood, and forage parties went out to find the precious material, which was stockpiled and issued to units on a daily basis.

The blowing of the causeway had also cut the pipeline from Johore Bahru, and this meant that the toilets were not working. Boreholes were sunk in the sacred Changi lawns. Washing was less of a problem. We were only a few yards from the sea, and we went down morning and night in organized parties. From here we could see the ships passing through the straits into the naval dockyard nearby. For the first few weeks a concentrated stream of ambulances passed in and out of camp, bringing wounded from the various hospitals, and we had the thrill of renewing acquaintances with many we had given up for dead. We had to evacuate our comfortable quarters to enable the hospital to be enlarged, and move to an open space nearby where we were accommodated in tents. The Australian ambulance drivers did a thriving trade in black market cigarettes and other little luxuries, and brought tales of atrocities on the civilian population in the city, of heads lining the streets, and Chinese being taken to the beaches, there to be tied in groups with barbed wire, sent into the sea, and machine gunned down.

I took the opportunity one day of visiting the dump where we had had to store our surplus kit shortly after arriving on the island. It was a shambles, and the 'vultures' had already stripped it clean. All I managed to find among the debris were a few personal letters. A few days later I accidentally knocked a pith helmet from the bed of the man sleeping next to me. As I apologized and picked it up I noticed the name and number inside. It was my own. That was the only item of stray kit I ever saw again.

All food was collected in as soon as we reached Changi and put into divisional stores, from where it was allocated to units on a daily basis. Biscuits and canned food lasted only a few days, and then the Japanese began to issue rice rations. This was our first acquaintance with the food that was to be our staple diet for the next three and a half years, and the result was astonishing. Our urge to urinate rose spectacularly, but the complementary bodily function disappeared completely. Twice a day we would visit the boreholes by the Changi cinema and squat there for half an hour or more without result. Going through the motions without the motions so to speak. 'Have you been yet,' became the standard greeting. MOs were inundated with requests for number nines (laxative), but most were refused, the MOs saying that the system would adjust itself in time. In about a couple of weeks, the maladjustment had indeed righted itself, while the 'record' as far as I know was forty-one days. It is one of life's little ironies that the record holder would in less than twelve months succumb to dysentery.

Our new campsite was quite near to Changi village which, at this time, was still inhabited by the original occupants, Malays and Chinese. Rumour had it that one young lady of generous nature was still making a comfortable living accommodating the PoWs, many of whom had gone into captivity with a considerable wallet tucked away. The village also provided a convenient point of trading with the outside world, now that the daily trips of the ambulances were tailing off. We were almost all ensconced in British Army tents and had made ourselves fairly comfortable. In the corner of the camp area was an empty Chinese house, which was converted into officers' quarters and Medical Inspection room. Here the incorrigible MO busied himself with attempts to fabricate ersatz whisky from a variety of most improbable raw materials, sweet potatoes, rice, and anything else which came readily to hand. His experiments continued for the whole of the time that we were there but, as far as I know, nothing even remotely potable ever resulted. Far from his being disheartened, the failures only increased his enthusiasm and he pressed on.

All this time we had been totally ignored by the Japanese. They were still acutely embarrassed by the sheer physical size of their haul, and were still checking the amount of loot left to them in Singapore. As for us, they seemed to be considering just what they could do with us and how they should deal with the teeming city of Singapore. The camp, up to this point unmarked and unguarded, was being encircled with dannert wire by working parties of our own troops, who erected gates and staked out the perimeter.

Eventually, when this was finished, a body of Sikhs, the majority of whom had thrown in their lot with the Japanese, took over guard duties, standing sentry at the gates and patrolling the wire. They were not in the least popular with the licentious soldiery, who took every opportunity to taunt them with what was universally regarded as their lack of 'loyalty'. It was required of us that every time we crossed a road from one part of the cage to another we should punctiliously salute these Sikhs, and this did not go down too well, especially with the officers, who went to great pains to avoid a meeting with them. As the main cookhouse was in the old sector, they began to have their meals sent in instead of crossing the wire. When the cage was complete, the interminable ceremonies of 'lining the route' began and lasted for a week or two. Almost every other day, we were required to stand on both sides of the main roads from Singapore, facing into the centre. For hour upon hot hour, we would stand there in the blazing sun, long lines of khaki stretching into the distance either way. From time to time we would be brought to attention as the word came down that the convoy was approaching, only to relax again as it was found to be another false alarm. The sun beat down. Eventually, for the final time, we would stand for attention, and would rigidly face the front, staring into space. A convoy of staff cars would sweep slowly and majestically through, each packed tight with bespectacled, golden beaming Japanese officers, all bestarred and red tabbed, gloating over the fallen might of the despicable British Empire. Usually the convoy included a movie camera or two, so presumably our handsome faces illuminated the gloom of many a Nipponese fleapit in the old country. During the two or three weeks that this ritual continued, we must have been inspected by every field officer in the hemisphere, and I strongly suspect that many of them came back for a second, and even third showing.

Meanwhile, we had established a tolerable routine. After a breakfast of boiled rice the morning was spent in various fatigues, cleaning, collecting firewood, digging latrines and other such tasks. Lunch was again boiled rice, with the addition of a weak stew, or perhaps a spoonful of boiled fish or corned beef to help it down. After dinner we endured a period of 'compulsory rest' until tea-time, tea being a somewhat similar meal to the midday meal.

We were now observing Tokyo time and, shortly after six in the evening, darkness fell with the tropical suddenness to which we had become accustomed. The transition from daylight to darkness was all but unmarked by any period of twilight, and the variation in the time of nightfall varied so little throughout the year as to be almost imperceptible. We had for the most part no artificial light after dark but found that the brilliant moon gave quite enough light to be able to read out of doors without undue strain, or to be able to play cards in comfort. Otherwise, from tea to lights out at ten o'clock, we would sit in groups talking. All around was the hum of insects while from the swamp behind the camp would come the sound of the symphony orchestra, which was provided intermittently by the bullfrogs. After a period of quiet, one lone bass voice would call tentatively, another answer and more join in, till the swelling crescendo of croaks almost made conversation impossible. Then silence would fall and the whole performance would start again.

Our main trouble was boredom, finding something to occupy our minds after the morning chores were over. One afternoon we were playing what we fondly imagined to be bridge, for most of us had a pack of cards, when I became aware of the Intelligence Officer, a county player of some repute, standing behind me, engrossed in the play. Obviously wanting to be put 'in the picture,' he enquired pleasantly.

'Looks a good game. What do you call it?'

'Bridge, Sir!'

'Good God. Is it?'

He spent the next two or three afternoons teaching us the rudiments of the game, and many times over the next few years I gave thanks to him silently.

Most card games, especially the army varieties, cannot sustain interest for long without the aid of a cash incentive, and this we certainly could not supply. Bridge has its own, inbuilt, interest and we spent long hours whenever we could safely do so with this game, which helped to keep us sane. The Japs seemed to have a pathological hatred of the game. To them all cards were the hated bridge and many times, when playing patience or rummy, the cards were swept to the ground by a passing Jap, screaming 'No bridge, no bridge!'

Cards were not a sufficiency in themselves and other interests had to be found to keep our minds active. Classes of all sorts were started and anyone who had the slightest knowledge of a subject was pressed into service as an instructor. I was pressed to pass on my schoolboy French to some dozen devotees and classes were begun in almost any imaginable subject. Some, like my language laboratory, took only a few days to peter out.

From those that succeeded grew the Changi University.

Other prisoners who had a leaning towards amateur theatricals joined forces with those who had had actual experience and, in no time, concert parties and plays were in full swing. Although the various units each had their own camp theatres, intercommunication was quite free and posters advertising the various productions were displayed at vantage points around the camps. Sufficient musicians had retained their instruments to enable several orchestras to be formed. Several of these instruments were later carried laboriously the length and breadth of Thailand and the Far East, and provided hours of priceless entertainment. I once saw, in the mountains of Thailand, where all kit had to be carried on one's back or left behind, a soldier staggering under the weight of a large piano accordion. It was not his own. It belonged to his best friend, killed in action, and he was determined to hang on to it, allow it to be played whenever the occasion arose, although he himself could not play a note, and to return it eventually to England and the family of his friend.

The weather was kind to us. Singapore has an even, warm climate with no overabundance of really heavy rain. Most downfalls were seized on with delight as an opportunity to have a shower and a rubdown with the soap which, at that time, was still well in evidence. Serious sickness was negligible, the most prevalent being dengue, a highly virulent but not fatal fever, known as sand-fly fever, and a fungoid growth between the toes, which rejoiced in the name of 'Singapore Foot'. Malaria and dysentery were not yet the menace that they became in later months; indeed at this time they were fortunately quite rare.

Diet was uninspiring, monotonous but just bearable. The only possible permutation was to supplement the food with one of the coconuts borne in clusters on the palms that dotted the camp area. Officially, these were regimental property, as the officers had been quick to spot the possibilities of these toothsome morsels, and the nuts had been placed 'out of bounds' to unauthorized personnel. To be caught with one was a court martial offence. In spite of this, there was no lack of daring night raids and the sight of discarded husks in the morning bore witness to the number of nuts that had vanished the previous night.

Now that the camp was completely wired, contact with Singapore was virtually cut off, but items of food and precious soap could still be obtained via the daring spirits who crept out through the wire at night, and visited the local Malay village. In addition to visits to the 'lovely' maiden there, who still carried on the oldest profession, the seeds of the soon to be thriving black market were sown. One group of entrepreneurs was discovered in full swing by the Japanese and carted away. A few days later they were returned unharmed, with the remark that as it was the first offence they would not be shot – this time.

A few sporadic attempts were made to escape, and some got over the Straits of Johore and on to the mainland. As far as we knew, all were soon recaptured and returned to Changi. However, our deceptively peaceful existence was fast coming to the end. The Japanese, having recovered from their embarrassment at the rich prize that had fallen into their hands, were now ready to consolidate and to start re-organization in and around the city. For this they needed labour and, in March, an advance party was sent to Singapore to prepare the way for a larger contingent.

In early April we paraded, 300 strong, to march back along the road we had traversed two months before. We had to carry our own belongings this time and we waited at the wire for the 'poached egg' (probably a permit) without which we could not leave the camp. Eventually we set off, our heavy kit swollen by numerous articles scrounged in true army style during our stay in Changi. Along the road on either side were nondescript dwellings which had been knocked up from a variety of materials; wood, corrugated iron, canvas, many bearing improvised name plates: 'Journey's End' and similar names. Out of the cantonment we swung, past Birdwood Camp, now a charred and derelict shadow of its former self, and on past the newly-formed military cemetery, already containing an alarming number of graves in neat, orderly rows. The road, weeds already growing over the sides, looked forlorn and neglected. Past Changi jail, faces at the bars, faces of the civilian internees who were now interned in the squat ugly building.

A halt was called.

'Fall out and make yourselves comfortable. The Nips are providing transport from here.'

The transport proved to be a small fleet of British Army vehicles and we were soon bowling in style through the streets of the city, now free of debris and looking surprisingly tidy and spruce. Our destination was a hutted camp on River Valley Road, one of several built to house the expected hordes of refugees, which in the event never materialized. The place was completely derelict. The advance party was already in occupation of the central block and we were housed in another line of huts, rather like the tail of a letter L, near the Great World amusement park and fronted by a street of Chinese houses.

A working party was actually in the process of wiring us off from the street and from the Singapore River with great coils of dannert wire. Those lucky enough to have cash took advantage of the temporary lack of security to visit the houses and enter into spirited trading, while the rest of us sat on our packs and gloomily watched them as they tucked into hot fresh crusty rolls and golden yellow butter. Our stomachs rebelled noisily.

Chapter 5

River Valley Road

In contrast to our Changi billet, the camp that was to be our home for the next six months or so seemed to be quite luxurious. The site on which it was built ran alongside the dank and noisome Singapore river and was bordered on the other side by streets of Chinese-occupied bungalows. It was more or less L-shaped, with a central square around which all available space was crammed with wooden, attap roofed huts. Attap, the universal roofing material of the tropics, consists of palm leaves bent over a bamboo strip and lightly stitched together. A strip of attap really consists of a makeshift tile some two feet in length. The roof timbers consist usually of thin bamboo poles and when the attap strips are attached to these poles they overlap every few inches and, if properly done, form a waterproof cover even against the torrential rain experienced in the tropics. In most of the camps we occupied the attap had been skimped with the result that water dripped everywhere, but in the River Valley it was adequate.

Apart from the roof the remainder of the huts frames and sides – were of good timber and solidly constructed. They were about 150-feet long with open doorways at each end and a gangway running the whole length down the centre. On each side of this were shelves some six-feet wide, one a foot or so above ground level and another about six feet up, and reached by a series of wooden ladders at intervals along the huts. The lower one had thus enough room to sit comfortably but not quite enough to stand upright, whilst the upper was a little less roomy. The stampede was to claim a bed on the lower berth. Too late, the snags were discovered – the main one being that each time one of the upper élite moved the unfortunate occupant of the lower berth was covered in a shower of fine dust.

Another unwelcome bonus was the nightly visitation of bed bugs, which quickly became a plague. They would drop with a soft 'plop' on the bare flesh of the lower occupant and as fingers, probing for the predator in the dark, made contact the soft, bloated body would burst and then would come the all-pervading acrid almond smell always associated with the pest. I imagine we carried them into camp with us and they, finding the conditions much to their liking, quickly multiplied. Others swore that they had been hiding in the cracks in the woodwork for months, anxiously awaiting our arrival.

There were at first no roads in camp and the hard-baked earth between the huts was turned into ankle-deep mud by every rainstorm. Later, duckboards were made and put down to obviate this nuisance. Water was laid on from the mains, but the pipes were of very small bore and the farther from the main gate, the lower the pressure. We had one tap to serve several huts, both for washing and drinking and, at popular times, our supply being farthest away died with a sigh, after which apologetic murmurs and gurglings were all that could be obtained. There was no artificial light, so at the perpetual six thirty nightfall considerable ingenuity was employed to lighten our darkness. A variety of oil lamps were fabricated from bottles, jars, boot polish tins and other containers. Thanks to them the huts were filled with an oily, smoky, choking fog, picked out with small pinpoints of light. By these we attempted to play cards or read. On moonlit nights it was far easier to read out of doors, for the moonlight in the clear air was bright enough to read even the smallest print.

In the first few days we were able, with the general consent of the sentry, to slip across the road to the Chinese houses, the first of which had set up as a kind of corner shop. Bargain lines of corned beef, condensed milk, tins of jam, and tiny fresh bread rolls were amongst the items always available. I had almost forgotten the sheer delight of biting into hot crusty bread thickly spread with butter. Hordes of itinerant sellers would throng the outside of the wire and brisk trade was carried on through the barricades. To all this the sentry would turn a benevolent blind eye, for perhaps a couple of hours or more, then for no apparent reason, perhaps it was near the time for a change of guard, he would leave his post and charge wildly, rifle butt flailing, swiping indiscriminately at British and Chinese alike, even knocking some of the unfortunate traders half senseless. The enterprising merchants, if they managed to escape the onslaught, would flee in all directions and peace would descend. After a few weeks wire trading was strictly forbidden and no more visits to the little 'shop' took place.

Meanwhile, in camp we were being grounded in basic army drill and Japanese words of command. *Kiotske* – Attention, *Kire* – Salute, *Kashila Migi* – Eyes Right, *Nowori* – Eyes centre, and many more. Quite the most favourite, and one which remained top of the hit parade for years, was *YASUME*, which meant 'stand at ease' or 'rest'. On parade, we at first numbered off in English but the nasty suspicious Japanese mind, always on the lookout for mickey taking, seemed to think that in the British Army the numbers eight nine and ten were not usually followed by Jack, Queen and King. We were ordered to learn Japanese numbers and to number off in Japanese. This did not come easily, as it was difficult to achieve the staccato, machine-gun pace required of us. As a temporary expedient, men learned one number only and the same men stood in the same position on the front row each day. Honour was satisfied on both sides.

Eventually we were considered smart enough to represent the Japanese outside camp, and one morning we were marched out to make our acquaintance with the field which achieved immortality as the 'Cabbage Patch'. This was to become some sort of Jap HQ and, prior to the commencement of building operations, a large quantity of sand was to be accumulated as one of the basic materials. There was plenty of this all over the city in the form of the now unrequired sandbags that had protected various public and other important buildings. As the war was now over and Japanese rule was to last for a thousand years there was no longer any need for such precautions. We found at the cabbage patch a fleet of new two-wheeled carts and we were lined up with these, ten or so to a cart, and spent the next couple of hours learning how to handle them to the Japanese satisfaction. We dressed, redressed, marched, and wheeled till we were dizzy, so that we could indulge the Japanese passion for ritual, with its attendant yelling, shouting and show of authority. At last, the 'Shoko' arrived, and we were passed worthy to haul the glorified trek carts through the streets of the city. The River Valley Construction Co. was in business.

For the first few days, we worked at a municipal estate, comprising tall blocks of flats, at Tiong Bahru, where we loaded sand from now defunct air-raid shelters. The carts loaded, 'Yasume' was announced, and the prisoners went on the scrounge. Some disappeared into the flats, where they were entertained to tea and refreshments, whilst those outside were no less well treated. Tins of corned beef, milk, jam, portions of cheese and other delicacies were thrown down from the upper windows and scrambled for in the dust, a not particularly edifying spectacle. Sense of pride seemed to die during those weeks, and the Japanese guards would stand impassively and stare at the spectacle of the high and mighty white man descending to animal depths, their thoughts masked in their heavy lidded amber eyes.

Meanwhile, at various doorways smiling orientals appeared with trays loaded with tit-bits of food and cups of steaming tea. It didn't take long before it became known where this was likely to happen, and hardly had the shout of 'Yasume' died away before a shoving, bustling queue had formed at the doorways.

As the eats appeared, the queue would shuffle forward, each man taking a cup of tea and something to eat, and then moving to the back of the line in case there might be a second helping. This continued until the supplies ran out, when a yell from the Jap in charge would send us scurrying to take up our positions with the trucks, to return to the cabbage patch to unload. Two trips per morning and two per afternoon.

When the sand at the flats ran out, we moved farther afield, calling at various private houses, or at the General Hospital where all blast walls and air-raid shelters were being removed, and already a fresh coat of glistening white paint was replacing the sombre camouflage grey and black. One private house we visited belonged to the millionaire proprietor of the famous 'Tiger Balm' and at 'Yasume' time we were invited into the exquisitely furnished house, there to be served china tea with slices of lemon in delicate china cups.

All this time, we were only one of many labour battalions at work all over the city. Others were on such tasks as clearing up the damage caused in the recent battle, helping to extend the municipal airport which was being pushed out into the sea, or preparing and building the Japanese War Memorial at Bukit Timah. By and large, the discipline was free and easy and the guards were commonly accepted as 'decent Nips'. We had now come to appreciate that the Japanese referred to their country as Nippon, and they were Nipponese, usually known as 'Nips'. The alteration of the name Singapore, to 'Syonan' was one alteration that was never accepted by us.

By far the most profitable of the many jobs was that of clearing out the huge waterfront godowns, as the warehouses were called in the local dialect, and competition was fierce for a place on these parties. Workers were transported by lorry to and from the dock area and the 'perks' which began to trickle back to camp with them soon became a flood, whole cases of food even, being smuggled in. Most went undetected, but one lieutenant, who was unlucky enough to be caught with a water bottle full of sugar, received savage treatment. This unfortunate officer was later accidentally killed when he fell from a moving truck in the centre of Singapore, but the two incidents were not connected.

The classic story was told of a Nip, ordered to stop the pilfering in his command, who put a tin of condensed milk in the centre of an otherwise bare godown floor and covered it with his cap. He then settled down to wait out of sight of the door so that he could catch anyone who tried to remove the milk. Two hours later, he decided to give up his vigil and retrieved his cap, only to find that the milk was no longer there (This was, to the best of my belief, an original story. In 1979, reading a book on the early days of the railways, an identical story was quoted, dated in the middle 1800s.)

Much of the food went straight to the cookhouse to help give variety to the issued rations, but other items of a strictly non-food variety stayed with those who had 'won' it and 'shop' was opened after tea. The loot was all put on sale, and the sight in the battalion working on a 'good' job reminded one of a Woolworth store, without entirely losing sight of Fortnum and Masons. Perhaps the most energetic of all were the Malayan Volunteers, an organization similar to the British Territorial Army, and formed from the planters and businessmen of Malaya. Their knowledge of the ground and, usually, their command of the Malayan and/or Chinese dialects gave them a great advantage in locating and bartering for the goodies available. On entry to their hut at night you were assailed by a babble of noise and blinded by unaccustomed light. Most things were on sale in the 'shops'. There was a tobacconist, with dozens of brands of cigars and native cigarettes. These were usually packed in paper, the cover bearing a representation, or perhaps a misrepresentation, of well-known English brands. I once started to make a collection of various brand packets, rather in the manner of a stamp collection, but lost interest when the total grew to over 100. There was a chemist with an elaborate hand-painted sign, 'I buy and sell all kinds of drugs'. Grocers and confectioners were too numerous to count. There was even an enterprising laundry, with the motto, 'Persil whiteness guaranteed', and a range of tariffs depending on whether or not the customer provided his own soap. Small cafes and itinerant vendors dispensed a liquid from four-gallon cans, still redolent of the gasoline they had recently contained, steaming hot and described as 'hot, sweet and milky'. This was usually paraphrased as 'hot, sweet and filthy' by those unlucky enough to try it out. Other huts had different ranges of merchandise on sale, ranging from fresh bananas and pineapples, legitimately purchased by Johore working parties, to cosmetics, books, articles of clothing, sugar and a host of other items. During our stay in River Valley, the prices rose inexorably as stocks ran down in the city and, as Singapore was gradually stripped bare, the plethora of merchandise faltered and vanished from sight. In the camp itself conditions gradually improved during the year. A system of drainage leading into the river had been dug and a network of duckboards had been laid, so that the recurrent problem of ankle-deep mud was eliminated.

More water pipes had been run in and banks of showers and wash points had already been established at various points in the camp, but the old problem of small bore pipes still meant that you were likely to be left high and dry, just when you had liberally lathered yourself under one of the showers. It was better to sneak out after lights out and risk the wrath of the guards for a shower in peace.

Many English books, picked up by working parties, had found their way into camp and those who had not been able to lay their hands on any had been able to swap or purchase copies, so that attention was turned towards the formation of a camp library. A special hut was allotted to serve this purpose and the building was also in constant use for debates, lectures and exhibitions of one kind or another. One of the most popular was an Ideal Home Exhibition in which we were asked to submit our ideas of the type of place we would like to have on returning home. Some excellent plans were forthcoming. As for the library, we had to deposit a minimum of two books, and were then allowed to withdraw one book per week. A wide range of literature was available, but most people at this time tended towards the lightest of tastes and the lighter works of fiction were always hard to find, being usually all out on loan.

Several debating societies were formed and there was no lack of enthusiastic debaters on a wide variety of subjects. Lectures were also arranged and most huts had at least one lecture per week, subjects ranging from 'Cricket and cricketers', 'The history of the London Buses', 'Customs of Malaya', 'The Malayan Campaign', 'The History of Japan', 'Life in the Colonial Service' to 'How I escaped from Singapore'. Obviously the last speaker hadn't quite.

Concerts, which began shakily, were soon in full swing, with several good and well-established turns. They were originally given on makeshift stages in the huts, but as the Nips objected to the noise near the main roads, the venue gradually narrowed, till at last an empty hut in the centre of the camp was turned into the River Valley Theatre. Admission to the shows was allocated to various sections of our camp, and another camp that had been established across the river at Havelock Road, by rota, to enable everyone to see them. A repertory theatre was also established, under the guidance of Major Jim Swanton, and the first two plays were rapturously received. I had just finished typing the scripts for the first major production, 'Outward Bound,' when my own stay at River Valley came to an end. Whether it ever reached production, I never knew.

Many of us made our first acquaintance with the game of bridge and, with the installation of electric light in July and August, bridge schools sprang up everywhere, and camp tournaments were organized. The official allocation of light was two per hut, and the more scrupulously conscientious battalions hardly ever exceeded ten 'bootleg' lights, unlike the Australians, who had soon fixed up an over-bed light to every bunk. The lights would build up to a peak as more and more men brought back bulbs and cable that they had scrounged until, at last, the sorely overloaded system would break down, plunging the entire camp into stygian darkness. Then a purge by the outraged Nips resulted in a hurried reversion to the norm of two lights per hut for a few days. Chaos reigned on average once a fortnight.

All internal administration was carried out by ourselves. Camp HQ consisted of a Camp Commandant and a Camp Adjutant, who acted as liaison officers with the Japanese. We had an excellent interpreter who smoothed over many an awkward incident and defused many an explosive situation. We had an Admin Battalion, concerned with the collection and distribution of rations, camp bakery, hygiene, sanitation, drainage and the like. In turn, each battalion had its own admin party, comprising of batmen, clerks, sanitary orderlies, cooks etc. At least, that was how it started out, but the staffs were subjected to various and increasing purges as more and more men were required by the Nips for their working parties.

Anyone found in camp whilst the official working parties were about their allotted tasks ran the risk of interrogation and, through inability to communicate, a beating. To get round this, passes, printed in Japanese, were issued for sick, camp workers and others with official business in camp during the day. These were printed in the Japanese characters and varied slightly, possibly for the different categories. Not being able to read Nipponese, the officers handed out these passes indiscriminately. We never knew quite whether we were sick or working, just flashed the passes and no one seemed to query them, so everyone was satisfied.

For the rest, work started at nine, dinner break was from one until three when work was resumed until six o'clock. Roll call under the Nips took place at eight and lights out was at ten. Sunday was a work day but every Thursday was an official rest day.

Thursday was usually occupied in dismantling beds and 'furniture' in a search for bugs. In the few weeks from these pests first being discovered in camp they multiplied to such an extent that no hut was free from them. At night the air was filled with the sound of slapping, scratching, shuffling, flapping of blankets and muffled cursing as the tormented victims suffered. Was that one on your leg? No, it's on your stomach now. Your back itches. An exploratory finger catches something soft, presses and the familiar sickly smell fills the immediate vicinity. Another one gone, but a dozen more to take its place. Nip out of bed, shake the blanket, slap, crush and kill, and in the morning, count the red blotches on stomach and legs that show where the little monsters have been at work.

Which is why, each Thursday found us hard at work, dismantling beds and applying boiling water and creosote to all the nooks and crannies, squashing the enemy as they emerged. Forty a week was an average catch and might ensure a good night or two's sleep. Blankets were strung on the perimeter wire in the sun. The practice rather backfired on me when one night at lights out I retired to bed, only to find that out there in the dark were my blankets, still adorning the wire. Prowling sentries made night venturing from the hut rather hazardous, but it got rather cold at night and I risked a quick dash. I lay back on my bed and drew the blankets up to my chin, only to erupt with a piercing shriek.

Clinging like grim death to the underside, and brushing my bare stomach, was a cold, clammy chameleon.

The other main occupation on Thursday mornings was that of pegging underwear on the line and carefully inspecting for lice, an occupation commonly known as 'reading the papers'. In the afternoons it was a quiet game of cards, a read or a trouble-free rest on the newly assembled and bug-free beds. And, of course, the Test Match. Cricket hit the camp hard about the end of May. Someone in a tour of the godowns exhumed a few boxes of tennis balls. Boxwood bats were made, and we were in business. The idea caught on and by July every hut, indeed every section of every hut, had its own cricket team. There were inter-hut, inter-battalion and inter-regimental matches every evening. Every battalion had its own pitch, and play began straight after tea, until failing light made further play impossible. The Nips would turn up for Roll call, their shouts being met with 'keep quiet' and 'put a sock in it' by the watching crowds. After all, how could you expect a Jap to comprehend that a game of cricket was more important than a 'Tenko'. Eventually, however, the guards would become so inflamed that a gradual drift from the pitch took place, Roll call taken, and with the salute the frustrated players and spectators would rush back to the pitch with whoops of joy and play resumed.

The craze grew to tremendous proportions. Every spare piece of ground was pressed into use as a pitch. If a ball was hit over the wire even the most law-abiding prisoner would nip smartly out to retrieve it as soon as the sentry had turned his back. Tennis balls were prized beyond gold or rubies. The highlight of the week was the regular Thursday match at the 'Oval'. A pitch had been laboriously dug over and prepared with specially selected marl, under the expert supervision of Jim Swanton. For weeks it had been watered and rolled, rolled and watered, until, completely devoid of grass as the whole camp was, it at least bore some semblance of a level plane. Most cricketers would have viewed this gravel strip with something approaching horror, but it was here that the crowds assembled every Thursday to see the England vs Australia needle matches. Play may not have been strictly orthodox, and the drains did nothing to improve the outfield, but to the enthralled prisoners of war it was no longer River Valley – it was Trent Bridge or Melbourne, and even there they could not have been better entertained.

So time slipped comfortably by. If this was prisoner of war life, it wasn't so bad. In any case, it was only a matter of weeks before the end came. We had all heard of the famous landing in the north of Malaya, and even now, it was said, a British army was fighting its way down the mainland to relieve the island. We could wait and, meanwhile, life was passable.

Chapter 6

The Mask Slips

Gradually, almost imperceptibly, the scene began to change. Up till now we had always been allowed a fair amount of freedom regarding the size and composition of the working parties. There had been at first no restriction on the numbers left in camp and the two-hut hospital was always well filled in addition to the men given light duties by the medical officers and allowed to remain in camp. Here, as in every camp we ever had, the care of the sick was left entirely to our own medical personnel, and the medical officers and medical orderlies were not required to go out on working parties, but could follow their own vocation. It now became the practice for the more seriously sick to be evacuated weekly to Changi and, as the numbers available for working parties began to drop, the first of the soon to be familiar purges on the sick began, whilst the numbers of cooks, camp orderlies and suchlike were drastically cut. All accompanied by the most profuse apologies. The Nips really hated to be so severe, but of course more men were needed at work.

Dysentery of the bacillary type was the most prevalent disabling disease but in May a few cases of beriberi, a vitamin deficiency disease, occurred, whilst in June a case of cholera among the crew of a ship in Singapore harbour threw the whole camp into a shambles. Everyone was hastily inoculated with anti-cholera vaccine and gradually the scare was forgotten. Another widely distributed complaint, also caused by vitamin deficiency in our diet, was lovingly called by its sufferers 'Changi Balls'.

The skin around the scrotum dissolved into weeping sores during the day and hardened to a cardboard consistency during the night. We were, as always, short of medical supplies, and the only remedy the medical staff could contrive was raw Lysol, applied to the affected parts, neat. The recipient usually took off from a standing start, describing a graceful parabola, and open-mouthed spectators outside the medical inspection room applauded heartily as the Olympic record for the long jump was exceeded time and again. One night, I remember a patient lying back on his bed, an idiotic grin of pure delight on his face as he dabbed gently away with the contents of a purloined box of Ponds.

'When I tell my wife what I did with her favourite face powder,' he said, 'she'll never believe me.' Usually the condition cleared up of its own accord after a few weeks, as suddenly as it appeared.

Work was becoming more varied and farther away from camp. The Cabbage Patch had been transformed into a Jap HQ and the godowns were empty, no longer requiring our expert attentions. Work on the war memorial and the airport was still going on. In June a party was selected to go to Formosa. They were all fully inoculated and medically examined before leaving but, to our surprise, they were back with us again the next day, having spent twenty-four hours cooped up like chickens in the hold of a Japanese tramp steamer. They stood by for several days then departed again, this time for good.

Rumour, never idle, was that we were all leaving the camp, which was closing down. The most persistent of these tales was really delightful. A rest camp had been prepared in the Cameron Highlands in Malaya and, having finished our work in Singapore, we were all to be transshipped there, to spend the rest of the war recuperating. Such was our naivety, that this was widely believed to be true, even after we had finally landed at our ultimate destination. In early June, the second camp at Havelock Road was established, separated from ours by the dank, foul Singapore river. The two camps were separated by a wooden bridge, closed to all without a pass, so that social contact between friends was impossible. Our hospital, however, served both camps, so that sometimes old ties could be renewed in 'dock'. In a sort of no man's land between the Havelock Road camp and the river was a line of store huts, soon visited at night by a few hardy types, who braved the evil-smelling mud and slime to attain their goal. It took the Nips a while to realize what was going on, by which time a large and varied assortment of swag had been surreptitiously transferred across the river. A unit of the Imperial Guard, taller men than the average Japanese, was put on duty, or at least that's who we understood they were. Electric lights were installed around the huts and left burning all night, but still the raids continued. Eventually, of course, the Nips made a capture, and one morning we saw them striding through the camp, dragging a PoW behind them on a length of rope. They disappeared through the gate and that was one prisoner we didn't see again.

Exception was taken to the appearance of Sikhs on guard duty on the camp perimeter, the Sikhs in Singapore having gone over to the Japanese to a man. One evening, the usual fun of sentry baiting was in full swing when suddenly consternation reigned. A Sikh and two fully-armed Japanese appeared from behind, having marched through the camp. Grabbing two or three of the jeerers they marched them off to the guardroom. They were only released in the morning, after much sweating and a hard night's work by the interpreter.

It was about this time that Gunner Everall, a member of the 85th Anti-Tank Regiment ran into trouble. The usual treatment for running foul of a Nip was a slap or two in the face, the treatment they would expect from their own superiors for any misdemeanour. Apparently, the captain would slap the lieutenant, the lieutenant beat the sergeant, the sergeant knocked the living daylights out of the corporal until, finally, the poor bloody private kicked the barrack-room cat. Then all was forgotten, honour having been satisfied. Everall had always vowed that if any Jap hit him he would hit the Nip back, and eventually he did just that. He was literally dragged to the guardroom and there roped tightly to the trunk of a tree where every Nip who passed took a playful swipe at him with the butt end of his rifle, or with a clenched fist. One hand only was untied twice daily, so that he could eat his meal of plain boiled rice and cold water. Otherwise, he was left roped for fourteen days, urinating where he stood, his legs foul with his own waste. He was then released and returned to camp, and when I saw him two years later the rope burns on wrists and ankles were still plainly visible.

Late in the summer, we were presented with forms of undertaking not to escape. These, said the Japanese, would be signed by each and every man. The wording was in the form, 'I solemnly swear on my honour that I will not under any circumstances attempt to escape'. 'Impossible,' said the Camp Commandant, 'It is a soldier's duty to try to escape should an opportunity present itself. We cannot and will not sign such a document.'

'In that case,' said the Nips, 'you will be punished.'

When asked what form the punishment would take, the horrors of the Selerang concentration were outlined. Sometime before, a similar document had been presented to the troops in Changi, where they also refused to sign. When the time limit set by the Japanese expired, the troops were told that they would all be placed in confinement in Selerang Barracks, there to await a change of heart. The entire population of the Changi cage, 15,000 men, was moved into an area consisting of four barrack blocks surrounding a bare concrete parade square. With them they took all equipment for cooking, etc. and even live animals. They were packed cheek to jowl, on balconies, on the roofs and under canvas on the parade ground, where cooking also had to be done, hard by the latrines which had to be hacked in the solid concrete. The Black Hole of Calcutta was not even in the same street. For five days they were kept in these indescribable conditions – dysentery and other diseases rampant and spreading like a bush fire among the tightly-packed men. Finally, with the numbers of sick and dying threatening to outstrip those of the healthy, the medical officers disclaimed all responsibility if the situation was allowed to continue. The paroles were signed 'under duress' and the concentration was broken up.

In Havelock Road a similar parole was presented at the same time as the one demanded of us. They also refused to sign, and the whole camp was brought out on the parade ground, made to kneel and to continue kneeling until the signing was effected. After some hours they too signed under duress.

The Commandant of River Valley asked the Japanese for a direct order to sign, after which the completed forms would then be handed over. The British Commandant, in a message to all troops, said that he took full responsibility for the decision and that no action would be taken against us on our return to Britain for this unprecedented action. We signed.

Rumours of the total closure of the camp grew stronger. No one knew where we might be going, except for the wishful thinking about the Cameron Highlands and, on the whole, no one really cared. It was obvious that there was no more work for us in the area, rations had been cut and parties from the city told us that the civilian population was also going short. Shops which six months before had been bursting at the seams were now desolate. We heard murmurs of sadism and cruelty from the other PoW camps and we knew that some of the Indian troops, in particular the Gurkhas, who remained fanatically loyal to the British cause, were having a very hard time of it.

Occasionally we heard of purges still going on among the Chinese civilians, and the celebrations to mark the six-monthly anniversary of Japanese rule were marked by rows of Chinese heads on poles in the streets. These were placed at strategic points where the greatest publicity would be given to the message that civil disobedience did not pay.

Several visits of inspection were made around the camp by the Japanese Officer Commanding, rejoicing in the name of General Fukuye. Has nickname among the prisoners of war takes little imagination. All had to be spick and span for his visits, and as he went around the camp all men had to turn to face him as he passed, bowing from the waist. Patients in hospital had to sit to attention at his approach, while those too ill to sit were graciously allowed to lie to attention.

Late in September, the first issue of Red Cross stores arrived from South Africa. The camp was now half empty, due to the regular evacuation of the sick to Changi and the detachment of various working parties to other camps. The stores were received in bulk, and the whole issue for all camps in the area was sent to River Valley for distribution. Two huts in the centre of the camp were allocated to hold the supplies and it was a sad commentary on our already lowered moral standards that it was deemed necessary to erect a double barbed-wire fence, guarded by an NCO and twenty men, solely to protect the stores from depredations by our own men. We had our first issue of a quarter of a pound of sugar, a tin of jam and some vitamin sweets and were told that the main issue would be made as soon as a schedule had been drawn up of the total inventory and the allocation to each camp.

Early in October preparations were put in hand for the camp's final closure. A record card was prepared for each man, showing his home address, next of kin, number, rank, name and civilian occupation. It was widely suspected that the latter was to enable the Japanese to allocate us to various jobs of war importance, and hundreds of us became labourers and shop assistants overnight. We were issued a PoW number, which we had to carve on to a wooden tag and hang around our necks, and the issue of Red Cross stores was speeded up to try to give each man a fair share before he left. Field postcards were issued for us to fill in to get a message home, our first opportunity to write. Of course, by then, no mail had been received from home. The wording on the cards left much to be desired, but we were told that if we added anything beyond the words allowed, or tried to alter the cards in any way, they would be destroyed. My card arrived home in June 1944, a year and eight months after writing, and was the first real intimation that I was one of those who had survived the capitulation.

On 9 and 10 October an issue was made of items of clothing and boots. There were not sufficient to supply every man, and so lots were drawn. All the items were of South African origin, as was the supplementary issue of jam, sugar, bully beef, M & V ration, tinned milk and eighty Victory V cigarettes. Parties were to be despatched in lots of 650 and, on 11 October, we paraded, each man carrying his own kit – his entire worldly possessions. We were to be known as C working battalion. There had been much controversy as to how much of our cooking equipment and other paraphernalia of camp life we should attempt to take with us.

'It is not necessary to take any,' said the Japanese. 'The camp you are going to is fully equipped for your needs.' Although we had as yet not had any great experience of the worth of Japanese promises we decided, fortunately, to take as much as possible and several fully-laden trucks set off for the station. Shouldering our kitbags and packs we swung out behind. River Valley lay behind. What lay in front we happily could not guess.

We had entered the camp as the main body of 85th Anti-Tank Regiment. We left as C Battalion, a motley collection of RA, RE, RAOC, RAMC, Infantry and Malayan Volunteers, with no ties and knowing few of our neighbours in the column. We strode on through the hot stifling afternoon sun, through the streets of Singapore to the railway terminus. Here we found a train of enclosed steel boxcars of the type usually employed for the transport of rice and other such commodities in bulk. They were already loaded with cargo and on top of this our kit and equipment had been slung. The remaining space between the pile and the steel roof was our travelling quarters and in we clambered, thirty to a car in addition to all our personal effects. There was no room to stand, no room to lie down and very little room to squat, but by the dint of much pulling and shoving, and not a little swearing, we at last made ourselves as comfortable as possible. The sun beat down on the steel roof and the temperature climbed into the region of the unbearable but, mercifully, the steel sliding doors were left open and we arranged amongst ourselves to take it in turns to sit in the open doorway and dangle our legs over the edge. With a hiss of steam and a train-long clanking of buffers we were off up country.

The famous Johore causeway was something of an anti-climax. We had heard so much about it, those of us who had not been on the mainland before, and seeing it for the first time, the narrow, low stone structure seemed barely wide enough to support the railway line. It seemed far too insignificant to warrant the enormous importance that had been attributed to it the previous February as we waited the final onslaught. We pulled up that evening at Gemas, an important junction where the east and west coast routes diverge. We were allowed on to the platform, Japanese sentries being posted where they could command a full view of the train. I volunteered to obtain a few boxes of matches from the kiosk, which was strangely open for business. I addressed the incumbent in my best Malayan.

'Ada korek api?' No response. Evidently the Malays in Johore do not understand Malayan. After vainly trying to get through to him I retired to the train, having met my match. It was the last time we set foot on Malayan soil. A series of yells and animal grunts from the guards herded everyone aboard and we were off again. We took the west coast route via Ipoh and Kuala Lumpur. We saw little sign of life on the parallel road and even less sign of the vicious campaign, which had been fought over the ground some six months before. The bridges which had been blown, had all been swiftly repaired by the Japanese engineers using timber in a lattice-work construction. The resulting structure, though ramshackle, was obviously doing the job required. The road and railway ran together for much of the way, and it seemed that rarely had both road and rail bridges been destroyed at the same point, usually one or the other, occasionally neither. If impressions were correct, it would appear that, in the haste of the withdrawal, the job of holding up the Japanese advance had not been carried out with the efficiency that we had been led to believe.

The track was, for the most part, a single line with passing loops at intervals. Here the driver collected a key on a large bamboo ring from the signalman. This gave him the authority to proceed and, at the next double-track section, he handed this over to the signalman to be collected and used by the next train going south. In theory, and no doubt in practice, this rendered a collision impossible.

Vague impressions followed as we sped north; Ipoh, cool and clean in the morning light; Kuala Lumpur with ornate domed station, pinnacles reaching for the sky; Penang island just offshore, somnolent in the shimmering haze. We sweated in our steel prison, cramped and tired, unable to lie down, and able to perform our bodily functions only with the aid of a couple of stalwart men to hang on to arms and legs as we hung out of the side of the cars at 30 or 40 miles per hour. We crossed the border on 13 October, the date that seemed to have been haunting us. On 13 November, we left the Clyde and on 13 January at 1300 hours we disembarked at Singapore, then on 13 October we entered Thailand (Siam). Our first stop at a Thai station was a complete contrast. The Malayan stations had been quiet, with few of the locals to be seen. Here all was hurry and bustle with the large straw hats overshadowing the sombre black and white of the garb, another contrast with the brightly-clad Malayans. We didn't know where we had stopped, for the station name boards were to us just meaningless hieroglyphics. The people paused fleetingly in their darting hither and thither to gaze for a while at this trainload of white-skinned 'invaders' then continued on their way. Here and there, traders stood with baskets of assorted merchandise – soap and Players cigarettes. We would have been eager to buy, but they gazed with scorn on our Malayan dollars, while to us at this time, a *tical* was just something you used to have on the sofa in the front room in the far-off days of peace. We looked longingly, but settled for taking a can down to the engine to beg some boiling water from the engine driver so that we could have a brew up. We moved on, through the flat countryside, where even the houses seemed different in the few short miles from the border; here we saw the occasional buildings with brick construction and tiled roof.

Our next stop was for us the end of the line – Bampong. We crawled wearily to the bare earth and stretched our aching legs, shouldered our kits and straggled out into the little township. The houses here were all of wood with palm-thatched roofs. The street was deserted apart from one mangy dog, lazily scratching a flea-bitten ear. The sun hung heavily in the cloudless sky. There was a faint stirring of memory as I gazed on that forlorn sight. Incongruously my mind went back to boyhood Saturday mornings at the cinema. This was like the familiar Wild West sets, and any minute the sheriff's posse would come thundering round the corner and draw up in front of us in a lather of sweating, stinking horseflesh. The dog continued to scratch wearily. There were apparently no horses in Thailand, only fleas, flies, mosquitos, oxen, scrawny ducks and chickens – and flies.

At the end of the pathetic main street we turned right and the camp came in sight, half a dozen bamboo and attap huts lying drunkenly askew in a sea of water and thick glutinous mud. One or two tattered scarecrows, green of complexion and with lacklustre eyes gazing from dark hollow sockets, came forward to meet us. Welcome to Thailand.

Chapter 7

Welcome to Thailand

After River Valley, the impact of Bampong was, to say the least, frightening. The camp was full of walking dead and there was an atmosphere of gloom, almost of despair, everywhere. The residents had been brought up from Changi in August to prepare a staging camp for the following flood of workers who were to bring to fruition the long cherished dream of a railway linking Bangkok and Rangoon. The Japanese were already pushing hungrily into Burma, their eyes on the rich prize of India glittering in the distance, and supplies were vital to the success of their undertaking. The sea route was long and hazardous, and would be even more so when the Allies began to recover from the shattering blows of the past few months. The railway was the obvious solution.

It had been surveyed long ago and now, despite the serious lack of modern engineering tools, the supply of hands was inexhaustible, or very nearly so.

The advance party just hit the end of the rainy season, and the camp was soon a quagmire, the posts of the huts sinking into the mud, so that, in places, the attap roofs nearly touched the ground and the beds were only just above water level. The place abounded with mosquitoes, and malaria was soon endemic. Stray food lay around the edges of the huts where remnants of mess tins had been tipped over the edge and, on this, the flies, great bloated black monsters never absent from the Thai scene, thrived and multiplied. Dysentery also began to take its toll. When I made enquiries as to whether anyone I knew was in the camp staff I found that Donald, the Orderly Room Sergeant, had indeed come up with them, but had already fallen victim to dysentery, as had a dozen or so more. The remainder all looked ill, dispirited and tired.

We were ushered into an empty hut and staked our claims to space. We were to be there only for a few days, and had nothing specific to do until we moved on. Although not allowed into town we could move freely around the camp area and visit the *padi* fields, about a quarter of a mile away, to draw water for washing and laundry. We liked the look of the brown-skinned people, but noticed with surprise that the males were ostentatiously armed

Padre Harry Thorpe, an Australian chaplain who ministered to prisoners of all nations. He re-baptised Stuart Young, who was not alone in seeking solace in religion during his arduous captivity.

Stuart Young as a newly conscripted soldier in 1940.

Stuart and his brother Bob in a photograph taken in 1941. Bob served in Italy.

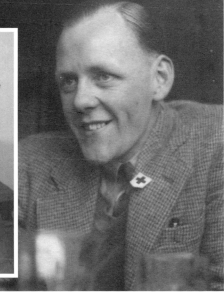

Stuart in 1946 after four years as a guest of the Japanese.

Ronny Graham who elected to stay behind at Bampong but died of dysentery in November 1942.

Frank 'Tommy' Thompson was shipped to Japan by the Japanese but the vessel was diverted to the Philippines where he was caught up in the fighting and never heard of again.

Alan Pratt, Bill Bailey and Stuart Young. A photograph taken in May 1946 and originally annotated by Stuart as 'comrades in distress'.

HQ 85th Anti-Tank Regiment RA. The photograph was taken in Clacton on Sea in October 1941 not long before deployment. Stuart captioned the original 'Lambs to the Slaughter'. Gunner Stuart Young is second from right, back row.

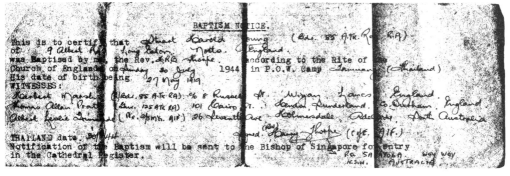

Baptism chit signed and dated by Padre Harry Thorpe.

Official baptismal certificate completed by Harry Thorpe and sent to Stuart Young after the war.

ONCE

I BUILT A RAILROAD MADE IT RUN

I MADE IT RACE AGAINST TIME

ONCE I BUILT A RAILROAD

NOW IT'S DONE

KANCHANBURI CEMETERY

Post-war photos of the Burma–Thailand railway. From author's original manuscript.

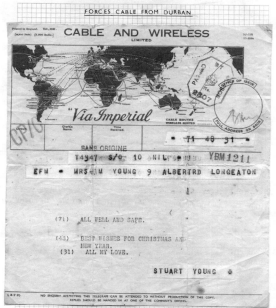

Telegram sent by Stuart while in Durban in 1941 on his way to Singapore. Note the interesting annotation on how these were composed.

FORCES CABLE FROM DURBAN

CABLE AND WIRELESS LIMITED

"Via Imperial"

SANS ORIGINE

EFM — MRS M YOUNG 9 ALBERTRD LONGEATON

(71) ALL WELL AND SAFE.

(43) BEST WISHES FOR CHRISTMAS AND NEW YEAR.

(31) ALL MY LOVE.

STUART YOUNG

IN ALL DESPATCHING OFFICES (POST OFFICES) LISTS OF SHORT PHRASES NUMBERED 1 TO 100 WERE ON DISPLAY. SERVICEMEN COULD SELECT 3 PHRASES. NUMBERS ONLY WERE TRANSMITTED BEING TURNED BACK INTO A MESSAGE FROM A CHART AT THE RECEIVING END. NO OFFICE OF DESPATCH SHOWN — HENCE FRENCH 'SANS PRINTING OCT 1941 14500 PADS ORIGINE'

1941

Official notification that Young was a prisoner of war in Japanese hands – issued sixteen months after his capture.

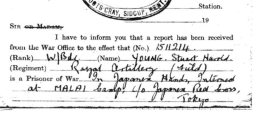

MISSING

Tel : Foots Cray 2291   Royal Artillery Record Office,
(Field Branch),
Foots Cray,
Sidcup, Kent.

Date 17.3.43

To: MR. B.H. YOUNG.

Dear Sir,

According to the records in this office your Son 1511214 GNR. STUART HAROLD YOUNG Royal Artillery, was serving in Malaya when the garrison of Singapore capitulated on 15th February, 1942. Every endeavour is being made through diplomatic and other channels to obtain information concerning

No. ___ Army Form B. 104—83A.
(If replying, please quote above No.)

R.A. RECORD & PAY OFFICE
FIELD BRANCH
9 ___ 1943
FOOTS CRAY, SIDCUP, KENT

Record Office,
___ Station.
___ 19

SIR OR MADAM,

I have to inform you that a report has been received from the War Office to the effect that (No.) 1511214
(Rank) W/Bdr. (Name) YOUNG. Stuart Harold
(Regiment) Royal Artillery (field)
is a Prisoner of War In Japanese Hands, Interned at MALAI Camp, C/o Japanese Red Cross, Tokyo.

OFFICIAL NOTIFIC— ATION 16 MONTHS BY WHICH TIME MANY HUNDREDS ALREADY HAD DIED IN CAPTIVITY

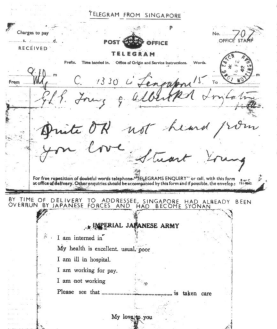

Top: telegram sent by Stuart Young from Singapore prior to his capture. It is delivery stamped Nottingham 16 February 1942, by which time Singapore was in Japanese hands. Bottom: postcard issued by the Imperial Japanese Army to allow PoWs to inform their families of their circumstances. Stuart Young noted that only one of several he posted was ever delivered.

Photos of Selerang Camp in 1942. From author's original manuscript.

The tables turned. Japanese prisoners working under British supervision after the war. Described by Stuart as a 'favourite picture'.

Telegram sent by Stuart's mother to welcome him home and delivered to him at Gibraltar in October 1945.

BUCKINGHAM PALACE

The Queen and I bid you a very warm welcome home.

Through all the great trials and sufferings which you have undergone at the hands of the Japanese, you and your comrades have been constantly in our thoughts. We know from the accounts we have already received how heavy those sufferings have been.   We know also that these have been endured by you with the highest courage.

We mourn with you the deaths of so many of your gallant comrades.

With all our hearts, we hope that your return from captivity will bring you and your families a full measure of happiness, which you may long enjoy together.

George R.I.

September 1945.

'Welcome home' letter from Buckingham Palace to liberated prisoners of the Japanese.

with wicked looking knives and ornately decorated pistols, stuck in the sash around their waist. This, we were informed by the old hands, was because the Japanese had not conquered Thailand, which remained officially neutral, but were in the country by treaty. The Nips kept pretty strictly to their own camp areas and to the main roads, any of them straying too far afield being quite likely to be found with their throats cut, as indeed was one shortly before our arrival. Guests they may have been, but honoured guests most definitely not.

On the day we were preparing to move out, one of my oldest friends, Ron Graham, stated his intention of reporting sick with stomach trouble. We had been together since the first day at Sheffield in 1939, and our allotted army numbers were almost consecutive. Knowing him, I was not altogether surprised when he said that he had heard that all the sick were to be sent on by river in a day or two, and this was his way of getting out of the long walk ahead. The hell camp claimed him too, and I heard after the war that he was dead inside two months in that hole. This sort of thing happened so often to those who tried to work things out their way that a sort of fatalism grew up among those in Thailand. Never volunteer for anything, and, likewise, if detailed for a move, never try to get off the draft. If your number was up, well that's it and there was nothing you could do about it. I suppose this was another manifestation of the widespread 'Tid apa' complex, but most people lived by this creed.

We set off that morning along a well metalled road, moving northward. It was a flat but pleasant country and, after walking all morning, we passed through a little village and then halted for a meal. Later, in the heat of the afternoon sun, boots began to come off as the new leather produced a bumper crop of blisters. Some sat by the roadside and, producing knives, slashed out toes and heels from the new footwear that had been issued only days before. The craze spread, and dozens of pairs were ruined beyond repair before we made a halt for the night. This was at a hutted camp near the little town of Kanchanaburi, shortened almost at once to Kanburi, which name it retained for the rest of our stay in Thailand. We stayed there for two nights, while we rested and our blistered feet were treated. Then we again paraded for the off.

'Just take a small pack and a blanket,' we were told, 'the rest of your kit will be taken up by boat, and will be waiting for you when you get to your destination.' We were grateful for this opportunity to lighten the load, and surplus kit was dumped on the ground in a big heap. Some of it was never seen again, and that which did finally catch us up took well over six months to make the 120-kilometre journey.

We swung out into the road and in a minute or so were walking down the main, indeed the only, street in Kanburi, past the paper mill that was the town's only industry outside of agriculture, smoke issuing from its tall chimney. There were a few shops open and the locals looked at us with interested, friendly faces. We reached the end of the street and swung to the left. The metalled road ended abruptly and we found ourselves almost immediately in semi jungle.

We had not gone far before we realized that we were walking along a raised embankment, with bamboo and scrub below us on either side. Even then it was some time before it struck us that this must be the start of the projected railway. The column extended into a straggle, about a mile in length, with a party of Japanese at the head and two with fixed bayonets sweeping up the stragglers in the rear. We soon mapped out a plan of campaign, which was to walk smartly up to the head of the column and then stretch out on the embankment side until the prodding bayonets and the shouts of 'Kurra' and 'Bagero' convinced us that it was time to get on the move again. This process, we found, was just long enough to brew and swallow a cup of tea.

That night we stayed in a curious walled enclosure at a place by the name of Raja. We saw nothing of the town, but the townspeople and the ubiquitous saffron-robed monks moved freely among us as we lay in the open air. We stayed there another twenty-four hours before moving off again along what was little more than a jungle path. We walked all day and, in the fading light of the evening, came upon a well-worn earthen slope, leading down to a sluggish river. A flat-bottomed boat and boatman was waiting for us and we ferried across in small parties, some Nips going across with the first few and the remainder bringing up the rear. On the far bank, in a little clearing overshadowed by feathery fronds of bamboo, we made camp and the cooks, in a little world of their own on the riverbank, performed miracles again to produce a meal. We dropped off to sleep in the velvety gloom, ignoring the whine of the mosquitoes; all was peace. An hour or so later, we awoke to a steady downpour, our blankets soaking, the water splashing from the bamboo fronds and running in little rivulets over the tops of our groundsheets. We struggled vainly to rig up lean-tos from bamboo and ground sheets, but the rain trickled through and ran down our necks and we sat huddled in damp misery till morning. The rain ceased when we set off but the wrung-out blankets weighed a ton. The morning seemed endless, my head reeled and my legs got weaker and weaker. The track ahead was swimming hazily, and even though I had seen the sort of treatment meted out to the dropouts, I had just decided I couldn't move another step when 'yasume' was called. I dropped flat, too whacked to even undo my pack. We stayed about an hour and I felt sufficiently recovered to make it without undue difficulty to our next stop at Tarsoa. A meal was already waiting and I fell asleep exhausted, astride a bamboo pole in the rice store.

The following morning the trail we were following, never very brilliant, had vanished entirely in a luxuriant growth of trees, bamboos and creepers. The Japs had drawn their parangs and were hard at work slashing out a path for us to follow. We might have imagined that we were breaking entirely new ground, had we not noticed that, from time to time they would halt, their eyes searching the treetops. We followed their gaze and saw, strung from tree to tree, an army field-telephone wire. Evidently the signals at least had been here before us, and it was their line that we were following. We slithered downhill and toiled up, slipping and sliding, our cheeks whipped by springy canes and our legs ripped by thorns. Suddenly, we came on a plank bridge across a tinkling crystal-clear stream. A halt was called and we lay on the banks, splashing our burning faces and drinking our fill of the clear water. Little more than six months later and that same stream was a putrid stinking river of instant death, a foul cholera–ridden sewer.

It was already late afternoon when we pushed on, and as the trail took a sudden downward turn we burst into a little clearing, some fifty by a hundred yards. In the dim fading light we could see the framework of four huts, just the bamboo skeletons with attap clothing their roofs. The silence was eerie, and the jungle pressed close on all sides. 'Tonchan,' said the leading Nip. Tonchan, 120 kilometres from Bampong and the end of a seven-day journey.

We dumped our kit under the attap roofs. From one corner of the site a trail led again downhill, presumably to the river, and the cooks vanished to prepare the evening meal. Half of one hut was claimed by the officers, while the other ranks jostled for places in the rest. It was already quite dark when we were told that the meal was ready, and we followed the precipitous track for what seemed about half a mile to the river's edge. The advance party from Tarsoa had brought up a quantity of tea, rice, and four marrows, and from this a meal had been prepared for over 600 men, boiling the rice in water from the river and cooking on bamboo fires in the open air, there being no buildings erected as yet.

It was already pitch dark before we began our meal, which we ate by the light of fires we had constructed in the centre of the camp area. We settled down to sleep that night on the rocky ground, the night air alive with eerie and unaccustomed animal sounds. It was our first night in the jungle proper. Even Changi and River Valley Road already seemed like the most unimaginable luxury.

Chapter 8

Tonchan Takes Shape

In the days that followed, our first camp tasks were to complete the huts and to build more for other work battalions that were following us up from the camps in Singapore. A hut also had to be built to house the Japanese guards, who at first were living some distance away in tents. This hut, overlooking the entire camp area from an eminence nearby, turned out to be a magnificent structure of several rooms, the whole supported on stilts and having an imposing flight of steps leading up to the main doorway. A separate cookhouse was added and, some weeks later, a stream was diverted through the Japanese lines, by means of improvised bamboo pipes, to provide showers and baths. Both shower and bath were necessary because the Japanese considered the Western idea of bathing to be indescribably filthy. Your Japanese will under no circumstances enter his bath until he has been well scrubbed from head to toe and is scrupulously clean. The Japanese area took several months to complete, in contrast to the couple of weeks or so allotted to the building of the PoW quarters.

Meanwhile, we erected bed shelves in the original four huts and lined the side with bamboo matting. The other huts were started and duly occupied by the newly-arrived H and K Battalions. In one of those typical displays of friendship, encountered from time to time in PoW life, a hut that had to be shared, through lack of space, with C Battalion was barricaded halfway down to prevent free access from one battalion area to another, presumably to prevent 'borrowing' of kit when its owner was not there to guard it. Two huts were erected on the edge of the site to accommodate the officers, and some hundred yards or so away, in the edge of the jungle, a lone hut was put up to act as camp hospital, should it be needed. We had an RAMC Medical Officer and a couple of orderlies in camp and daily sick parades were allowed.

The basic material for building was the omnipresent bamboo, which grew in profusion around the camp. There was the tall willowy variety which is so familiar in ornamental gardens in this country and which, we were told by experts, was the female variety. The other type grew in thick clumps some forty or so feet tall and was covered with stout, ugly looking spines, some thicker than a man's finger. This type could grow to a diameter of a foot or more across, and the clumps grew so thickly matted and interlocked that even if every stem was chopped through at ground level the whole mass would remain upright and had to be hauled down by teams of men, sweating as they pulled on the ropes. You had to keep a weather eye open and be quick to get out of the way of the clump as it swayed majestically before falling to the ground, for a slash by one of those wicked thorns could lay open a man's arm or leg to the bone. It is strange to remember that bamboo is nothing more than a species of grass.

When finally cut and trimmed to size, we found its uses to be innumerable. Poles with a diameter of some four to six inches were selected and used for the uprights and frameworks of the huts. The thinner, willowy ones were lashed horizontally to the roofing beams to take the attap strips, and attap, after all, is only strips of split bamboo on to which palm leaves are fastened. Even thicker canes than those used for building were split and bashed into a sort of flat sheet, from which the beds were made. They were made into a continuous runner fastened some two feet above the ground, on which the prisoner of war lived, ate and slept. The centre sections of some of the thicker canes were poked out and the resulting pipes were used as conduits for water, or half sections for urinal troughs. Latrines were of necessity constructed of bamboo, but seats were dispensed with. After all, a sliver of bamboo can slice like a surgeon's scalpel.

Flat sheets also made capital duckboards. Pieces were fashioned into knives, forks, spoons and combs, whilst some of the outsize segments did service as buckets when furnished with a plaited grass handle. Hammered and split, native fashion, bamboo could be separated into thin flat canes for making mats, rugs of a sort, rice sacks, baskets and dozens of other useful items. It provided, at least initially, all our fuel for cooking and boiling water and the young shoots themselves could be cooked and eaten. It was averred, though never put to the test as far as I know, that the silky covering of the bulbous new growth made excellent condoms.

The camp guards were at this time not very much in evidence. The party consisted of a nucleus of Japanese under the command of a tough little regular army sergeant, one Hiramatsu. From the beginning his belligerent non-compromising attitude to all and sundry earned him the nickname of 'Tiger', a name which stuck to the end. In the early days, one of his men went sick with malaria and, there being no food available for useless mouths, no matter their nationality, 'Tiger' went to his bedside and left at his head a loaded revolver. The hint was taken and the unfortunate returned forthwith to duty. In spite of his fearsome reputation I always had a grudging respect for this earthy, forthright character. I firmly believe he did the best he could in a situation not of his choosing and not altogether to his liking. He was harsh but fair, as he understood the word. I believe that he paid for a year of indescribable horror with his life as a war criminal and probably went to his last rest wondering what else he could have done in the circumstances.

The remainder of his staff were conscripted Koreans who, while wearing Jap uniform, carried no badges of rank and were considered as having no status by the pure Japanese. By far the worst treatment (with a few notable exceptions) came from the Koreans, who soon got their baptismal names changed for ease of recognition. The Pig, the Silver Bullet, the Frog, and Donald Duck were some of many who strutted, swaggered and raved along the camps of the Kwai Noi. Each morning they would parade in front of the Jap hut, face the east, sing the ritual hymn, say a few prayers and salute the flag. Then, after breakfast, the Koreans fetched the working parties.

In our part of the camp we attempted to lick it into shape. The greatest problem was sanitation. First efforts to dig latrine pits failed when solid rock was struck a few inches below the surface of the ground. Just below the camp a cliff dropped sheer to the river, which swung in at that point. Platforms were hung over the cliff, the refuse falling into the river as we squatted on the trembling bamboo. Our own cookhouse drew water from the river every day for cooking but, as the cookhouse was upstream of the latrines, this did not offer any great cause for alarm. However, presumably camps also drew river water downstream, while if those further up had similar ideas on hygiene the consequences can be imagined.

Fortunately, after only a day or so, softer ground was found inside the jungle and huge pits were dug. It was intended that they should be forty-feet deep but this was found to be impracticable, so the deepest possible were excavated. Sides and roofs of bamboo and attap were added to keep out the flies. Vain hope. In twenty-four hours the pests moved in and, shortly after, the cesspits were seas of heaving maggots. Months later I struck up an amiable conversation with a fellow-traveller as we squatted, regarding the loathsome bloated insects as they covered the sides, sheeted the roof, hung in festoons along the material that held the structure together and buzzed infuriatingly round our bodies.

'Are the flies like this in England?' he asked cheerily.

I could only murmur, 'Well no, not quite.'

Elsewhere, the flies were the same problem, They infested the huts, crawled over your face and alighted on the food you were trying to eat. Once I counted the number of times that a fly settled on a spoonful of rice that I was transferring from dixie to my mouth. Eighteen times it came back before I finally dislodged it. Precious though a spoonful of rice was at that time, that was one that was consigned to a swill pit.

Food was poor and monotonous, mainly rice boiled in river water, about three quarters of a half-pint mugful per man. About half a mug full of thin watery vegetable stew and a mug of milkless, sugarless tea completed the meal. In the early days, before vegetables were brought up, there were times when only a spoonful of peanut oil or something similar was available to help down the rice. Sugar, until the advent of the canteen, was unheard of and was almost never issued to the cookhouse, whilst milk was one of those luxuries only to be dreamed about. Occasionally, in later days, pumpkins were issued as vegetables and a thick yellow stew, almost thick enough to stand a spoon in, was the result. The times we had meat in the first six months or so could be counted on the fingers of one hand, and still leave plenty over.

Medical supplies were limited to two or three items, of which magnesium sulphate or epsom salts were in greatest supply. Full of good intentions, we were issued with a prophylactic dose of quinine each night to keep away malaria, but this finished before the first week, as it was realized that there simply wasn't the quinine available or ever likely to be, for the Japs could offer no guarantees of further supplies. In conditions like these I was staggered one day to observe a highranking officer, after carefully looking round to see that he was not being observed, pull a large tin trunk from below his bed. He opened it, and it appeared from where I stood to be crammed with jars of Marmite. He carefully took a spoonful, replaced the jar and slid the trunk back.

That was one man who was not going to suffer from beriberi. I wondered who the hell carried the trunk up there and whether he shared the spoils. It must have weighed a ton.

It was inevitable that sickness would hit the camp and it wasn't long before it did. With the hordes of flies, the nightly visitations of mosquitoes and the general lack of nets for sleeping at night, malaria and 'squitters', the popular name for diarrhoea, became rampant. The pitifully small stocks of quinine were used for the one, the magnesium sulphate for the other. A stiff dose of epsom salts, lay off eating for twenty-four hours. Purge the system and hope for the best. This was all the struggling medical staff could do, and in many cases it worked. However, on 16 November, little more than three weeks after our arrival at Tonchan, Gunner Allen reported sick with 'squitters' and was admitted to the little hospital. Less than forty-eight hours later he was dead.

We were shocked beyond belief. This was the first time that anyone's death had impacted on us. He was one of us and we didn't die. But he did and he was followed in quick succession by others: Parker, Raine, Spary, Ross, Clarke, Crawford and Parker were all committed to the hastily-opened little cemetery behind the hospital before the end of the month. More followed in November, culminating in three deaths on one day on 29 November. By the end of the year, there were twenty-three wooden crosses in the little plot. We laid them to rest in the regulation depth trenches laboriously hacked out of the rocky ground. Although coffins were out of the question, each man was lovingly laid to rest in a shroud made from empty rice sacks or army blankets. The service was read over each by a senior officer and there was still time in those early days to observe the niceties of protocol. The service was always attended by a Japanese in full uniform, sword and white gloves. This was usually Staff Sergeant Hiramatsu, who would stand respectfully in the background and salute as the victim was laid to rest. I had the job of collecting the pitifully few personal belongings from the hospital and giving them to an officer of the man's regiment in the hope that, somehow, they would be returned to his family after the war. For my pains I became known around camp as 'The Ghoul'.

Among most of those early deaths, bacillary dysentery was listed as the cause, but by the end of the year malaria was gaining ground. There were two types; B2 or benign, which recurred time after time, but, apart from fever and weakness, caused no other serious effects. In little over twelve months I had twenty-one attacks. The first time I was sent downstream to Tarsoa, where I spent three days under observation before returning to Tonchan. I still recall the second day, when the Medical Officer with his assistant took my temperature the second time.

'Ah,' said he in his best Harley Street manner, 'A classic case of malaria, subnormal temperature alternating with above normal.' I was given quinine and sent back to work.

The other type, malignant malaria, with its sub-division of cerebral malaria, which struck at the brain, was a killer. The death toll mounted as drugs grew shorter. Men were sent by the 'Tiger' on anti-malarial work, draining stagnant water and splitting the stumps of cut-down bamboo so that water, the breeding ground of the mosquito, should not collect. On Christmas Eve, a party that had been on this work across the river brought back a thirty-foot python they had killed. After skinning it, so that the Koreans could amuse themselves making snakeskin knickknacks, the carcass was hung on a little ornamental bamboo fence, which we had erected in front of our huts. In those days we even had time for that. We helped ourselves to 'steaks', frying, boiling or grilling them according to taste. It was heavenly, all things to all men, but my recollection is of a strong resemblance to rabbit.

The river was unofficially tapped for supplements to diet. The angling fraternity, with the aid of makeshift lines and bent wire, came up with some form of flat fish which tasted delicious. The Medical Officer tried frantically to get us not to eat the stuff and gave dire warnings of potential blindness and future sterility. Not quite so delicious were freshwater clams of some sort, which were brought into camp. Well stewed, they never tasted like anything else but old car tires. Enterprising fishermen put down night lines and were rewarded with catches of huge, revolting, black fish which they hung up on the end of their hut. Some, even when they had been decapitated, were about the size of a well-built man. God knows what they tasted like, but as they eventually vanished from sight, they were presumably eaten by someone.

The thought of these oversized sardines lurking on the riverbed was most unnerving, especially as most of us went for a swim after duties. A sensational story went the rounds in the camp concerning one of the monsters, which apparently threw a line on to the bank one night, baited with a tin of condensed milk. It then pulled in a PoW, who was never seen again. Unfortunately the story could not be confirmed.

On another occasion, outside a hut belonging to H Battalion, I saw a kind of lizard tethered to the hut timbers. It must have been fully five feet from snout to tip of tail. It was there for several days before it finally disappeared, presumably into someone's inside. Actually, I did later discover the taste of lizard and found it to be not at all unpalatable.

All this time, there had been no attempt at all to wire us in. Access from the camp to the jungle was free but there was nowhere to go. We were strangers in a strange land. There was a price on the head of every escapee should the local inhabitants care to turn us in. How far were the British lines northwards? Were we still in Burma, or even in India? We knew we had lost the Dutch East Indies, but did we still have Borneo, Celebes, New Guinea? We had no idea, so with no money, no food, no knowledge of the language and the people, escape never looked to be possible. True, some brave souls did try, but with the exception of a handful in the latter months of captivity, who vanished in mysterious circumstances, I know of none who were not eventually brought back.

There was a radio operating somewhere in the vicinity, and in the early days news was passed to all and sundry in the camps. However, some individuals could not resist the opportunity of gloating over the Japanese who, of course, wondered how the prisoners got news, sometimes before they themselves had. This could shortly result in a visit from the Kempetai, with fatal results for the radio operator should he be discovered. It was decided to issue news to other ranks laced and diluted with the most preposterous rumours. In this way it was hoped that even the most gullible of the Koreans would not swallow as gospel the fanciful yarns they were fed. But many of us did. The column which was sweeping down Malaya to our rescue, whilst we were in Singapore, became an almighty force liberating the Phillipines and the British were sweeping all before them as they burst back through Burma. These, and other equally ridiculous stories, were eagerly devoured as they swept the camp. It was impossible to separate the wheat from the chaff, but at least the hope that the rumours engendered boosted our sagging morale.

But to really do this, something more than a rumour was needed. Permission to build a stage was obtained from 'Tiger', and attempts to float a concert party were put underway. Some of the most unlikely latent talent was uncovered – sketches, songs, recitations, and instrumentalists blossomed, some of them remarkably good. Costumes were fashioned from all sorts of scrap material, dyed with tea and various jungle leaves and flowers. The front row at shows was always reserved for the guards, who were themselves as starved of entertainment as we were. When the first 'females' began to take the stage in mosquito-net skirts, with tow wigs, 'Tiger' insisted on inspecting them to make sure that all was not what it seemed. We usually closed the proceedings with the National Anthem, all standing in respectful silence while the small camp orchestra churned it out. After a couple of shows, the Nips tumbled to the significance of the tune and it was banned forthwith. What to use as a substitute? Several melodies were suggested and rejected for various reasons but, at last, 'Auld Lang Syne' was tried and accepted by the Japs. They seemed to know the tune as well as we did and we were told that it was their Naval Anthem, serving them in pretty much the same way as 'Anchors Aweigh' did for the Americans. If that was so, it could well explain their enthusiasm for the tune.

This was Tonchan in 1943, but as the year went on the death rate accelerated, the food remained foul and inadequate and the cemetery steadily filled with rows of little crosses. But life and death was not confined to Tonchan Camp.

Chapter 9

The Railway

Within days of our arrival at Tonchan we found the real reason for our being there and parties were sent out into the jungle to make a start on the work.

It was the tail end of the rainy season when we marched up in late November and the following three months were to be completely dry. In spring, following the dry period, intermittent thunderstorms increasing over the months in frequency and severity ushered in the monsoon, when torrential rain poured on the jungle twenty-four hours a day and turned the baked earth into a thick glutinous, squelching mud. Then the rains slackened off, watery sun appeared and the next three months saw gradually increasing dry spells leading to the rainless time we were now entering. The storm during the night at the river crossing on the march up was the only really heavy rain of our first few months.

Much of the inland transport in Thailand was by river. When we first arrived at Tonchan, a houseboat was moored at the river edge, which was presumably a recognized crossing place and even fordable after the dry season. It vanished shortly after our arrival, probably cleared out by the Japs, who wouldn't want any contact with PoWs. However, we were only one of many camps that had been established on the Kwai Noi and all had to be supplied with tools, food and the like, not for odd houseboats, but for thousands of men. The river was not enough and besides, when it dried in a month or so to little more than a trickle, there was every prospect that a laden barge would not make the trip at all. So a road had to be built to enable lorries to reach every camp on the line.

Our task was to build a section back to Tarsoa, until we linked up with the men from Tarsoa building forward. In the opposite direction, (northward) the next camp forwards were building back to meet us. There was nothing elaborate in the operation, just a clearing of bushes and undergrowth, a rough filling in of craters and the removal of any trees standing in the way. This was done by chopping them down to ground level and removing the stump. For this purpose, the Koreans had a certain amount of explosives but, having received no instructions in their use, had absolutely no idea of what to do. The limit of their inventive genius was to scrape a loose hole beneath the stump, drop in the dynamite, light the blue touch-paper and retire forthwith. Result – a large bang, a shower of earth and one stump still firmly embedded in the ground. The offending stump was then, as a rule, laboriously dug out by hand.

Within days, however, a road of sorts had been constructed, the first trucks began to roll and the supply line was open.

Almost simultaneously with work on the road, work began on the real objective, the railway. Originally scheduled to take eighteen months, there was at first none of the bestial slave driving that characterized the period after April, when the 'Speedo' campaign began, although the work was always long, hard and backbreaking to men who were becoming progressively weaker through poor food and disease. In all, some 46,000 Allied personnel were employed on this work; some 16,000 died and thousands more returned home after the war completely broken in health.

The force was divided into five groups and we, from Tarsoa to the Burma border, were known as IV group. Below us, based on Nakompatom, was II group. III and V were working from the other end and I group was never mentioned, if indeed they were employed on the same work.

The biggest and probably most well-known structure on the railway was the bridge over the River Kawai, erected by II group, where the permanent way crossed the river. It was a spidery lattice edifice, built tier upon tier like a pack of cards with sleepers and rails laid straight on the top tier, no duck boarding or side rails, just a set of rails floating through space. It was a colossal undertaking with the materials at their disposal and was built at the cost of a number of lives. The first time I saw it was when we crossed on our way down country and I metaphorically take off my hat to all who worked on the job.

We in C Battalion had no bridges to build if one discounts the single-storey trestles that crossed a swampy patch of jungle near to camp. Most of the work in our sector was that of making embankments and blasting cuttings.

For the embankments, the line to be taken was marked by a triple line of canes, one marking the centre attached to two sloping canes left and right, which marked the outer extremities, the joining piece marking the top. For miles the damn thing ran and the complete inventory of equipment was several hundred flat wicker baskets, a similar number of chungkols, or draw hoes, and a number of pick-axes. Long lines of men waited with baskets whilst those with chungkols drew earth into them, then they walked to the centre pole to dump the earth and returned for more. As soft earth by the track gave out, the chungkollers moved out into the jungle and the men with the pickaxes were there to loosen the earth for shovelling. Gradually, as the thousands of basketloads per day were dumped, the embankment grew upwards and outwards as the poles were buried along the route.

On either side of the work stood the Korean guards, rifles at the ready, eyes everywhere, to see if one of the white coolies dared to stop for a few seconds to wipe the sweat away or to rest for a precious moment his aching back and limbs. The cries of 'Bagero' and 'Kanero' rang in the humid air and the unfortunate recipient of these terms of endearment would, if a trifle slow in dodging, receive a fist in the face, a rifle butt across the side of the head or worse. A savage kick in the crotch was the favourite gesture of love and respect from the little Oriental gentlemen. Should one of the British officers who were allowed to accompany the working parties venture to protest, he too was made to stand to attention and forced to receive the love taps of the guard. Many an officer returned to camp at night bloodied but unbowed, having been thoroughly beaten.

A halt was called throughout the day only to allow the men to partake of a cup of tea, mid-morning and mid-afternoon, and for one hour, midday, for 'mishi', the interminable rice and stew. Otherwise, the men were expected to keep on the move. The only thing that made the work at all bearable was the game of 'Beat the Nip' that went on. Work stopped momentarily each time the Nip, gazing all round, had his back to you. Men with baskets would place two on their heads at the same time. Not with any idea of working harder for the Greater Asia Co-Prosperity Sphere, but the bottom one would only have a line of earth which showed at the front where the top one fitted and the top one, if the tall PoW towered over the diminutive Nip, would have the same, so that virtually no earth was being carried at all. Eventually the penny would drop, the offenders would be lined up and punishment administered but, of course, during this, work in the immediate vicinity virtually ceased. Another ploy for a few minutes' breather was the sudden urgent necessity to visit the lavatory. 'Benjo Nippon.'

'Okega', and into the jungle out of sight and, if lucky, out of mind, for a while at any rate. But, in the main, the work was a long hard slog and the men returned to camp at night thoroughly worn out. Even on the way home work had still not finished, for the party was required to walk along the newly-built embankment to take the place of non-existent rollers, and help it to settle.

Where the ground rose in rocky crags and promontories, cuttings had to be driven. The loose soil, if any, was removed, exposing the rock beneath. Each party was divided into pairs and provided with an eight-pound hammer and a metre-long bar to act as a drill. The bar was placed on the rock, the hammer swung and, if the bar holder was lucky, hit the bar square on the end. The bar was rotated a fraction. Hit it again, rotate, hit, rotate, hit. Accidents were quite numerous at first, for many men were having their first experience of hammer swinging, and brave was he who took on an unknown quantity as partner. At first, the Nips said that each pair should drill one hole as their day's task, and following a rest, could then return to camp. The idea was that when the drill had been sunk to its full depth into the rock, the Korean in charge would verify it, drop a stick of explosive down the hole, and when the resulting spoil had been cleared, the whole process could be repeated, until the required depth had been reached.

The offer of early return to camp worked like a charm. Gangs who had been lethargically swinging, trying to spin out the work to last the day, accelerated and holes were finished even before the midday meal. Next day, the Nips were apologetic. Two holes per man, then go home. As this was done, three holes per man. What was not taken into account at all, was that the hardness of the rock varied appreciably, so that as the number of holes per day increased, some were still able to complete their stint, while others, 'No finish, no go home', were still out, protesting muscles screaming with fatigue, at nine, ten, eleven, or even later. It was a real hell of a job.

Early in the new year, the Japs decided that as there were so many officers (even with two per working party there were still many left in camp) an officers' working party should be formed to push on with the jobs. There was consternation and protest, but to no avail. Out to work the officers went, Geneva Convention or no, and were put to the same backbreaking tasks as the rest of the work force.

The Japs could speak no English, and most commands and instructions were passed on in sign language, resulting in many misunderstandings, and resultant bashings. I had struck up an acquaintance in the very early days in Tonchan with one Jack White, a Eurasian from Singapore, who slept a bed or so away. Born of Scots father and Chinese mother, he had spent his early days in Shanghai and had become fairly proficient in basic Japanese. Quite early on, hearing an altercation behind the hut, he looked out to see a PoW at attention in front of a raving Korean and had gone to see if he could help. That was enough. He was invited to become official camp interpreter. He confided his fears and doubts as to whether he should become involved, but I offered no advice. After a while, he told the British Commandant that he would do what he could, and from then on he was in constant demand. The Japanese language has no words ending in consonants, and so the nearest they could get to 'White' was a resounding 'Oo ay toe'. At all times of the day or night the stentorian cry would issue forth, and away Jack would run to sort out some fresh tangle, returning often with bruised or bloodied face, but having done his best. We lost touch when, for ease of contact, he was required to live nearer the Japanese quarters. Many of the prisoners called him Jap happy; indeed, he was largely distrusted by both sides but without him our lot would have been far worse.

So the line reached tentatively out to Tarsoa to the south, and Konyu to the north. We had little communication with these camps; a few sick were from time to time sent down to Tarsoa which was supposed to have better 'hospital facilities' than we had, and we heard stories from up above. The evacuation of sick to Tarsoa brings to mind a member of our battalion who was taken ill with appendicitis. We had no means of operating and so requested that the Japs take him to Tarsoa. 'Agreed,' said the Japs. 'Tomorrow.' On the morrow he had to be taken on a sort of litter to the side of the river where the Japs assured us that a boat would call to take him downstream. No boat arrived and, the whole day, the lad lay, nearly unconscious and in great pain in the sun. 'Tomorrow,' said the Japs, and he was returned to camp, to be jostled down to the riverbank again next day. No boat. 'Tomorrow,' said the Japs, but it was becoming obvious that, for the unfortunate prisoner, tomorrows were rapidly running out. The Medical Officer decided that the only hope of saving his life was an immediate operation, and the only surgical instrument available was a penknife. The appendix was removed but the expected, indeed the only possible, result was that the prisoner died that evening.

The terribly hard work under the broiling sun, the starvation rations, the primitive sanitation, the lack of proper protection at night, all took an ever-increasing toll. Much, even in these circumstances, depended on the individual and his attitude of mind. Those who were determined to survive and determined to return home overcame some fearful obstacles, while others, who in the seemingly never-ending ordeal, lost their sense of belonging, died quickly and of comparatively mild doses of the diseases that others overcame. A typical example is that of two sergeants, friends during the whole of their service and still together as coolies on the Railway at Tonchan. They contracted dysentery together and were admitted to the grim hospital ward together. The reputation of this dark little building by now was such that men said, 'If you go in there, you won't come out again,' a slander on the harassed, overworked medical staff who were doing their best to work miracles. One sergeant accepted the verdict of the majority and settled down to die.

The other said, 'I'm going out when I've got over the "shits", to be with the lads again.' So for the first time they were separated. Both went down to little over three stones in weight, and clung on to life for weeks. Eventually the one succumbed but after nearly three months the other was where he intended to be, back with his friends. I had often heard of the phrase, 'He turned his face to the wall.' Now I saw it actually happen, as men who had given up all hope turned their backs on life and decided to die.

Of the several dozen crosses now in the little graveyard, one factor seemed common to nearly all – the age. All but one or two were in the age group twenty-three to twenty-six, while the older men, and there were plenty of them, seemed to cling more to life. I had my own theory about this, but I have never seen it offered by anyone else. It seemed to me that the majority of those dying were born during or just after the First World War and I wondered if it could be due to the fact of rationing and general poor food at this time. Their mothers would be on short food rations while carrying, and they would be lacking in vitamins during their formative years, so that perhaps stamina and physique were deficient. Be that as it may, the fact remains that the earliest deaths were nearly all of this group in Tonchan.

It is a popular trait of the British soldier that, no matter what he has to suffer, he always fancies his vocal prowess. In the early months of 1943 the men would come in from work exhausted and ready to drop. After a meal they lay back on their beds and someone would strike up a well-remembered chorus from back home. The men next door would join in and before long the whole hut, two huts or even more would be thundering out song after song until the repertoire, and it was a long one, ran out and they would gradually lapse into uneasy slumber.

The Japanese were far from amused by the row and would rush into camp. 'No Sing Kurra'. Like the RSM at Changi they could not see that a defeated army had anything to sing about, and actually saw something immoral in the outburst of song. It was politely explained that the British Tommy has always fancied his vocal (and other) prowess, and that it was almost impossible to prevent him singing. In the end they came to accept this, and after a time no more was heard of it.

What the Japs could not accomplish, however, could be done by other means. One night a dog fell into the latrines. It was a 'pet' of the Koreans; at least, they amused themselves by titillating it with a stick until it reached a climax, and venting other amusing little spiteful tricks on it. God knows where a dog came from in that country. This poor beast swam frantically up and down the noisome heaving morass of the latrines, 'Yelp, glug. Yelp, glug.' At last it was lassoed by some prisoners, heaved out and freed. The terrified beast scuttled away under the huts, and cowered somewhere under the beds on which friends and I were lying.

Next day the Koreans threw the dog in the river, where they fended it off with poles until it drowned. Below us, those in the Tarsoa camp were drawing water from the river for cooking.

One of the results of the general conditions was that the conversation at night turned completely from 'subject normal'. Never during that year on the railway did I hear mention of the opposite sex except when reminiscing of home. The conversation was entirely of food, of meals past, meals present, and meals yet to come. What we would do when we went out for our first meal at home. Menus were discussed in great and loving detail, the names of dishes rolling off the tongue in ecstatic delight. In the middle of this gastronomic make believe one night a sergeant said, 'Wish I was at Blackpool. There was a little Jap at Blackpool used to make the most wonderful little rice cakes. Wonder if he's still there. When I get home, I'm going round to see. If he is, I'll buy three dozen – and stuff 'em down his throat one by one!'

Another story that stuck in my mind was told by a cockney of his days pre-war. 'So I was leaning on this wall in the West End, when a rozzer comes up and says "Ere, what you on then?" "Working guv," says I. "Come off it. None of your cheek. What you on?" "Working guv!" So he runs me in. I was working, too. Across the street was this 'ere theatre showing that new play, "Who killed the Count". All up in lights it was, bold as brass. They was paying me two quid a night to see that the "O" didn't go out.'

So far, apart from the steady toll that was filling our little cemetery, our life, though arduous, was just bearable, consisting greatly of a battle of wits with our little, grinning captors. But the rains were starting, the monsoons were coming, and it was perhaps as well that we had no idea of the dreadful conditions and diseases that were in store for us in the next six months or so.

Violent thunderstorms were beginning to fill the nights with fire and noise and we woke one morning to find one of the huts half demolished by a large tree that had been toppled during the night. Fortunately, no one had been seriously injured. The camp began to empty, as working parties were detached to smaller camps nearby since work in the vicinity of Tonchan was completed. They went to Kanyu, to Tonchan South where we had halted by the banks of the little stream on our forced march north, and to the Sawmill camp nearby.

The worst part of our captivity was upon us.

Chapter 10

Lazy, Hazy Days of Summer

No clothes could possibly stand up to the treatment they were given in the jungle. Soaked with sweat and dirt, never washed, for even had there been time or opportunity, there was no such thing as soap to be had, they literally disintegrated. Even those who had reasonable shirts or shorts left them in camp whilst working, from the first days in the jungle, and made themselves loincloths with pieces of cloth. These were lovingly nicknamed 'Jap nappies' and rapidly became the only garb a well-dressed man would care to be seen in. Boots rotted away in the steamy foetid atmosphere, and for a while this meant no work, for how, we argued, can anyone walk about barefoot in the jungle? The Japs universally sported a kind of rubber baseball boot with separate compartment for the big toe, their jungle boot to facilitate tree climbing. One or two pairs of these found their way to the PoW lines, but usually it was no boots, no work. Until, that is, a party of Australians on their way up country called into the camp for a meal. Dozens of sun-bronzed toes wriggling in the dust.

The following morning we were all paraded outside the huts and kept waiting while the Koreans swept through the sleeping quarters and emerged bearing in their hands any footwear they found in the huts. Steadily the pile grew, for although there were many who were genuinely bootless, others, by good luck or good husbandry, had more than one pair. There was hell to play, and 'Oo ay toe' worked overtime. Eventually all was calm, but no one ever again missed work solely through bare feet. Even boots had their dangers. One morning, my next-door neighbour awoke and plunged his feet deep into his boots beneath his bed. He screamed and tore them off again. A scorpion had taken a fancy to them in the night and had been annoyed at being rudely awakened. Fortunately, a Thai scorpion's sting, although painful, is seldom fatal, and a badly swollen toe for a few days was the only result.

We were now receiving pay for our labours, the princely sum of one tical (6p) per month for private soldiers, and three ticals (17½p) per month for NCOs. Officers were also paid about ten ticals per month, and this money could be spent in the camp canteen. This had been started in the new year when, entirely out of character, the Japanese had given a Bangkok Chinese merchant permission to bring supplies up the river and sell them to the camps. The merchant had an unpronounceable name, but was known to all and sundry as Pong, or Boon Pong. He supplied camps with salt, thick, gooey native sugar, hands of tiny bananas, cooking oil, duck eggs, native tobacco, known along the river as Sikh's beard, and many other items. The most highly prized were perhaps the eggs, and many a dozen were fried at night in the corner of mess tins after dinner. True, one or two exploded in a rainbow of riotous colours as the shell was cracked but, in the main, they were manna from the gods. An egg was five satangs, there being 100 satangs to the tical. A hatful of rock salt, which had somehow to be ground or crushed before it could be used, about the same, a hand of bananas ten or fifteen, and other items, similar prices. Change was a problem, for we were paid only in brand new, specially-printed occupation money. A system of debit and credit was worked out, pay being given in toto to the canteen officer, and purchases being made against this. The canteen was run by a Captain Pete Hunt, who coped extremely well.

Pong also supplied many other items to the camps, items which the Japanese would not have been entirely happy about, a steady supply of drugs to help the overworked medical staffs, radio valves and batteries for the clandestine radios that were operating near most camps. These were organized by a former (and later) BBC engineer who risked life and torture to get the news to the camps. Pong was not the bland smiling moneygrubber that he seemed to the Japanese, and ran a courier service for goods and contacts between the camps and the Bangkok espionage network that was operated, so we were later told, from police headquarters. It was widely believed after our release that the chief of police was also head of the British secret service in Thailand. Be that as it may, there is no doubt that Pong supplied all the camps on the river with thousands of ticals' worth of goods on credit, merely on the word of the Camp Commandants that he would be paid after the war. He was, in full, and was decorated by a grateful government for his selfless devotion to the river camps.

The goodies that he brought were especially welcome in the hospital, for the Japs had ordered that the sick were not to be paid and also had to subsist on half rations. 'Tojo has no use for idle hands,' they told us. 'No work, no eat.' In practice, the rations for the whole camp, fit and sick, were cooked in the same cookhouse and, although the issue for the hospital was less, the whole was divided up equally when cooked. In paying our cash to the canteen, a small proportion was given over to the hospital to buy extras, mainly eggs, for the sick men.

The storms increased in intensity daily and often we went out in rain, worked all day in rain and returned in rain at night. The food orderlies had to descend the steep trail to the riverbank to collect a large basket of cooked rice and four-gallon petrol cans full of dark brown liquid that the cooks called tea. In spite of this, it was an eagerly sought after job. There was always the probability that in trying to ration out the rice (Cook would say 'Half a mugful' or 'Three quarters of mugful' according to the amount of dry rice issued to him) there would be some left, and the orderlies were first in line. For the rest, it was customary for first served to go straight to the back of the queue and start a second line, commonly known as the 'Leggy queue' from the Malayan 'lagi' for more. They would stand there surveying the diminishing basket of rice, while consuming their own portion. If it became evident that there would be none left over, they would slink disconsolately away, otherwise they would shuffle forward like Oliver Twist for what few grains remained. Another perk of the orderlies was the 'toast'. Army dixies were worn out and the cooks were using native cast-iron kualies, flattish slightly dome-shaped pans some three-feet across, to cook rice. When the cooked rice was scooped out, a coating of burnt rice remained to be scraped off the kuali and, coming off in large sheets, this toast was a highly-prized delicacy, though what it must have done to tender stomachs can be imagined,

On the long haul back up to camp, the slope slippery with mud, it was usual to rest at the QM rice stores, some halfway up the hill, and then continue to the top. One day we went down to find that, in the night, the river had begun to rise with the volume of rain. Trees, bushes and other debris raced down, and that night our cookhouse had joined the rubbish on the flood. The meal had been cooked in the open air. The following day we were hastily assembled for a fatigue party to evacuate the rice stores, at which the river was lapping. This roaring, turbulent stream full of tossing trees and junk was the same that, only weeks before, we had been able to walk across without getting wet knees. Now it was forty or more feet deep and rising before one's eyes.

We hadn't time to worry about the remote possibility of the campsite being flooded, for that night we were told that we would be moving again. Tonchan was already taking on a forlorn, neglected look for, during the past few weeks, there had been almost daily parties moving to Tonchan South and other camps in the vicinity to carry on with the task of linking up the sections of railway with the camps on either side. We weren't particularly sorry to leave. We didn't imagine another camp could be much worse than this, where we had lost so many of our friends. We could not have been more wrong.

Tonchan South had been built on the spot where we had stopped by the bank of the crystal gurgling stream, on our march up country, and where we had slaked our thirst. That stream was now a filthy, sulphurous and mud-coloured rivulet, loathsome to look at. The camp, apart from the usual Nip quarters, was a tented enclosure created from captured British Army tents, presumably from Malaya. However, a small tent had to house at least twelve men, sometimes more, so that the end men protruded from the end of the tent. Moreover, to make the 'accommodation' stretch a little further, the cunning Nips had split each tent in two, so that you either had an inner, or a flysheet as cover. It was difficult to know which was the worse. With inners, every time you touched the roof a leak started, and a steady drip, drip, drip turned your blankets and prized personal possessions into a sodden mass. In the other, having no side walls, the incessant rain sluiced under the sides and, until these were built in with bamboo, purloined planks and any other type of material that could be won, life was cold, wet and miserable. Blankets were of necessity placed on the bare earth, for no beds had been erected. Very few materials were available in that weeping wilderness, and there was no time in any case for building home refinements, the majority of men being out at work from dawn to dusk.

The rain was now coming down almost incessantly for twenty-four hours a day. The shivering, emaciated prisoners, after a night's sleep in sodden bedding, were parading in the early morning gloom in the pouring rain, working all day in the downpour, and returning to camp at night in the never-ending sluicing to spend another night, wet and miserable in saturated blankets. Dysentery, that ubiquitous scourge, was rampant, and all day and all night, a never-ending trail of men could be seen wending their weary, pain-racked way to and from the latrines. These were, of necessity, in the jungle some little way from the camp living quarters, and the miserable dejected sufferers plodded their way through the ankle-deep mud and the rain, to spend up to fifteen minutes squatting on the bamboo platforms, while it felt as if their entire insides were slipping out through the bottoms of their bodies Often, after reaching halfway back to camp, another spasm would rack their tortured frames, and they would retrace their steps, over and over again, without ever reaching the comparative comfort of their tents.

It was one of the paradoxes of the English temperament that, in spite of the fact that they had been out in the rain all day, and that the tents were not that much better, if a man had to go out for any reason after work at night, the first thing he would do would be to reach for something to protect his almost naked body from the rain. Even in those circumstances it was amusing to see them reaching for one of the rare groundsheets, even though a wet Jap nappy was the only clothing they had to protect. I suppose it was a sort of reflex action.

The three cookhouses, C, H and K, were situated on the banks of the stream and used the same filthy water for such things as making tea and boiling rice. They struggled in the rain, with sodden bamboo for fuel to prepare breakfast in the dark, make a midday meal for those working near enough to camp to fetch it, and to get an evening meal for the returning working parties at night. Rations on the river had never been plentiful, and now they seemed to be even less. The usual dole of cooked rice per man was down to about half a half-pint mug per meal, with the usual nondescript watery stew to help it down. The canteen was still in operation, and one of the most prolific items, the ubiquitous duck egg, was still available. I happened to be cooking one in the corner of my mess tin one night, when my neighbour began to drool over the tit-bit.

'If I buy an egg, will you cook it for me?' he asked eagerly.

'Here's the mess tin and oil. Help yourself, ' I replied.

'I don't know how to fry eggs,' he vouchsafed.

After some fifteen months as a PoW, words failed me.

Another night I was awakened from my slumbers by a hand shaking my shoulder. Apparently someone wanted to see me by the main gate. I went over, to find a scene of indescribable excitement. All was hurry and bustle. F Force, newly arrived from Singapore with 3,000 men, were marching up country, not as we had done following a barely discernible trail through almost virgin jungle, but marching along the trail we had cleared, and with their possessions on their backs or in trek carts. They had called in for a meal from our cookhouse, the idea being that they would move by night so that they did not interfere with operations on the way. Also, the cookhouses along the way were not being used in the middle of the night, so they could be impressed into providing a meal for the marchers. It appeared that they were moving into Burma to help complete the railway from the other end. After a quick meal, they disappeared into the night but not before I had had a quick word with Jim Swanton, who was the officer in charge of this particular contingent and who, finding out somehow that I was in this particular camp, had enquired after my health.

It was a week or so later that one of the sergeant majors from H Battalion was admitted to the little camp hospital, suffering from stomach pains and diarrhoea. The following day a word was whispered round the camp, bringing a chill to the hearts of all who heard it. Cholera. Another was admitted to the hastily-allocated isolation ward, quickly followed by a third and another. Two days later the sergeant major had died. His body and all his possessions were burnt on a fire of bamboo, the flames of which could be seen all over the camp.

The Nips beat a hasty retreat from the camp, erected a fence between us and them, and posted an armed guard on the only connecting gate. Considering the fact that medicines and suchlike were said to be absolutely unobtainable, it was remarkable that in a case affecting the Nips themselves this did not apply. Within twenty-four hours ample supplies of disinfectants had been received, pits dug and filled with disinfectant-soaked sacking at every entrance to the camp and between the British and Japanese lines, and supplies of anti–cholera vaccine had been rushed into camp. We had, of course, been vaccinated against cholera at Singapore, but we were told that this was only effective for six months or so, and that a booster dose was vital. The whole camp was lined up for the jab, followed by a second dose six days later, but this was a long-term policy and did little or nothing to lessen our chances of being unwilling participants in the fury that was now upon us. Even in this nightmare, one could still find humour. One of the 18th Division, a huge Irishman named 'Paddy' Byrne, was the camp butcher, not that he was particularly overworked, but on the rare occasions when we had a meat issue it was brought up live, on the hoof. With one mighty blow from the back of a felling axe, Paddy could kill one of the decrepit Thai oxen outright. The remainder of his time he spent on general fatigues in the cookhouse. He was in front of me in the inoculation queue, a great hulking figure making two of me. We shuffled forwards, dab with antiseptic, shuffled forwards and came up to the needle, wielded none too gently by a Jap orderly with British assistance. The one in front of Paddy received the jab in stoical silence, but it was too much. With a sigh Paddy measured his length, unconscious. He never was a brave man, in spite of his size. He was on the *Empress of Asia*, which was sunk outside Singapore. To the right and left of him, troops were losing no time in bidding adieu to the old tub, diving into the sea in all directions. Not Paddy. He clung to a rope like grim death and closed his eyes. Then, urged to let go and drop, he finally condescended to slide fractionally at a time, down the rope into the briny. If he is alive now, he still has the deep scorch marks on his arms and legs that he bore at Tonchan South.

The deaths mounted: two, six, ten a day, increasing all the time. A still was set up to make distilled water for a saline solution which was injected into the arm of the victim, in a vain attempt to still the enormous loss of body fluid. The cholera victim loses fluid through the mouth and by passing water and liquid faeces all at the same time. The flesh literally melts off the bones. One day, as we were going out to work, the man on the next bed to myself said he was staying behind to report sick with diarrhoea. Even after the rigours of the last few months he must still have weighed about twelve stone at the time. When we returned to camp in the evening, the change in him was frightening. His face, now putty coloured, had fallen in and resembled one of those Amazon shrunken skulls. The cheeks had collapsed, the mouth receded from the gums and the eyes looked black and lacklustre from cavernous sockets. He appeared to have lost several stones in weight even in the ten hours or so we had been out of camp, and shortly afterwards was removed to the isolation hospital. Few came back from there, and he died next day, less than forty-eight hours after feeling 'slightly ill'. His belongings were removed to be burnt, and we drew disinfectant to slop liberally round the tent. Such were the conditions in which we were then existing that, although he slept next to me, I never even knew his name.

The burning of the dead had to cease, purely because it was impossible to find enough dry fuel to stoke the insatiable fires. Burial pits were dug as far from the camp as possible, and night and day the burial parties struggled to keep pace. All were volunteers, both in the wards and the fatigue parties, and all knew the risks they were taking. A ward orderly one day, he had every chance of taking his place in one of the beds the next, but none faltered. The MO and his staff were indefatigable, and the stills worked night and day to provide the distilled water. No one, it was ordered, was to use water at all without it being well boiled first. No drinking, no washing, no contact with unboiled water. Most of us brought back from work what little fuel we could collect, and four-gallon cans of water hung almost permanently over fires at the door of every tent. And still the admissions never faltered. We all looked carefully for the watery discharge with white flecks, the 'rice-water stools' that were the first symptom of the disease. For no one wanted to go into 'dock', a virtual death sentence. Tests showed at last that the source of the outbreak seemed to be in C Battalion cookhouse, and all the cooks except the chief, BQMS Weedall, were changed, lest one of them should be a carrier. Stringent precautions were taken in the preparation of food, and every avenue that could be foreseen was stopped up. At last, the back of the outbreak was broken, the rate of admissions was checked, and we could say that the epidemic was over. In a few short weeks thirty members of C Battalion had succumbed, even more from the rest of the camp, and the total death roll was well in excess of a hundred.

Hard pressed as we were, the camps of natives in the area were even worse. These, Malays, Tamils, Javanese or Sumatrans, had been brought up in their thousands by their Japanese masters, with fanciful stories of good working conditions, easy work and good pay. They were dumped in stinking unsanitary camps with no facilities and worked to death. Their endearing habits didn't help, the usual method of evacuating the bowels being to squat in the mud just outside the door of the hut and do what comes naturally. They were already dying like flies when cholera struck. A fatigue party from our camp was sent to a nearby native hellhole that had been nearly wiped out and had no fit men left to bury the mountain of dead. Before leaving, the working party were strictly forbidden to touch any personal possessions they might find lying around, let alone bring anything back into camp, for it was at the height of our own outbreak.

They found a pitiful sight. The huts were filled to capacity with living skeletons, dead and dying – corpses and those tenaciously clinging to life, cheek by jowl. In the centre of the camp, the working party was set to work digging a huge pit, many feet deep. They then had to collect the corpses and, to their disgust, toss them into the pit, one on top of another. As they worked, Indians were dragging their palliasses to the side of the hole, lying down there to await the merciful release which they felt could not be too far away. Some few demented souls even leapt into the pit and lay there among the dead, waiting for the grave to be filled in.

It took several days and more than one pit to completely clear the camp and accommodate the pile of dead. One hole had been nearly filled in when a guard noticed a gaunt arm protruding from the soil. He hit it repeatedly with the butt of his rifle until the bone snapped, whereupon he trampled it into the ground.

Here and there in the disgusting confines of this charnel house a few pathetic items of discarded rations lay around. Flies buzzed around this forgotten hoard, and it could not be imagined that in this disease-ridden, infected, godforsaken place anyone would have given the stuff a second glance. Amongst the food was a quantity of dried fish, locally known as 'banjo fish' from the shape it assumed when gutted and dried (another type of fish was similar to a gutted herring, or kipper and rejoiced in the name of 'flapper' or 'modern girl'). One of the working party picked up some tinned food and some 'banjo' fish and smuggled the loot back into camp. That night he cooked and ate the fish. Three days later he was dead.

At about the time that the outbreak started our work force was augmented by a party of mixed Dutch and Indonesians. They didn't move into our camp but made a separate encampment immediately adjacent and when the cholera started they fenced themselves off from the British troops and led, apart from work, a completely separate existence with all contact barred between us. They considered us, I suppose, a little dirty in our habits but we only saw them from over the fence. From long association, they knew the difference between the poisonous and the non-poisonous shrubs and trees, whereas we were scared to experiment with the various leaves and flowers, hungry or no. They would come back from work with haversacks bulging with berries and other provender, and we would watch them add these to their diet and consume them with every evidence of delight. In the matter of personal hygiene there was also a wide gap. Being used to toilet paper, of which there was none, we kept a store of leaves for this purpose, probably the same leaves that the Dutch were using as a supplement to diet. We became adept at choosing the best suited for the purpose. This was too fragile, this too glossy, while a banana leaf would split, letting through your finger with the direst of results. The Dutch, as was their custom, took with them to the latrine a bottle of water with which they swilled themselves down after going through the motions. There was an apocryphal story of two Australians who watched this party piece with more than a passing interest.

'I'm going to have a bash at this,' said one, and vanished in the direction of the latrine clutching to his hairy breast a full water bottle. Some hour or so later, his friend, becoming disturbed, set off in search of the missing digger.

'You all right Blue?' he asked anxiously in the gathering gloom.

'All right be buggered,' came Blue's voice somewhere in the darkness. 'I've got a bootful of water, a handful of shit and I still haven't wiped my arse.'

Perhaps the best commentary on this was that, during the whole episode, not one case of cholera was reported from the Dutch camp, while over a hundred British troops died.

Cholera over, we still had sickness of one sort or another to make sure that the medical staff had no time to be bored with life. Dysentery and malaria were still rampant, Mag Sulph and insufficient quinine the only drugs available. Now deficiency diseases, due to the incessant and almost unrelieved rice diet, began to rage with ever-increasing severity. Rice in its harvested state is packed with vitamins Bl and others, but unpolished it is a mealy brown colour, stodgy, filling and unappetizing. The vitamin content is entirely in the husk or skin. The rice eaters of the world demand polished rice, gleaming white, podging you out for an hour or so, and then leaving you as hungry as before the meal. With the chaff that is polished off goes all the goodness. The nearest parallel in this country is the difference between wholemeal and white bread, though that is not exact. The polishings are collected in sacks as waste or perhaps to be made into vitamin foods or tablets of some sort. Anyhow, white rice we got.

Vitamin Bl deficiency, and lack of other essential vitamins resulted in a variety of ills. Chief among them was beriberi which, in common with nearly the whole camp, I suffered. The ankles swell and ache. The swelling increases and steadily the legs and feet fill with fluid. The limbs become puddeny and the skin distends tight around the gross appendages, looking glossy, almost as if varnished. A thumb pressed into this bloated flesh leaves a dent, which does not fill out as the thumb is removed, but remains impressed in the putty-like flesh for an hour or more. Eventually, unchecked, the disease reaches the abdomen, the chest, and eventually the lungs, whereupon the victim literally drowns. Not so common was cardiac beriberi which had no swelling. The possessor of this charming disease, while appearing quite healthy, just dropped down dead while walking, or passed away in his sleep. As these twin scourges became more and more widespread, the Nips allowed sacks of the discarded rice polishings to be brought into camp. We would rather have had the vitamin tablets, with which they were freely supplied, but any port in a storm. The sacks were left at the MI room and were available to all. No asking, just take your mug or some other receptacle and help yourself. They were vile. They were revolting. They were packed with vitamins, but ugh! They were in a fine powder about the colour and consistency of snuff, or even finely-ground pepper. And how they clung. No ivy ever clung more tightly than those damn rice polishings did to the roof of your mouth when you tried to swallow them. Scoop up a spoonful and place it in your mouth, it stuck to your palate. Stir them in tea, they were completely insoluble, sticking to the side of the mug, and again to the roof of your mouth. Then try scattering them on your meal of insipid rice. You swallowed the rice, leaving the polishings – guess where? Right again. And the taste was revolting, bitter and acrid. But somehow they had to be ingested if one was to survive.

Arthur Carling, once a strapping young Tyke from West Yorkshire, now had severe beriberi, which was filling his chest with fluid, and so I had fetched him a mug full of polishings from the MI room. He heaved as he vainly tried to swallow the nauseous stuff.

'It's no good, I can't face it Stuart,' he said at last. He emptied the remains of the polishings on the ground. He steadfastly refused to take any more, in spite of the pleadings of all his friends, and as he got more and more sick, he was taken down to Hospital in base camp. We heard a few weeks later that he had died, drowned by the encroaching fluid that reached up from his ankles to his lungs. Those who persevered with the treatment found the fluid melting away, and the normal sylph-like figure reappearing.

Pellagra, another deficiency disease marked by angry red scabrous patches, appeared on legs and arms. As far as we had experience of it there were no other ill effects, fortunately for us, for it was only after the war that we discovered that it can and often does result in insanity and death. Tropical sores were prevalent and were turning into gangrenous pus-filled ulcers. Strips of cloth soaked in the never-ending Mag Sulph were the only dressings, but when they became too bad for even the Nips to insist that a man went out to work he was sent down river to a 'rest camp' from where, if he was unfortunate enough to recover, he was sent up country again for more work on the railway.

For this never ceased, and the 'Speedo' campaign had started, as high command, needing an urgent lifeline into Burma, ordered that the track must be finished and would be finished by August. More and more sick men were sent out to work. The maximum number allowed to be sick was laid down daily and, if the requisite numbers for the working parties were not forthcoming, into the hospital would stalk the camp officials. Along the rows of sick men, a hand on the forehead carelessly – 'No sick. Worku' and, in spite of protests, worku it was until the parties were made up.

More and more were dying, simply through the lack of will to keep alive. They had no interest in eating, none in keeping themselves clean, or as clean as possible in the circumstances. One I saw one day, sick, but more mentally than physically, was being scrubbed in a can of water by his friends

'You won't have to do this much longer,' was his mournful parrot cry, 'I shan't be here much longer.'

He wasn't. It was easy to give up that summer, the longest six months in the life of anyone who lived through them. There were times when the 'washday' smell of the boiled rice in the baskets waiting to be served out was so overpowering that you just could not face the stuff at all and sat, watching others wolfing down the last few grains, while to bring a spoonful to your own lips, brought on a retching and nausea that was indescribable. Fortunately, this feeling lasted only about twenty-four hours or so, because a diet of fresh air at that time was not exactly the most nutritious.

One day, I volunteered to be one of a party to meet Pong's barge at the riverside at its nearest point to the camp, about a mile away. I was supposed to help carry a skip of eggs back to the camp in the normal way, slung on a pole between two men. I had had a short spell in camp on light duties, but felt fairly fit – until I started to walk to the river, let alone carry eggs. After about half a mile I collapsed with the exertion, and had to sit there with my carrying partner while the rest went on. I was not sorry when eventually reaching the riverbank to find that Pong had not kept his appointment, and that the carry was off till the next day.

Such was summer 1943, but bad as it was for us, it was even worse for the native camps. Our chronic sick were evacuated to Non Pladuk, even if they were later sent to work again. We had the heroic and untiring efforts of the MOs and their unflagging orderlies. We had the Major Brodies and the Colonel Lilleys, men whose fame spread far beyond their camps for the efforts they put in for their men, now alas both dead. The natives had no one working for them. They died in their thousands, and their camps, neglected, were soon overtaken again by the jungle, and remained silent foetid pestilence-ridden oases in a pestilence-ridden land.

Chapter 11

Over the Hill

The camp at Tonchan South was on a plateau, a sheer drop to the side ending in a plain, on which was to run the railway. Just outside the camp boundary to the east, ran the 'road' to Tarsoa, now a morass of thick glutinous mud which clutched lovingly at the wheels of all vehicles that tried to pass, dragging them in axle deep, and even more. When this happened in the camp environs we would be fetched out of bed at any hour of the night to free the drowning vehicle, heaving while ankle-deep in mud and half-drowned with teeming rain.

Down the cliff the work on the railway was proceeding at full speed. Track-laying was approaching from the south, and the bed had to be ready when the track laying gangs reached our area. It was speedo, speedo, speedo, screams, curses, bashings galore, embankment, cutting, trestle bridges. Men worked till they dropped with fatigue, worked from first light, and walked home in the dark for, by this time, camp, anywhere from the screaming, ranting, raving speedo, was home.

Eventually, as the rainy season drew to its close, the track reached Tonchan South. The sleepers were of mainly unseasoned wood, the rails filched from stores in Malaya, and the gangs worked with incredible speed. The rails were fastened to the green sleepers with dogs, not with the chairs usual in this country, and these were driven in by hand, one to each sleeper. Immediately the line was past, it was in use. Rail cars, army lorries with tyred wheels replaced by flanged, scurried back and forth with supplies, with food, any and every type of cargo. At last the quagmire of a road was unnecessary. As far and as fast as the rails were laid, they were followed by the motorized traffic so that the railway was in use to the utmost as soon as possible.

The speedo continued unabated. The rail link was needed to supply the army in Burma, and nothing was to be allowed to stand in the way of its completion. By using the motor trucks, the camps and the advance gangs could be supplied, the track helped to settle, and the bridges and trestles along the line subjected to test. We were now employed on lifting and ballasting the line where any slight subsidence occurred, re-aligning the track, and general maintenance and repair. At last all seemed to be coming to an end and the line was far to the north, approaching a meeting with the gangs moving down from Burma.

'The big loco is coming to try out the track tomorrow,' the whisper went round, 'the ninety-tonner from Bangkok.' Sure enough, we were at work as usual when a whistle from around the bend indicated the arrival of the monster. We were motioned to clear the track and took the opportunity of a few minutes sit-down while we could. At least there was nothing that Nippon could give us to do until the giant engine had cleared our section of track. Round the bend into view lurched the snorting, hissing monster, inching slowly and cautiously forward. This was the consummation of all our efforts but, while interesting, the rest was more pleasant than the view.

The monster crept past, inch by inch, engineers hanging from both sides of the cab, scanning the track ahead, followed by a railcar of knifebox pattern, with Koreans at the controls. There were no coaches on the engine itself, and the miniature procession was soon past and nosing down the track in front. We were waiting for the command to restart work, the loco, five, ten, twenty yards ahead, when, with a soft sigh, the sleepers and a section of the track vanished beneath the surface of the ground and the loco, belching steam, lurched, and came to rest precariously at the most crazy angle. Pandemonium. Shouting, yelling Nips ran forward to inspect the tragedy and we were completely forgotten. The railcar reversed, Nips pumping like mad, as it rocketed off in the general direction of Tarsoa and all stations south. After a time it re-appeared with sliding jacks, reinforcements of manpower and a wide variety of equipment of all kinds. We lolled on the side of the track, chins cupped on hands, interested spectators of the unaccustomed scene. We had expected that we would have to do the heavy work, but it was evidently too important for us. Far from feeling insulted at this lack of confidence in our capabilities, we were content to leave it to the undoubted experts and take a rest. For a couple of hours or more they worked like galley slaves, to the accompaniment of the barrage of yells and shouts, without which any child of Nippon is unable to imagine any physical labour being carried out. The sweat rolled from their bodies, staining their shirts black, while we lolled back, taking our unaccustomed ease. At long last, the jacks had raised the monster locomotive and eased it back on to the track, the job was done. Cautiously the Giant felt its way on to more solid ground, gradually it increased speed and, to wild Nipponese cheers, it inched down the line and out of sight round the bend.

Then it was our turn again. Apparently the loco would return to Tarsoa that evening, and the track must be put right before the return. We were put to work raising the rails and filling with ballast under the sleepers. We were now the ones to toil like demons, until with a toot on its whistle, the ninety-tonner came back again, this time at a fair rate of knots, on its return journey down the line. It passed safely and we returned to camp.

That over, the tempo of work slowed, and it was evident that our stay at Tonchan South was coming to an end. We knew that we wouldn't be kept in idleness for long. The question was, what now?

Even at Tonchan South, there were moments of relaxation and, dare I say it, beauty. True, there was no time there for entertainment, as such, and even the games of bridge with which we had whiled away a few nights at Tonchan were absent. There was a library of sorts operating and I read a few books.

The wildlife was more in evidence than at Tonchan for some reason. There we only heard gibbons as they whooped their way around camp, saw traces of wild pig on the side of the road, and caught the python. And one day, when the cookhouse had moved up the hill to escape the floods, I saw a nine- or ten-foot green bootlace snake slide downhill and under the mosquito netting where the cooks were preparing dinner, the cooks all leaving, gracefully at the same time, by the opposite side, like a shot from an 'Our Gang' before the war. Not a word was spoken, as the snake swept majestically straight through, and on to the river. The cooks returned and continued as if nothing had happened.

At the start of the rainy season, and at Tonchan South, we heard the sound of some tree insects, filling the air with their shrill mating cry, like the sound of demented circular saws. There was the little lizard with the peculiar call, a 'ticking' that went on interminably, like granny winding up her alarm, then a diminuendo down scale sort of 'cuckoo' cry. This was soon twisted to a name that fell more readily from the tongue, by the brutal and licentious soldiery, and no doubt the commandant of River Valley would have been proud to know that we had named wildlife after him.

One day, as I lay in my tent, the rain ceased for a few minutes, and a watery sun peeped wanly out. A crumb of earth shivered, and rolled aside, and from the hole so uncovered, crept a small insect, looking as wet and bedraggled as I felt. It moved a few steps, hesitated and unfolded a pair of soggy-looking wings. From the hole in the ground issued another ant-like creature, and another, like soldiers on parade, the same number of steps, the same hesitation, the unfolding of wings, a few more steps and the take-off as the wings dried and shimmered iridescent in the sun. Soon the clearing round the tent was full of the flying creatures, and they continued to emerge for some twenty minutes to half an hour. Then suddenly they had gone. All was silence again, and the rain poured down once more.

The gibbons were heard again in the early morning, their mournful whooping cry sending a shiver down the back of all in camp.

'Sign of a death when you hear them,' said the superstitious. If so, we should have heard them twenty-four hours a day, not just in the pre-dawn gloom. The little gekko still kept up spirits with his strict injunction to do just what we would like to tell the Nips. In fact, one 'tenko' when we were all drawn up ready for counting, and dared not move a muscle for fear of reprisals, one burst into full cry, and cheeks puffed, and colour returned to normally sallow cheeks as the assembled 'squaddies' tried their best to refrain from bursting out laughing.

In the ground lived little land crabs and timid little lizards who would poke a cautious snout above the ground and cast a wary eye around the vicinity. At the first sign of movement they would withdraw or, if they had completely emerged, dash back headfirst, somehow turn inside the burrow which must have been quite large inside, and the snout would poke out again. The trick was to make a noose of creeper, place it round the hole, and wait. When his neck emerged, pull, and you had him. Jimmy Findlay, who was a butcher in civilian life, cleaned and prepared them for me, and fried they were just like a bit of chicken. Bit was right, for they were only two or three inches long.

Into the Jap cookhouse went larger game, the occasional wild pig, and other meat. A friend of mine, who had a pal in the Jap cookhouse, was one day given some roast meat which had been sent back uneaten. He thoroughly enjoyed it, until told it was roast cat, when he promptly returned the lot. The thought of cat, wild or tabby, was too much.

When the railway had passed the camp, rations for the Japs and British were delivered by rail and left at the foot of the plateau from which a stiff climb led to the campsite. Strangely, when the Japs came looking for a party to drag the rations up the steep climb there was no lack of volunteers. The route to the Japanese cookhouse lay through the British lines but, by taking a detour, the baskets could be carried down between any two of the huts, between which there were usually blankets hanging out to air. As each two men negotiated the course between the 'washing', hands would reach out furtively, and the baskets reached the Jap cookhouse up to a third lighter than when they had left the railway side. Anything Japanese was considered 'fair game', and the story was told, presumably true, of one enterprising merchant stealing a four-gallon can of cooking oil from the Japanese store and selling it back to the Jap cookhouse. He was reputed to have pinched and re-sold the same tin some four or five times without the Nips ever realizing what was going on.

As the road dried out a certain amount of traffic was restarted on it. We had a very occasional issue of meat, usually the peculiar saddle-backed hogs that are transported in wicker baskets all over Thailand. This used to be cut up small and included in the vegetable stew that was our usual diet. A wild whoop at mealtime would indicate that some fortunate gourmet had been lucky enough to find one or even two oxo-cube-sized pieces of fat and gristle in his watery stew. I must have had some in my time, and still have the trichinosis to prove it. At other times beef, if you can call it that, came up on the hoof. Poor emaciated beasts, they reminded me of the art teacher who, according to Mr Punch, demanded of the Hansom cab driver 'Call that a horse. Rub it out and do it again'.

They were brought up by an elderly Thai, equally decrepit, who did not as we are accustomed to, drive his beasts, but led them from the front. He left one beast at each camp on the road through. There were at this time a few Australian troops in camp, and whatever one can say about the Aussies 'unenterprising' is not a satisfactory epithet. Two would-be tycoons lay in wait as the Thai ambled past and the long straggle of angular beasts made up the rear. When satisfied that the herdsman was out of sight, they quickly hustled off the rear beast and, before the poor animal could say 'Tojo for Prime Minister', he had ended up as steaks, on a hastily-erected shop counter. The first I knew of this was as I was returning to my tent; I passed the emporium where the two entrepreneurs were leaning, a placard proclaiming 'Best Steaks 50 satangs each'. With the aid of two pals, we raked up a dollar-fifty between us. We had recently been paid and canteen supplies had dried up, so that night we fed on best steak. Well, hardly best, even after half an hour's battering in traditional manner, it was still slightly reminiscent of old boot leather, but delicious old boot leather.

Some few weeks later, another herd was on its way through, and the British were not to be outdone. They also laid in wait and duly abstracted the last beast. The Thai had either been forewarned, or was not as daft as he looked, a not too difficult feat. He raised the roof, and soon appeared, thundering down towards the British lines, the Jap guards trying vainly to catch up. All they found was a lazy scene, one lad with a guitar, the rest giving renditions of old ballads in close harmony. The area was searched in vain, and well searched. Eventually, the Thai was helped on his way, loudly protesting, with a few bayonet jabs in the better upholstered part of his anatomy, while the grumbling guards returned to their posts. No sooner had they gone than the choir disbanded, the top of the swill pit was uncovered, and a half-suffocated cow was dragged from the smelly depths. It all added flavour to the meat ration that night.

The black marketeers were flourishing, and trade with the Thais was brisk. Anything of value that hadn't already been sold, or taken by the Nips, was traded over the wire, and when the supply of valuables began to dry up the greedy ones were not above stealing to fatten their wallets. Blankets, preciously hoarded mosquito nets or precious boots would mysteriously disappear and those shadowy figures who were always willing to take the risk of being caught by the Nips for trading over the wire would fatten their pile a little more. In the hospitals of the various camps we heard of men who would go into the sick with offers of water at a dollar a cup, payable if necessary after the war, standing and pouring the precious fluid from cup to four-gallon can. This never happened in our camp, but our black marketeers grew fat on their piles, with all sorts of fruit, canned foods, proper cigarettes, and other items of the most unimaginable luxury. Once I saw one drop his wallet into a latrine. It fell from his shorts as he sqatted there. Rather than lose the money, he climbed down the bamboo structure, to the loathsome mass below, and retrieved his little fortune from the filth and the maggots. For 'the love of money is the root of' – many things.

Chapter 12

Goodbye to Tonchan

Now that the railway was operating past the camp, the heat came off, and conditions became easier, The latrine rumours, which had been conspicuous by their absence for some time, returned in full force. The gallant band of British soldiers who had been fighting their way down the Malay peninsula in the early days at Changi, turned up in the most unexpected places, coming down through Burma to cut the rail link, driving the Nips out of Java, retaking the Philippines, and fighting their way across Indo-China. There was a radio set operating in the vicinity and snippets of genuine news were interlaced with these fantastic tales. Most people believed nothing at all. The Nips, too, had their own tales, and one Korean told us with great glee of the Jap submarine that had sailed up the Thames and bombarded London. A similar story told of Sydney we found later to have at least some basis of truth.

Towards the end of that miserable summer the camp began to break up, the less fit going back to base camp for treatment, the workers going up country to places where there was still need of our attentions. Some of those going down were to join parties going out of Siam. We envied them, but not later, when we found the full horror of the prison hulks, the treatment and the losses. I learnt after the war that at least one friend of mine, a Corporal Pharoah, after being torpedoed on one of these hell ships, spent several days on a raft, watching others slip off one by one in the daytime heat and nighttime agony, as gradually their senses left them and they became raving mad. Eventually picked up by the sub which had earlier attacked their ship, the survivors returned to England just in time for Christmas, and he was good enough to write to my people who had had no word, and give them the situation as he knew it, reassuring them that I was still alive.

The remnants of C Battalion started to march up country, and spent the night at Kinsayu, now a deserted camp, peopled only by the ghosts of the many who had died there. This was the camp commanded by Colonel Lilley of the Sherwood Foresters, one of the most beloved officers on the river, a man who fought tooth and nail in spite of all personal suffering, for his men. He was never afraid to stand up to the Japanese if he knew his cause was right, and the troops under his command unfairly treated. He paid for his concern with his own health and did not survive the end of the war by many years.

At Kinsayu, after a meal, we took to the river, being ferried in a small fleet of the little 'pom-pom' Thai motorboats, piloted by their Thai owners. We chugged laboriously upstream. At places where the river entered swift running rapids, the underpowered boats were unable to cope, and the boatmen would stand on the prow of the boat, push a pole in the riverbed and, twining one leg round the pole, walk the length of the boat to the stern to help the straining engines. It sounds an impossible feat in retrospect, but they accomplished it with consummate ease. Little wildlife was seen, except for what were commonly believed to be alligators, sunning themselves on occasional sandbanks, diving for cover at our approach. I still have the feeling that they were some sort of iguanas, and still do not know whether or not they have alligators in Siam (there are). After passing all day on the river, we arrived at the foot of a gloomy cliff, and climbed up to a camp of about four small huts, with the Jap quarters adjacent. This was Rin Tin, another camp wiped out by cholera. Our present quarters were some little way from the original camp, which had been burnt down as a precaution when it had been abandoned earlier.

The rations landed, the motor boats vanished into the gloom the way they had come, and we had a meal of rice and tea and settled down for the night. The next day we started work. The railway had been joined some weeks before, with much ceremony, a reputed golden spike the last nail in the last sleeper. Knowing the acquisitive habits of the average PoW, I often wondered if the spike was still there twenty-four hours after the ceremony, or whether it had even then been 'flogged' to some enterprising Thai with an eye to business. We were at Rin Tin for maintenance work. For some days we chopped trees into small billets to feed the insatiable maws of the locos for in that country they were all wood-burners, and their appetites being colossal, stockpiles of wood were being placed at intervals along the line to replenish the ever-empty tenders. When the piles we made were considered sufficient we began to establish a stock of small stones at the trackside for ballasting the sleepers.

The stones were obtained from half a mile or so inside the jungle, in much the same manner that we had built the original embankments, chungkol and basket, a hundred baskets per man per day. The same games to outwit the Nip, double baskets with a thin line round the bottom edge, and it still worked as well, the Nips not seeming to have learnt anything in the last year. We tipped the stones in a pile at the edge of a light railway which led downhill. They were loaded on to trucks, flat bottomed with a loose 'box' container. When full, one man sat on the stones, another hung on behind clutching a steel bar which actuated chocks on the wheels to act as brakes on the downhill journey, and then the car was pushed back uphill for another load, having to be manhandled off the lines to let loaded cars, on their way down, pass. It soon became a game to see who was the fastest, most daredevil driver and the mad crews would thunder past, the brakeman waving his bar in the air to demonstrate that the brakes were not being used. Spills were ten a penny, as neither track nor car wheels were designed for a cresta run, and eventually one of the drivers broke his arm, and a modicum of sanity was restored.

In a few weeks the jobs were completed, and it was evident that the Nips had no idea what to do with us. For several days we were split up into squads, each under the command of a Korean, and sent out into the jungle to do foot drill 'a la Nippon'. We spent hours drilling to Jap commands but it was better than working. At the end of the week, we had a passing out parade, and the best squad was complimented. The contrast between this 'holiday' atmosphere and the events of the past six months was unbelievable. For a day or so we did nothing at all, and we were off again, this time by train, back to Tonchan main camp.

For the first time we saw the ever-changing panorama of the line built at such enormous cost in human suffering, if not in comfort, at least from a fresh angle. We passed the enormous cuttings, some with precariously overhanging slabs of rock perched high above the embankments, the bridges and trestles spanning the low-lying swamps. It was an awe-inspiring sight, and a strangely sobering one, for it is said that for each sleeper on that line one worker lay dead.

We detrained at Tonchan, now eerie and deserted. Forlorn, collapsing huts sagged perilously, and the jungle was fast encroaching on what was left of the camp we had founded. We visited the little cemetery, now palisaded, and gated, and the last resting place of over 130 souls. This was now hallowed ground, having been consecrated, together with all the others up and down the line by the Australian padre, Harry Thorpe. Harry, a jovial, likeable fellow, had attempted to join up as a padre but had been informed that there were, at the time, no vacancies in the corps. Not to be outdone, he enlisted as a private soldier, and came to Malaya and fought in the battle of Singapore. As a prisoner of war, he declared himself a minister of the church and was so treated by the Japs, who allowed him the privileges of an officer. Finding himself on the railway, he was eventually given almost a free hand to travel up and down the line, consecrating, holding services, baptizing and preparing for confirmation those who were desirous. He brought comfort to thousands, generally acting as father, mother and uncle to all, a toiler of strength. Whether it was so or not, I always got the impression that, though enormously popular among the British troops, he was never accepted quite so warmheartedly amongst his fellow countrymen, Since the war he has been a regular and welcome guest at the annual Festival of Remembrance, is a Canon in the Church of Australia, and has done wonderful work for children.

We stayed at Tonchan only a day or so, before shouldering our kit and hoofing it north again, this time only a few kilometres to a new camp at Tampi. Here we had a camp of four or five huts fronting the line, alongside which the road ran parallel. Under the aegis once more of Hiramatsu, the Tiger, we settled in for a stay of some months. Our new job, as we found out, was to survey for a new branch, hugging the river. At Tampi, the line was at the peak of a hump which the wood-burning locos, now running a regular schedule, found rather too much for their limited power. Trains were running daily in both directions and the timetable at that time seemed to be quite well adhered to. One train passed the camp at ten at night, and our hut was right alongside the line. I remember one night dreaming that the Japs had tied me to the line, my neck on the rail, and as the whistle announced the arrival of the ten o'clock, I found myself bolt upright in bed, sweating profusely as my colleagues on either side tried to hold me down. I had escaped, though, and the train clanked by safely some twenty yards away.

So we started work again, split into parties of about twenty. We walked along the track to a point where we dropped downhill into one of the old Konyu camps. Another hotbed of cholera, Konyu was the last resting place of hundreds more men, but the camp we saw looked quite innocuous. A grassy plateau feet above a sandy beach now contained only one hut, the same hut, knowing ones said, where the Japs used to have their Geisha girls for relaxation in the heyday of the camp.

On the beach sleepers enclosed a pool of warm water, fed by a hot spring, and if our transport was not already there, waiting for us, we were allowed to wallow in the warm pool, or swim in the little creek which led to the main stream.

Our transport was another of the ubiquitous 'pom-poms' and we were taken downstream to where the engineers were conducting the survey. Landing, we made our way up to the proposed site, where we had to cut a path along the hillside, parallel to the river, with, at intervals, swathes running up and down at right angles. Then we would rest for a few minutes while the engineers took readings from all angles, with much waving of arms and voluble Japanese. Then it was on our feet again and the process was again repeated until the Japanese were satisfied, and a new set of readings was taken. Before sundown, we embarked on the motorboat and returned to Konyu ready for our short walk back to camp.

One day we were surprised to discover, overgrown with shrubs and thickets of bamboo, a series of red and white poles left over from a previous survey over the same ground. Tags on the equipment showed that they were from a British survey of 1927 and had apparently been abandoned there in mid project. It could only have been coincidence that we were covering at this point, an absolutely identical route. We never discovered why the job had not been carried through to completion, but the usual crop of authentic explanations was not slow in coming forward. The railway, though feasible, was said to have been dropped on security grounds, the line being too prone to lay Malaya open to invasion from the north. Apparently no one had told the Japanese that they would need this railway to do the job. Another theory was that the project would have proved too costly in terms of human life. We fervently wished that someone had told that to the Japanese too. Whatever the real reason, there is no reason to believe that the poles are not there to this day, in mute testimony to an idea that was born twice and, as far as that section was concerned, never carried to fruition. In spite of our efforts over many weeks the spur was never built and to the end of the war, the trains puffed and groaned daily over the hump.

The day's work over, we returned to the river's edge, were picked up by the boatman and returned to Konyu, where we had another warm dip before climbing the hill back to Tampi. This relatively peaceful daily round was enlivened only once, when a prisoner, idling in the boat on the return journey, found a loose deckboard and, beneath it, the Thai owner's wallet containing about 200 ticals. We were having our baths when an enraged howl indicated that the owner had discovered his loss. After a furious argument with the Jap guard, we were lined up to be searched. A loincloth doesn't take a lot of searching and nothing was found. The evening was hot, and one or two took swigs from their water bottles while we were waiting. The rest stood around looking bored, bewildered, or both, and at last the irate, still unsatisfied, Thai was sent on his way bemoaning his loss.

Back at camp one of the thirsty ones borrowed a knife and, taking the bottom off a perfectly good water bottle, retrieved 200 soggy, dripping Thai dollars.

Our camp was small by previous standards but one of the most comfortable we had in Thailand. This was not a particularly hard standard to attain, but we settled down to make life as pleasant as possible. Trees grew in the campsite and, in the relative peace, wildlife came into the camp. Apes, more than once, were seen swinging from tree to tree across the campsite, and I stood in wonder one night watching a flying fox, as it scuttled up each tree, and limbs wide apart, parachuted down to the middle of the next, up which he scuttled to repeat the manoeuvre. The thick membranes joining his legs were clearly visible.

Food was improving and, with the less arduous work and better sanitation, came better health, increase of weight to a degree, and the return of a measure of virility. Conversation, previously obsessed to exclusion of all other subjects with food, returned to that subject, so beloved of the armed forces of all nations of the world. Full rein was given to the clothing of dreams of sexual excesses, embellished with all the arrogance of the soldier, who, to hear him talk, is the personification of all the great lovers of the past, often embodied in one weak, puny, unprepossessing frame. Talk, however, it had to remain, for there was no opportunity of putting the boast to the test. The occasional woman seen in Thailand was usually fat and overblown, stained red lips parting in an inane grin as she expectorated a stream of rust-coloured betel juice between stained and yellowing teeth. Either that or she was smoking a cheroot about three-feet-long.

There was little wonder that with the return of energy and imagination and, in the lack of other opportunity, tentative experiments in homosexuality were essayed. Mutual self-gratification became commonplace, and many went beyond this. I made a few gestures in this direction but a few abortive experiments soon convinced me that this was not my bent, so to speak. If only half of what I heard was true it is certain that many continued this practice until the end of captivity, if not beyond, but, for most, it was only a temporary expedient.

One day all hell was let loose in camp when the Nips discovered that someone had cut out a section of the wall in one of the PoW huts to allow a freer passage of air at night. We must be punished, said the Tiger. Sabotage of IJA property.

We quailed as we considered the possible consequences, It was only recently at Tarsoa that another 'Everall' case had occurred. A member of the Sherwood Foresters had vowed that if he was ever hit by a Nip he would hit him back. This duly happened. He, too, was tied to a tree for a week, bashed or beaten with the rifle of every passing Nip, dragged down and thrown in the river to wash every night. At the end of the week, battered, bloodied and bruised, with broken ribs he was thrown into a truck, spades on top, and driven into the jungle. The truck returned without him, and he was never seen again.

We need not have worried. The guards were sent out of camp by the Tiger, and stood at intervals along the railway line. We were paraded, carrying our full kit, and sent off at intervals to run half a mile along the road, the guards seeing that we did not drop to a walk. At the end of the route, we turned and, still running, made back to camp. The incident was never mentioned again, honour having been satisfied.

Sometime in October a train, moving south, stopped at the camp for a short time. It was crowded with British troops returning from work on the railway and going down to base camps. We were able to converse with them, and some acquaintances were renewed. We found that this was the last few remnants of F Force, that had travelled by night through Tonchan South the previous June. Then they were still reasonably fit and confident. They had gone across the border into lower Burma, and had suffered unspeakable hardships. Short of food, short of medical supplies, weather worse than ours, if that was possible, they had been worked to death by sadistic uncaring guards, and then the ultimate, hit by particularly virulent cholera, which virtually wiped out the camp in weeks. Of 3,000 men who went up, oblivious to the coming horror, only a handful returned. The few hundred survivors, though emaciated, were still cheerful, and overjoyed at the prospect of moving back into relative civilization. We waved goodbye until they had steamed out of sight on the road to Tonchan.

As the year drew to its close the surveying job finished and the work programme stagnated. Although food was better, medical supplies were still short and, worse, supplies of quinine, never very plentiful, were drying up altogether. The main source of supply, in the East Indies, had been neglected and production was at a low ebb. Short of supplies for their own troops, the Japs informed us that there was none to spare for PoWs. I was getting malaria regularly and had been since Tonchan. A few plasmoquin tablets were available and my life developed into a regular monthly cycle, ten days relatively fit without fever, shivers, and a course of plasmoquin, severe rigours and high temperatures with a few tablets of quinine, and then the crisis, the furious sweating, soaking blankets in perspiration, the gradual return of appetite, the return to normal temperatures, and the cycle began again, month in, month out.

One day, following such an attack, I was on light duties, which involved sweeping up around the Jap HQ and generally tidying up the camp area. My attention was attracted to a group of uniformed men marching along the road across the railway line. Shuffling, rather than marching, would perhaps describe their progression. There were about forty of them, dark of skin, dressed in tattered khaki, and carrying a strange assortment of weapons, rifles of sorts, staves, bamboo spears, and a selection of umbrellas.

A sound made me turn, and behind me stood the Tiger, on the steps of the IJA hut, mouth agape, and eyes literally bulging from their sockets.

'Nanda,' he queried, 'What soldier?'

I did my best to explain by gesture and pidgin-English-Japanese mixture that they were Indians who, at the fall of Singapore, had changed sides and were now espousing the Japanese cause. He stared again as they moved out of sight around a bend and, shaking his head disbelievingly, re-entered the office.

Christmas came and went, our second in captivity. We managed to put on a pantomime, greatly enjoyed by prisoners and camp staff alike. We had regular concerts, ably backed up by the camp orchestra, which consisted in the main, if not entirely, of trumpet, accordion and drums. They were able musicians and I still recall with pleasure being introduced to the Albaniz tango, beautifully rendered on the accordion.

Our work in the new year seemed to be completely divorced from the railway. Some days we went out into the jungle and cut bamboo, lengths of the tall graceful feathery-fronded type, or spent days sweating in the thickets to fell the tougher, hard-spiked, thicker variety. The hazards of bamboo felling have already been mentioned. We would return to camp tired, sweaty and blackened, skin cut and irritated by the saw-edged leaves and fragments of razor-sharp cut bamboo. The poles were tied into bundles, and taken down to the riverside. This was a heavy job, but always resulted in a swim before return to camp, which made it a little more bearable.

Perhaps the most sought after job was the finding, felling, and stripping of 'tie' trees. These were a particular type of tree distinguishable by trunk and foliage and whose trunk, between bark and wood, yielded a fibrous web which could be cut into strips and used as a kind of raffia for tying purposes. We first of all spent a day in tracking down the particular type of tree which was required, blazing the trunks, and noting the position of the trees by comparison with the track.

The following day we would go out to this area and commence operations. The best trees were those that had the longest and straightest trunks before the branches started; those with short or twisted trunks were not felled. Just occasionally, we, in our ignorance, would pick a tree which was infested by red ants who made a nest of the long leaves which they sewed together to form a sort of beehive shape. When the tree fell with thunderous roar, or even before, when operations were well under way, and the tree was beginning to shake, the nest would split, and a shower of two-inch long, fighting mad insects would descend on our bare bodies and go into instant action. They moved like quicksilver, nipping and biting even the most tender parts of the body and, if pulled roughly away, would leave the better part of their jaws firmly embedded in the victim's flesh. A hectic ten minutes or so could usually see the rout of the invaders, and we soon got into the habit of inspecting the upper branches carefully before attempting to fell any tree.

When the tree was eventually felled it was sawn off just below the first branch and the bark was carefully removed. This revealed the spongy, fibrous growth which was just below the bark. Cuts were made around the top, an inch or so apart, and the cut ends were then hammered energetically with the back of an axe. Under the hammering, the web split into various layers which could then be carefully peeled the length of the trunk to yield strips of a tape-like material some yards long. These strips were bundled into hundreds, and a good tree would yield over a thousand tapes. A couple of trees was a good day's work and the finished bundles were carried back to camp where they were left to dry and, in doing so, became immensely strong. Although we could not see that there was anything exceptionally urgent about this work, the regulations regarding the sick and the numbers allowed to be in camp were not relaxed; indeed, if anything they became even stricter. Only four people per working battalion were allowed to stay in camp, and the intensity of sickness was determined only by the thermometer. Those with the four highest temperatures stayed in bed, the others went to work. For instance, one day, my bout of malaria did not rate the charts. I went off to work with a temperature of 103 but the Korean in charge took pity and I spent most of the day sitting in the shade of a tree and making an occasional can of tea, while the others did the graft. Cases were commonplace of men with very much higher temperatures being sent out to work. Temperatures of 110 or even higher were not unknown and did nothing more than cause slight headaches or mild delirium in those concerned, vanishing overnight, while comparable temperatures in a more temperate climate would be quite unthinkable.

We found on the way to work that we often had to cross the bridges and trestles which abounded on the railway and it could be disconcerting to be caught in the middle of a stretch by the approach of a train. On one occasion we were caught in the middle of a quite high bridge and found that the only way out was to lower ourselves over the edge and hang on to sleepers while the train rumbled overhead,

The top layer of the bridges comprised only a line of sleepers on which the rails were laid and there was no catwalk or side wall to afford any protection. There had, of course, been occasions when men had been knocked off bridges by approaching locos, and at least one death in this way had been reported but not in our group where there was comparatively little in the bridge–building line to be done.

Another day we came on a hut in the jungle, still inhabited by Indian labourers who had been on the railway, and now appeared to have been deserted by the Japanese, their usefulness ended. They may have been engaged on wood providing, of course, and must have got rations from somewhere but there appeared to be little sign of industry on the days we saw them. Piles of swill and rubbish lay outside the door of the hut, attended by the usual swarm of flies, and we were shocked to see that the inhabitants would walk just outside the doorway and squat down to perform their bodily functions barely a yard or so from where they slept and ate, and with no attempt to cover up the result from the ever-present flies.

Early in the new year I was summoned to the Tiger's presence and wondered what the unusual audience was in aid of. Wishing to appear reasonably tidy for the great event I borrowed a pair of presentable shorts, for the sum total of my own clothing had been reduced to a couple of jap nappies and an Australian bush hat, somewhat flattened by my habit of using it as a pillow. Dressed in my borrowed finery I entered the Jap office to be confronted by the Tiger and Jack White who had been with us as interpreter since our first days at Tonchan. Nervously I approached the desk and saluted.

The Tiger eyed me up and down. The colour rose in his neck, the muscles of which began to swell. His face gradually crimsoned, and his eyes bulged. Half rising to his feet, he burst into a torrent of Japanese.

'Where did you get those shorts?' asked Whitoo, 'you are down as having no clothes apart from loincloth.' I explained that I had borrowed them for the audience. After a lot of argument between Whitoo and Tiger, peace was at last restored. It appeared that a kit issue was in the offing and my name had been put forward as a worthy beneficiary, having neither shirt nor shorts to my name. When I appeared in an exceptionally well-preserved pair of khaki shorts the Tiger thought I was taking the mickey, but when it was explained that the real owner did not appear on the list of deficiencies he was at last mollified.

The clothing issue, which materialized shortly afterwards, was our first since the Red Cross issue at Singapore, and we were a little mystified by this sudden outburst of generosity. We were soon enlightened. The second anniversary of the setting up of the prisoner of war camps was at hand and it was to be celebrated by all, by order. On the morning in question we were all paraded by 'huts' on the general parade ground. Each man was dressed in all his tattered finery, shirts, shorts, hat, and boots, if the latter were still in wearable condition. In parties of about twenty-five, under the command of a Korean, we were marched out of camp into the jungle, out of sight of camp, but not out of earshot. As we left camp the camp 'orchestra' of trumpet, accordion and drums was playing 'The British Grenadiers'. The chorus of this well-known ditty is not overlong, and the possible permutations are few, so that the four lines were played endlessly, over and over again. We sat in the jungle, listening to the bulging-cheeked, pop-eyed trumpeter and nimble-fingered accordionist as they repeated ad nauseam, 'Some talk of Alexander, and some of Hercules …'

For what seemed like hours we sat there until, at last, the signal was given and we came to our feet. Parties began to march back to camp and, as it came our turn, we swung smartly out on to the road and, heads back, strode proudly back to the parade ground.

The guard had turned out to line the gate and, on a bedecked dais, the camp senior staff were lined up, Tiger resplendent in full-dress uniform and ceremonial sword was taking the salute as each squad passed him and moved to its appointed place. 'Of Hector and Lysander, and such great names as these …' played the wilting band for the six thousandth time. They were obviously failing fast under the strain, but they soldiered grimly on.

At last we were all on the parade ground, facing the platform. The Tiger came forward with his aides and proceeded to carry out a full-scale inspection of troops. This was the reason for the kit issue. He passed along the lines of troops, gaze travelling over clothes and boots, back and front. The inspection over, he returned to the dais, took the salute again, and the band gratefully subsided into silence, having just broken innumerable world records for the rendering of the greatest number of consecutive choruses, etc. etc. I often wondered if any of them could hear that particular tune again without an involuntary shudder.

For the next half hour or so we were treated to a dissertation on the workings of the Greater East Asian Co-Prosperity Sphere, our place in the new order of things, the need to work hard for Nippon, and the benevolence of the Japanese in general, and Tojo in particular, in keeping us alive at all. The harangue was delivered in short sharp bursts, with suitable pauses to allow Jack White to interpret, while Tiger's eagle gaze swept the eagerly listening concourse to try to discover any possible expression of dissent. There was no overt display of emotion, and the lecture was duly delivered, Tiger once again took the salute and vanished, medals and sword all a jangle, into the Jap HQ. We were dismissed and the rest of the day, by gracious permission of Tojo, was a holiday.

The rainy season was now approaching again and rumours were around the camp that we were on the verge of moving again. The most popular destination was the base camp at Nakompatom where, railway finished, we were to luxuriate in idleness for the rest of our PoW days. In any case, work here was being gradually phased out; we had obviously enough bamboo and ties for the job for which the Japanese required them. Rumour, though overoptimistic, was not entirely without foundation and the day dawned when we stood on the parade ground, kit at our feet, waiting to leave the camp by train. We were not by any means sorry to leave the jungle with its mud, flies, mosquitos, dysentery and kindred diseases. I was weak with fever, as indeed were most others, there having been virtually no quinine in camp for well over a month. The train pulled in and we piled aboard. We were off at last.

We passed through Tonchan, Tonchan South, the cholera camp, and Tarsoa. We marvelled at the construction difficulties that changed with almost every mile, though we knew from bitter experience at what cost they had been overcome. Here was a bridge, there was an embankment, here was a cutting, overhung with jagged outcrops of rock, precariously balanced in the uneven sides. We swung out over the river, where the rails clung to the cliffside for miles on a lattice of wooden struts, seemingly supported only by thin air from the foaming, boiling river beneath. Across the bridge at Tamarkan, a marvellous timber structure, immortalized for all time as the 'Bridge over the River Kwai.' Would that life had ever been so pleasant as in that tinselled classic but, unfortunately, we were living real life, not a screenplay.

By now we were running over the last of the jungle and into the fertile coastal plain. When we finally halted we found we were at Tamuan, the little village where we had made our first halt on the march up from Bampong, how many years was it before? Incredible that only some eighteen months had passed since we made that epic march. We disembarked and formed up for the journey into the camp which consisted, at that time, of half a dozen of the familiar attap-roofed huts. After claiming a bed space, I went out in search of the MO to see if there was yet any quinine available to quench the ever-burning fires of the insistent malaria.

Chapter 13

Tamuan

The camp area was one of the largest we had yet seen. It was situated some distance from, and out of sight of, the village and was quite close to the river. We commenced work next day and marched down to the riverbank where we found the water choked with dozens of bales of bamboo, the same bamboo we had busied ourselves cutting over the last month or so. We had to haul these out and carry them, two poles at a time, to a dump in the main camp area where they were placed in huge piles. A little excitement was engendered when one of the men, idly swishing his hand in the water as he lay on a bamboo raft one lunchtime, withdrew it hurriedly with a yell. His finger was dripping blood. A skulking fish, thinking it was something tasty to eat, had had a quick nip in passing. Thinking of the way we swam in these waters, doing our little breaststroke with bait dangling for the taking, we could not resist a shudder. I never looked quite so kindly on swimming after that, though I never heard of any fish that did take the big bait, fortunately. How the victim would ever have explained things to his wife would have presented quite a problem.

After a few days we had emptied the river of bamboo and had a large stockpile in the camp, flanked by a similar pile of ties, which had come down by road. We were now informed that the next job was to erect about fifty huts to finish off the camp. We were split into parties and each gang was allotted one task towards the building of the huts. The first party dug two rows of parallel holes, some four or five yards between, about fifty-five yards long and some three yards apart. Meanwhile, others were cutting bamboos to size and these were dropped into the holes, and tamped down, by a third gang. Sloping poles were next erected on these uprights to accommodate the ridge pole, and then the long thin bamboos were attached to take the attap. Finally the last party climbed onto the roof and attached the attap, overlapped in the manner of tiles. The completed frames were then ready for the erection of beds and, with the fastening of the side panels, the hut was ready for occupation. After the first hut was attempted, a sort of prefabrication cut the time and the work, by quite a bit. The whole shape of uprights, cross pieces, and V-shaped roof poles was marked out on the ground, and the poles were assembled with pegs on this jig so that a complete section, ready assembled, could be dropped into a pair of holes and all sections were identical for the insertion of ridge poles and attap runners. For once we were able to show the locals something instead of the other way about.

The building continued for some weeks and, as fast as the huts were assembled, further intakes from up country were moving in and occupying them. A large hut was built to serve as hospital and between this and the main 'lines' a huge pond was dug and filled with water. This was then stocked with ducks which were allowed to flounder in and around the water by day, being rounded up and confined to pens at night. One would have thought that, in that atmosphere, their lives would not have been worth a satang but, strange to relate, they lived a happy and carefree life and their numbers did not seem to decrease unduly.

The hospital filled steadily with malaria and dysentery cases, two diseases which, like the poor, were always with us. A medical laboratory was established where it was found that, in addition to bacillary dysentery, the disease that had carried off so many of our number, we now had a new scourge to contend with in the form of amoebic dysentery. A certain amount of Emetine was available for treatment but this had to be reserved for the virulent cases while those whose stools showed only the cysts of the disease were left without treatment until the disease became acute.

We had become accustomed up country to the jungle ulcer and its horrible and drastic results. In the steamy germ-laden atmosphere of the jungle camps during the rainy season, even the most trivial bamboo scratch refused to heal and eventually a small running sore would develop on the site of the scratch. This rapidly grew and widened, becoming an open ulcer which spread with each passing day. The overworked MOs had little to treat the ulcers with; indeed, practically the only medicament was the ubiquitous Magnesium Sulphate, which had to serve to treat almost anything from dysentery onwards. Cloths, as sterile as could be effected under the circumstances, were dipped in solution of Epsom Salts and laid on the sores with little, if any, effect. The ulcers grew, stretching from ankle to knee, laying the bone open in the centre of the rotting, pus-laden, gangrenous flesh. Cleaning was brutally simple. A dessert spoon was sterilized and, while the poor unfortunate patient bit on a piece of wood, and clung desperately to the head of his bed, the pus and rotted flesh was literally scraped away from the affected part. There was no anaesthetic of any sort and the agony must have been almost unendurable. In spite of this rough treatment, and the application of the salts-soaked rags, the ulcers continued to grow until, in some cases, the whole of the leg from the foot to hip was one sea of rotten stinking flesh. The only possible thing if it reached this stage was to amputate the limb, and in IV Group this was usually done at Tarsoa where one surgeon had the reputation of being able to remove a leg in six minutes flat. If the patient was well enough to stand the journey, he may have been sent to Nakom Patom, where better hospital facilities, relatively speaking, were available. In either case, amputation was quite a risk, as even if the operation was a success the patient often succumbed to shock.

Now in Tamuan we saw the end product of this dirty, horrible human experience. One of the huts was occupied solely by 'amputees', over a hundred of them, some minus one leg from the knee, some from the hip, some without either leg, some even, though these were few by comparison, without an arm. These were the 'lucky ones', who had survived the terrible mental and physical ordeal, and they were now employed on light duties, mainly the making of cigarettes. On the railway, even these physical wrecks had been made to work under the 'speedo', being taken out on stretchers and made to pass rocks from one to the other. We never knew where they went from Tamuan when the camp later closed, but believe they went to Nakom Patom and eventually reached home.

The cigarettes they made were for the use of the Japanese, and the prisoners made do with the local fireweed, commonly known as Sikh's Beard, or Hag's Bush. We were privileged at Tamuan to witness the care which went into the preparation of this luxury which had adorned the canteen for so long. Going to work one morning, we saw a Thai cutting the tobacco from the patch in front of his hut and laying it out to dry. When we passed his hacienda on the way back that evening the dried and cured tobacco was already on sale. Presumably the canteen tobacco had the same careful and involved preparation. Having brought the raw material, paper had still to be procured to make a cigarette to smoke. A brisk trade in the leaves of our pitifully few books had been flourishing for the last eighteen months to the great detriment of the various camp libraries. The thick pages of Hodder and Stoughton went up in flames and great clouds of acrid smoke, while the thinner pages of Dickens classics fetched a little more on the market. Really sought after were the luxurious thin pages of the Holy Bible, which made up to five cents a sheet. A fellow with a couple or so bibles could live in luxury for months. In the camps where matches were unknown, and cigarette lighters less than useless, it was remarkable to see how, each morning, within a few minutes of reveille, the lights spread through the huts like magic, and cigarettes were lit up all over camp. It never ceased to amaze me how it happened.

As in other camps, a library was started after the first few months and this, although run on similar lines to others we had known, was on rather a grander scale. Deposit of two volumes meant that one could be continuously out on loan and I formed acquaintance with Lawrence's *Seven Pillars*, Gunther's *Inside Europe*, *Inside Asia* etc., and with Arthur Bryant, Phyllis Bottome, Howard Spring, Richard Llewellyn, Armstrong, Roberts, Buchan, G. D. H. Cole, and many more. For catholic reading, there was no shortage of good books and the library was the most popular rendezvous in camp.

We began to move outside camp as work on the building came to completion. Some of our tasks took us miles from the camp area and we found that at Kanburi a camp had been established, inhabited solely by officers. With the ending of work on the railway the relatively large proportion of officers had become a source of embarrassment to the Nips and, for the first time in nearly two and a half years, segregated camps were put into operation, as indeed they should have been from the first days of captivity. Even so, the officers, contrary to the Geneva Convention were still required to form working parties. Not all the officers were segregated at this time, we still had a few in Tamuan, though not nearly as many as before.

In addition to the normal administration, we had Padres and Medical Officers, and work had been put in hand for the building of an operating theatre. This was soon completed and in operational order, hung with mosquito or fly netting and, under the circumstances, kept as sterile as possible. In the next few months, several quite intricate operations were carried out with considerable success.

I believe also that at this time a dental unit was formed but I had no need to make personal investigation of this as I had had my teeth attended to when a travelling dentist, equipped with a foot-operated drilling machine, had visited Tampi some months previously and I still had the temporary fillings many years later. Luckily I had no extractions, for he had no form of anaesthetic, rumour, that lying jade, declaring that he had an assistant with mallet, standing behind the chair.

'When I nod my head ...'

Len Lever, a private in the LAD attached to the 85th, was unfortunate enough to be caught by a Nip, while talking to a Thai through the wire.

Len had a chungkol in his hand and the Nip, snatching it from him, hit Len, unfairly and squarely across the top of the head with the blade. His skull was fractured and the broken bone was pressing on the brain. He was one of the first patients on the operating table where the doctors removed the bone with a joiner's brace and bit, and let in a piece of aluminium mess tin, cut to shape, to cover the hole in the skull. Thanks to their amazing skill, Len was still alive and well when I saw him on the boat returning to England at the end of the war. Lenny had been well known since the early days at River Valley for his concert party appearances. His parody of 'The Old Cabbage Patch' to tune of 'Baby Doll' was known in every camp on the river.

In the first week of June we were more than surprised by the arrival in camp of copies of the *Bangkok Chronicle*, an English language newspaper. These were brought in and distributed by the Japanese, and were the first news sheets we had seen since the clandestine copies of the *Syonan Times* were smuggled in to River Valley by the working parties. From them we learned of the opening of the Second Front in Europe, which was given front-page treatment, though naturally played down more than somewhat. It was evident that the Nips expected the invaders to be thrown back into the sea with considerable losses and when, after three days, the beachheads were getting stronger, and it was evident that this was no second Dieppe, but the real thing, the papers vanished as suddenly as they had appeared, and we saw no more.

Probably the best featured story of the front page was the Japanese attack on Imphal, a long and arduous campaign, which the paper assured its readers was daily about to result in the fall of the citadel and the opening of the gates of India to the invaders. We heard garbled tales over several months of the imminent fall of Imphal but fortunately for all in that hemisphere, except perhaps, the unfortunate Japs, Imphal held fast against all that they could hurl against it.

Some of the other news in the *Chronicle* was little short of miraculous and was obviously intended for the unsophisticated native reader, or perhaps just for Japanese consumption. We read of the brave Japanese troops facing the Americans in the Aleutians. Short of food and out of ammunition, they kept up the fight for months, eating snow, and hurling rocks at the enemy. A Japanese scientist in the homeland had perfected, after many months' research, a new and highly-improved explosive, for use in munitions. One of the 'Hero Gods', using the ammunition on test, reported that, when engaged by American aircraft, he fired a burst from his machine guns and distinctly saw the American pilot shake and turn pale as he realized the efficiency of the new Japanese ammunition and its superiority over the American type. Another 'Hero God' was attacking an enemy destroyer when he ran out of ammunition. Nothing daunted, he turned his aircraft upside down and, again approaching the destroyer, drew his sword and cut off the head of the captain as he stood on the bridge, causing the ship to run out of control. It was a shame that the supply of news lasted only three days, we were learning such a lot.

In the camp the black market, which had flickered on and off for two years, really flourished. The daring racketeers regularly broke out of camp to meet their contacts, and the last few remaining valuables found ready buyers in the Thai village. Rings, pens, watches etc. changed hands, as did clothing, if any remained in saleable condition, the last of the mosquito nets, blankets and, if no one was willing to sell, the racketeers were not above stealing to continue trading and to swell their bulging wallets, Some Red Cross medical supplies were received in camp and vanished the same night, at a time when many men were still dying for lack of appropriate drugs. An immediate search was mounted before the chest could be taken out of camp to be sold and it was eventually found pushed down one of the heaving, stinking latrines, but most of the precious drugs were lost forever.

A trade was also established with the Nips, many of whom were suffering from VD. Tablets of soda bicarb were painstakingly cut down with a penknife, and the magic initials 'M and B' carved into them, when they were sold as genuine antibiotics for five ticals per tablet. Pieces of copper tubing, obtained from God knows where, were cut into rings, filed and polished, and 'Hallmarked' before being sold as 'gold' rings for very respectable prices. The notes with which we were paid each month were always brand new, straight from the Japanese presses but, in dealing with the Thais, these were treated with a disdainful shrug of the shoulders and shake of the head. To the Thais, nothing was money unless it bore across the foot the imprint of the British printing house that had produced it.

Apparently anything could be obtained to order and I was shown by Lawrence Turner, our ex-Intelligence Officer, a 'procuration' price list which he had been given. This listed in detail the price of sexual partners of various sorts from young boys and girls to selections of riper reputed virgins. There must have been a demand for this service though, judging by the brisk trade in 'M and B' with the Japanese, the risks of the sport were obvious to all.

One of the more daring spirits was reputed to have a girlfriend in the village and, at night, he would break out, don native clothing, and visit his girl's house, even, it is said, visiting the local cinema. Later, he was caught out, and spent some time in the punishment cell which was erected by the camp gates. This was a bamboo cage some four feet or so in every direction, with insufficient room to stand up or lie down. Later inhabitants were two brothers, also late of the 85th, who escaped and tried to reach the British lines overland. There was a considerable price on the head of every escapee and a white man in a brown country, without any knowledge of the language, stood out for all to see. They were betrayed and brought back to languish in the cage. Others who disappeared at intervals were not seen until after the war, when they turned up in most unexpected manner.

At the end of June I was hit again by malaria, the twenty-first time I had succumbed, and was admitted to hospital. Plasmoquin and quinine were now available again and soon I had recovered sufficiently to expect to be discharged in the course of the next day or so. While at the urinal one afternoon I noticed that my water was a sort of port-wine colour and mentioned the fact to one of the Australian medical orderlies who told me to lie on my bed and not move. However, nature being a hard mistress, I was again toddling outside when two husky orderlies rushed after me and carried me back to bed. The riot act was read and I was forbidden to get to my feet again. I didn't feel at all ill and was greatly puzzled by their apparent concern.

At the end of the ward, right next to the hospital offices, were two single beds, screened with bamboo. These were for the critically ill and rejoiced in the name of the 'death beds', which they quite often were. About teatime I was carried down the ward and installed on one of them, where I was told that I had blackwater fever and that immediate blood transfusions had been arranged for me. The disease, of which I had never heard until then, is not transmittable, but results from the breakup of the red blood cells due to the presence of malaria parasites and insufficient or irregular treatment with quinine to eradicate them. The shortage of quinine over the past months, coupled with my recurrent fevers, had resulted in the onset of blackwater, the red corpuscles being passed out through the urine and, I presume, resulting in a sort of raging leukaemia. With blackwater it is too late for quinine, which at this stage only accelerates the disease, but we had fortunately received supplies of Atebrin a day or so previously and I was started on this. The blood transfusion was received by courtesy of Major

McKinley, a whisky distiller in private life, and I commenced taking a drop of the hard stuff by drip feed.

After about a quarter of an hour I began to feel awful. I was hot, and waves of nausea swept over me. I called for the orderlies, the drip was immediately stopped, and I was wrapped in blankets, with hot-water bottles and hot bricks tucked in at strategic intervals. Half-delirious, I remember nothing of the rest of the night, save that I was incoherently and effusively thanking all within earshot and many others for taking such good care of me until I finally lost consciousness. Apparently the system of classifying blood was rather sketchy and the good Scottish blood I had been imbibing was incompatible, so that a violent reaction had set in. I survived the night somehow and, for almost a fortnight, I lay there, oblivious to the world, eating nothing and caring nothing. Then, on the thirteenth day, I awoke feeling ravenous. I called for, and was given, a huge bowl of rice and some form of stew, which I attacked with gusto, eating every last grain. Hardly had I laid my dish down than I was violently sick, vomiting back all I had so greedily devoured. I lay back, exhausted, but that first meal in nearly a fortnight was the start of a returning appetite, although it was still some weeks before I was eating normally again.

One night I made my first acquaintance with cerebral malaria. An Aussie was brought in about ten o'clock and put on the bed next to mine. He appeared to be in some sort of coma, and lay inert but, in about half an hour, he awoke and began to thrash around violently, waving his arms, and shouting all sorts of filth and obscenities. An orderly appeared with a syringe to give an intravenous injection of quinine but was totally unable to get the syringe into the arm of the cursing, struggling Australian. Finally, with the strength of a madman, he knocked orderly, syringe, and accoutrements flying, and reinforcements were hastily summoned. Eventually six or seven stalwart men managed to pinion his arms and legs and, still struggling, the heavy, straining body was subdued sufficiently for the injection to be given. In a few minutes, all was peace. We slept. Next morning, I was awakened by a gentle Australian voice querying, 'What time is it Cobber?' It was the raging giant of the night before, now a meek, unobtrusive mouse. I never again heard him raise his voice, or utter anything that would have been out of place at a Sunday school outing.

A regular visitor while I was in hospital was a lad from Sunderland with whom I had struck up a close acquaintanceship over the past year. Allan usually brought some little tit-bit to help coax back my reluctant appetite, an egg, fruit, or food in tins which obviously hadn't been obtained from the camp canteen, though this didn't strike me at the time. It wasn't till long afterwards that I found that his most treasured possession, a gold ring, a present from his parents on his twenty-first birthday, had gone through the wire with the sole object of providing me with a few pleasures to hasten my recovery. It was largely due to his efforts that I was at last removed from the 'death' bed to another position across the ward.

One of the effects of our experiences over the previous year or so was the evidence of vivid dreams and this gave rise one night to a rather comic episode, when I was convinced that I was running a coffee stall on University Boulevard at Nottingham. I was doing a roaring trade, until, turning with a couple of freshly-filled cups of tea in my hand, I found that the intended recipients and, indeed, all my clamouring customers had mysteriously disappeared. I was alone, two cups of steaming tea in my hands.

'Does anyone want a cup of tea?' I enquired plaintively and awoke suddenly to hear a voice in the darkness, saying, 'Yes, mate, I'll have one if you've got one to spare.' I lay back in my blanket and feigned sleep.

Another night I was back at work, being warmly welcomed by the entire staff expressing great surprise that I was home so soon. 'Only got weekend leave,' I explained to them, 'got to be back at Tamuan on Monday.' Dreams like these were experienced by everyone. At this time, one prisoner had to be on duty at the end of every hut during the night, taking it in turns. If the Nip guard approached the hut watchman would spring smartly to his feet and report.

'Yonju ichi mei,' he might say (forty-one men).

'Ni mei banjo,' (two men at the latrines) and woe betide him if any had slipped out of the far end of the hut for a quick one and there were less than he had said in the hut. While walking down the hut to check, one was assailed by a constant hubbub of conversation from almost every bedspace. It was just like the atmosphere in early evening, just after tea, the difference being that, at this time, all the busily talking men were actually fast asleep. A classic example occurred towards the end of 1944 when we were awakened by a terrific uproar, emanating from the hut immediately behind ours. We craned to see what the trouble was. The inhabitants were leaving by every available vantage point, doors, walls, even it appeared by the roof. In no time at all the hut was empty, save for one man, fast asleep on his bed, and shouting at the top of his voice, 'Snakes, look out, snakes.'

When I was finally discharged from the hospital, I was transferred to, of all things, a light duty ward. This alone showed how conditions had improved for such a thing had previously been unheard of. Here I renewed my acquaintance with bamboo. We had already learned how versatile this material was. Now we learned even more. We became expert in cutting it down into thin strips, splitting these into ribbons, which we then wove into a variety of mats, bags, baskets, containers and vases etc. We were initiated into the art by a venerable Thai, imported specially for the task. He could speak no English and we no Siamese but he patiently went through the various processes for us until, by imitation, we were able to turn out passable finished products. These were then taken away, presumably for the use of the Japs, or maybe even for sale in some oriental Woolworth store.

In the evenings, we played the inevitable bridge, this time with a couple of Dutch regular army sergeants, Voss and Busing. We enjoyed the game, except for the fact that they insisted in talking during the deal and play in Dutch, a language which we could not understand. They both spoke good English and we had the uneasy feeling that they were taking full advantage of our lack of linguistic ability. I tried to redress the balance by taking Dutch lessons from Giel Busing, but had not progressed very far before I was adjudged fit for duty and sent out on woodsplitting for the camp cookhouse.

Just before I left, a rather unusual episode occurred with one of my fellow 'light duty' members. All through our enforced dependence on rice as a staple diet, two or three visits to the latrines at night, to empty bladders, was a natural concomitant. After a few hours in bed one would awake with what was universally described as a 'proud' and, carefully disengaging from the blanket, rush outside for relief. One night, this unfortunate youth awoke, feeling the usual symptoms, staggered to his feet, oriented the offending member in the approximate direction of the latrine and, eyes still glazed, started off. He had barely vanished from sight through the door at the end of the hut when a mighty wail, born of pain, anguish, and fractured pride, rent the evening air. We rushed outside.

Just behind the hut he had caught his foot in a tree root and, still half asleep, had fallen flat on his face. Not only that, he had also fallen flat on another portion of his anatomy and it was not a pretty sight. Rapidly swelling to enormous proportions, it was already turning several interesting shades of black and blue.

The MO was hastily summoned, and he examined the, by now, enormous appendage in its unaccustomed mourning shade.

'Well, Lad,' he said, trying hard to keep the chuckle out of his voice, 'I've dealt with a lot of these in my time, but never have I had to cope with a broken one. You may very well have made medical history.'

Fortunately, in the medical chest which had arrived just in time to save my life, there were complete ranges of the latest antibiotics and a course of M & B soon reduced the swelling, which was due to a fractured blood vessel, and his fears for the future were allayed.

Chapter 14

Farewell to Up Country

My stay in the cookhouse was not very long, fortunately for me, for I was far from expert in axe swinging, and always had a horror of, one day, seeing a dismembered foot, or leg, join the piles of wooden billets which we had to prepare. A quick check each night, however, revealed that I still had two.

In addition to the British cookhouses, there were also those of the Australian and Dutch contingents, staffed by their own nationals, and one day I had the opportunity to witness the skill of a professional with an axe. One of the Australian wood party was a lumberjack and he was proud of his tools, especially his axe, which no one else was allowed to touch. He kept it gleaming and razor sharp. One day he was challenged by a couple of young fit officers. Two identical logs, some four-feet thick, were chosen for the contest. The officers attacked theirs on a saw bench with a two handled cross-cut saw. The grizzled veteran set about his with an axe on the ground. The chips flew as he swung methodically but, seemingly, oh so slow. The officers sawed frantically, sweat pouring from their brows. As the Aussie's log parted and he leaned on his axe, the officers were about halfway through.

When I got into the 'lines' I found the pattern of the camp had changed and was continuing to alter day by day. The number of men had fallen rapidly as parties were detached for duties outside the camp. Whole areas of huts were now vacant and, added to the original British and Australians, there were now even more Dutch troops. They had brought into camp their skill with native plants and, on return from work, brought back leaves, flowers and fruits, picked from bushes along their path. These they would concoct into 'hot' little sauces and pickles to help down the rice, and would line the path to the cookhouse, billy of 'sambal' as the concoctions were called, dangling from one wrist, leaving the hands free to shovel down the rice and stew which was still the main form of meal we had. With the arrival of a customer, they would place their meal on the ground, dole out a portion of 'sambal', pocket the five cents they charged, and resume their interrupted meal. Every day there would be up to a dozen of these vendors, each with a different-flavoured sauce for sale, and the advent of a new recipe was greeted with delight.

Rumour has it that, one day, the Dutch Colonel burst into the British Commander's evening meal, almost incoherent with rage. The Englishman cocked an eye in the direction of the intruder and raised an inquisitive eyebrow. The Dutchman spluttered and gasped, 'I have a complaint to make. The British troops are being insufferably rude to my men, and I may add to my country. They are saying that Queen Wilhelmina is standing outside Buckingham Palace, selling Sambal.'

'Oh really!' was the disinterested reply. 'What flavour?'

One thing for which I have always been grateful to this period for was the ability to wake up in the morning on demand. The ability of the mess orderlies to look at a basket of cooked rice and judge just how much an individual ration should be in order not to have too much left over, without at the same time running short, had been in doubt ever since the Changi days. Hence the 'leggy' queue. If, as often happened, the last few men arrived to find an empty basket, there was no alternative to going hungry because the cookhouse had issued all the cooked rice on hand and there just wasn't any more. The prudent mess orderly put his own ration aside in his mess tin before commencing to serve. It was, therefore, imperative to be, if not first, at least early in the queue and, in the early days at Tamuan, I found I was waking up while it was still dark and having a quick wash, just as the first tinny tone of the Japanese reveille split the peaceful air. I was thus on my way with mess tin as the sluggards were turning, bleary-eyed from their beds.

This became an ability to wake at any time required and for many years I found no need for an alarm clock. You can find some good even in the most unlikely circumstances.

In the closing months of 1944 the camp was running to a standstill. Parties were sent up the line again for repair work, ballasting and to fell trees and chop billets to feed the ravenous iron giants that daily hauled the trains to and from Rangoon. Not altogether with impunity, for air strikes were increasing all the time, and many trains were shot up and destroyed. Indeed, it was said that, at the end of the war, there were only about five locomotives still in full working order in the whole of the country. As I said earlier, most men were apathetic about being detailed for such parties and made no effort either to be put on a detail or, having been named, to avoid going. What was to be was to be and when your number was up that was it.

However, one Jock Bell of the 85th found one day that all his mates were on an up country party and asked me if I could get his name included, which I did. The party's train was attacked from the air and badly shot up. Only one man was killed, Gunner Bell. 'What can you expect, interfering with fate?' was the general opinion in camp.

We were beginning to see air activity for the first time around Tamuan. At the sound of aero engines we were rousted from the huts by Korean guards and made to take shelter, much against our will, in the monsoon drains, which ran around the eaves of every hut. From here, by craning our necks, we could usually see, high in the sky, the silver shape of a Flying Fortress as it sailed, unchallenged, towards Burma. The Nips would often loose off a few rounds of .303 from their captured British rifles at this symbol of Yankee Imperialism but, as far as we knew, none were actually brought down in this way.

One night an attack was made on the marshalling yards at Nakom Patom. The PoW camp had been sited at the very edge of the sidings, and a stray stick of bombs fell among the huts killing a number of prisoners. This was the first occasion we had heard of a PoW camp being bombed by our own forces, but this was solely the result of the Japanese housing PoWs in circumstances where they were contravening International regulations. So many times were they remiss, in working officers, in employing prisoners on work of military importance and many other instances. There were, of course, quite a number of other instances of prisoners being caught in air raids and in our little working battalion we lost a number in this way.

One result of this increased activity was that, for the first time, measures for the security of the camp were put into operation. We were set to dig a wide and deep ditch around the whole perimeter of the camp, some fifteen feet wide and of a similar depth. Day by day we toiled, digging and shifting soil and erecting a stout bamboo fence on the outer bank of the ditch. At each corner and by the solitary bridge leading out of camp were erected large towers surmounted by guard huts, each equipped with machine guns. Evidently, something was afoot and for the first time we were securely fenced in. Strangely, far from depressing us, our morale was lifted by the sight of these precautions. This had never been deemed necessary before for even had we left camp there was nowhere to go. For thousands of miles in every direction we were in an unmistakably foreign and hostile country. Many of the older sweats were reasonably fluent in Malay but no-one could speak Thai apart from the odd word.

Now we were completely fenced in and the cookhouses which were at first on the riverbank had long since been brought inside the camp boundaries. It was about half a mile to the river in which we used to swim, and a quite unofficial arrangement was entered into with most of the Korean guards. After duties they were quite willing, in the new amicable atmosphere, to take us down in parties of twenty or thirty, checking us out with the sentry on the gate and checking us back in on return before dismissing us for the night. This, after waiting for about half an hour of their own time on the bank while we disported ourselves. In the circumstance, this was quite appreciated.

One night I saw a large Australian body, standing to attention, while a Korean methodically worked over torso, arms and legs with the flat of a bayonet. It transpired that he was one of the Nips' bathing party that night and had forgotten his hat. The Korean let him cut back, alone for it, took the rest of the party in and dismissed them and stood chatting with the sentry to await his return. Over half an hour passed and, thoroughly alarmed, he went back to the river to find him. No prisoner, and he ran back to camp, frightened and convinced that he had lost one of his charges. Finding out which hut the man lived in, he went there and found the missing man, fed and content, asleep on his bed. He had tagged on to another party, and passed his Korean at the gate without saying a word. For perhaps the first and the last time, I had more sympathy with the beater than the beaten.

We received our third and fourth issue of mail, though by that time it had lain for months in the Nip HQ under pretext of censorship and was up to eighteen months old. There was supposed to be a limit of twenty-five words each letter, and that to be sent only by next of kin, so that most men got only one card, often bearing the same message as previously. Many got nothing at all while others, whose friends decided to risk it, were the envy of all, with a dozen or more long letters. Some were the unlucky recipients of 'Dear Johns' or heard in a roundabout way that their wives had given birth in their absence, which in no way improved morale. One officer got a letter from another member of the 85th who had escaped from Singapore, and was writing from Ceylon.

The week before Christmas our rations were suddenly and unaccountably cut to almost nothing. There seemed to be plenty of rice and, indeed, a stone grinding wheel had been 'won' from somewhere, on which relays of men seemed endlessly to be grinding down rice into flour. We were let into the secret on Christmas Day, which this year was a complete holiday. The cooks really excelled themselves. They had developed over the years their own way of dealing with rice, and had patented, some time before, a type of porridge for breakfast, and a way of making cakes with the admixture of ground rice, to make a change from the everlasting 'swill'. For Christmas, this was the result of their labours.

Tamuan Prisoner of War Camp

MENU

Xmas Day 1944

0800 hrs	Breakfast	Two fried eggs on fried 'bread'. Sausage. Potato cake. Sweet coffee.
1100 hrs	Mid-morning snack	Shortbread. Sweet coffee, snack.
1300 hrs	Tiffin	Roast beef, roast potatoes, gravy, greens, bread, mince pie, tea.
1800 hrs	Dinner	Soup, bread, chip potatoes, greens, pork pie, pudding and sauce, tea.
2000 hrs	Supper	Individual Christmas cake, sweet coffee,
Night cap.		approx 1/16th pt Thai whisky,

What matter that we had been on short commons for the past few days or that the bread, pork pie, mince pie, Christmas cake, and the like were, after all, only thinly disguised rice. The cooks and canteen staff together had done a marvellous job and, with a little imagination, we were able to forget our surroundings, if only for a few short hours.

That evening we went to the pantomime. For weeks past rehearsals had been taking place regularly and the chorus of heavy-footed, hefty officers had been miraculously transformed into a troop of gossamer light fairies to grace the production. To see them dancing to 'Waltz of the Flowers' by Peter Ilyitch was an experience not to be missed. The producer who, in the past, was reputed to have had experience on the West End stage, and the composer of the score, himself a professional musician, had worked wonders, and the result was a bawdy version of 'Dick Whittington', full of marvellous scenery and gorgeous girls. Well we could dream, couldn't we?

Of the hilarious script, only the closing lines remain entrenched in my memory, viz:

BUTTONS: Well, they've gone at last, and we're alone. I'd ask you to marry me, but my name, I couldn't ask you to share that.

FAIRY QUEEN: Why not, Sandy. What's wrong with your name?

BUTTONS: It's Summerbum. Can you imagine Ophelia Summerbum?

QUEEN: It's better than mine.

BUTTONS: Can't be. What is your name?

QUEEN: Ophelia Cox.

Curtain.

It was a smash hit, and we went to bed content.

After Christmas work slowed almost to nothing and a variety of projects were started in camp to occupy the troops and try to make life better for all. By the main gate, sties were built and a pig farm was commenced. It did quite well and a promise of better rations seemed to be in the air. Another party set up a small factory for making soap and the end result, although rather on the soft side, certainly worked. Still others made innumerable experiments in an effort to produce paper.

We were also, once again, shod, albeit after a fashion. For more than a year we had gone barefoot in the jungle. Then, in Tamuan, tentative efforts were made to find some sort of footwear, first by adapting old worn-out Nip rubber shoes, with twine made from grasses, then by carving sole plates of wood, and making a strap of sorts to go over the toes from old clothing should any have survived so long, or from strips of rubber cut from old tyres. So was born the ubiquitous 'Dap'. Many times since the end of the war I have looked in the window of a chemist's shop at the display of bright yellow boxes, and imagined the fast talking ex-PoW in the buying office of Scholl's, saying: 'Look. I've got this great idea for an exercise sandal. Can't go wrong. You'll make a bomb.'

Whether or not this actually happened I don't know but I lay claim now. We had them first. The camp at night resounded to the dainty clip–clop of hordes of size tens, backwards and forwards to the latrines.

We also had, about this time, our first issue of soap from the Japanese. Can you remember the old tablets of Lifebuoy, a pungent carbolic and wrapped in printed greaseproof paper? There must have been a Lever Brothers' factory somewhere in Thailand and it was apparently still in some sort of production, for this was the soap issued by the benevolent 'Tojo'. I unwrapped my piece and idly read the blurb. Headed by the Royal coat of arms it waffled on in the way affected by such screeds, but wait, what was this I read? 'The regular use of this soap is the surest guarantee of infection'. Having spent nearly three years in Siam I had no reason to doubt the claim.

The canteen was a flourishing centre of camp life. It was allowed to be housed in a permanent hut with fulltime staff. Combs, toilet accessories, peanut toffee, cups of tea and coffee were only a few of the amenities to be purchased there. It even boasted a small garden in front, a garden crossed front to back, side to side, and corner to corner by trim little paths. These, it was fondly hoped, would give immediate impressions of a Union Jack to any itchy-fingered American bomb-aimer who might chance to stray in our vicinity.

Every Sunday Church services were held in the open air. The Roman Catholic parade was held on a gentle slope by the duck pond, always well attended. The priest moved from kneeling figure to kneeling figure, taking confession, and I often wondered just what, in that environment, all those dozens of closely caged PoWs had to confess. Nevertheless, each Sunday they were there again.

The Church of England services were taken by Harry Thorpe, who was now resident in the camp. I was horrified to realize that, as far as I knew, I had never been baptized and was in no position to meet my maker, as I had so nearly done some weeks before. I hastened to remedy the omission and, with the help of Padre Thorpe, a godfather from Wigan and one from Adelaide, I was formally baptized.

So life went on but gradually the camp was emptying. Regular parties were sent away. Some, we knew, had gone to Singapore, there to be trans-shipped in small merchantmen, battened down in filthy overcrowded holds to Japan, Indochina, Formosa and other places for work in factories and mines. Frank Thompson, a friend of mine for nearly five years of army life, was on one of these floating coffins which was sunk. He was supposedly landed on the Philippines but whether he was embroiled in the fighting there or died from other causes we never knew. He was never heard of again. Harry Pharoah was also on one, as I mentioned earlier, and was lucky to be home for Christmas. Tiger, whom we had not seen since leaving Tampi, returned to camp in the New Year, a shadow of his former self. All his old bombast had left him and his eyes held a haunted look. He was reputed to have been on one of the ships which had gone down, but, whatever his experience, he was a changed man.

We heard of the fighting on the Philippines, of the sea battles in the Pacific, and of land attacks on various islands. News came through of the continued advance of our troops in Europe but so often had we heard fantastic rumours, that, much as we would have liked to, we hardly dared believe that these latest stories were founded on fact. Evidence there was, if we had cared to look for it, in the shape of continued and increasing air activity, and we knew that the railway was being regularly bombed, but we had become sceptical.

The most hated trio in camp at this time were the three Nip guards, Captain Susuki, Lieutenant Suke (known affectionately as the Konyu Kid) and the camp clerk, a vicious, pestilential little Korean named Uke. Every night at Roll call the whole camp would parade in the square and, as the officers approached, Uke would call us to attention and leave the platform to walk up and down the lines of men. Susuki and Suke, boots agleam, uniforms immaculate, white gloves, and ceremonial swords, would mount the dais and gaze down on the assembled camp. For up to ten minutes we would be kept there at attention while the two would scan every line waiting for someone to move. A sharp command and Uke would move in for the kill. His one joy in his humourless life was to thrash a prisoner of war and he took a fiendish delight in slapping and punching and kicking. To move was only to invite more; the only logical thing to do was to stand stiffly to attention and hope it wasn't too long before his attentions were directed elsewhere by the hawk-eyed pair above. The 'Kire' (salute) given, the same procedure as Susuki, hand to cap, did that little semi-circular shuffle and back to encompass the whole parade, and then the sport was over for another day.

Poor Uke unfortunately contracted appendicitis and the whole camp prayed for him. An abortive attempt was made to have him sent down to base for an operation, but the Nips were unable to organize transport. Finally, he was admitted to our own operating theatre post haste, for his condition was rapidly deteriorating. The following morning at first light, the news was all round the camp. 'The operation was a complete success.' He died.

One night we were aroused about 2am and required to parade outside our huts. As we stood there, we were aware of a tremendous upheaval around the camp; shouting here and there, men running, and a flashing of lights. Eventually, after some half an hour, a Korean arrived, and Roll call was taken. Sometime later, we were allowed back into the hut to sleep. It transpired next morning that Suke, on the prowl late at night, had surprised a shadowy figure in a remote corner of the camp where there were no huts. Being of a prudent nature he shot first and asked questions afterwards. The figure turned out to be that of a PoW who had been out of camp with the Thais, and Suke had killed him outright. He threw the body into a ditch and covered it with soil then, presumably, had second thoughts, reported the incident, and had the camp on parade to find out precisely whom he had killed. We heard nothing more about the incident, the body was discreetly buried, and a veil of silence drawn over the affair.

In the last few months at Tamuan, I contracted amoebic dysentery, fortunately for me at a time when there were reasonable stocks of Eraetin in camp. I was admitted to the dysentery ward in the hospital, run by a Dr Pavillard, a large jovial man with little Van Dyck beard. I was a bit put out on admission to see a patient in his consulting room bending over while Pav filled a syringe.

'Coming to coffee Pav,' shouted a head tucked round the door.

'Shan't be a minute,' Pav replied, 'Just let me finish my darts practice' with which he took aim with the syringe at the face grinning at him across the room. Bullseye, and the syringe hung quivering in a well-filled cheek. I needn't have worried. It must have been a special patient, for my five 'shots', about half the normal dose, but sufficient to keep the disease in check, were administered in comfort by an orderly. A week later I was discharged as fit.

In March we learned that the camp, by then denuded to a couple of hundred men, was to be evacuated. We had been told that previous parties had been forced to stand naked at the gates, while their kit was searched, before they were allowed out.

'The Kempetai,' the knowing ones said, 'looking for diaries and records of the conditions in the camps.' We all decided to quietly ditch our diaries in case of trouble. Mine, a lovingly kept record of Changi, River Valley and the railway, went down the latrines, as did many more. Some buried their records in various parts of the camp in the hope that, before many more months were past, they would be able to return and retrieve them. The officers, the last few of the many we had shared the last year and a half with, were removed to the officers' camp at Kanburi, and the remainder, under the command of Sergeant Major Christopher, paraded and marched from the camp to the railway. There was no search at the camp gates and our possessions were not searched again.

By courtesy of a Thai, working as batman in the Jap quarters, the camp radio was transported to the new location in the baggage of the Japanese officers.

Chapter 15

End of the Line

Our first stop was at Nakompatom where, in addition to a meal, we were obliged to clear the line into a siding to allow trains from up country to pass through. All were loaded and one in particular was very interesting. It was crammed with Indian troops, all wounded, and wearing bloodstained bandages. In addition to the inside of the trucks, they swarmed all over the roofs, miserable, dejected, each with bamboo spear or similar weapon, and most carrying the inevitable umbrella. This was the same type of body that had so shocked Tiger at Tampi, and now they were in full retreat. Indeed, from the amount of equipment coming down the line, it began to look as if the entire Japanese army was on the retreat. Surely the time was coming.

Once again we were moved on and this time the line came to a full stop on the high bank of a river which had once been crossed by a magnificent steel bridge. The bridge had gone, a heap of twisted ironmongery lying in the water being all that remained. A crazy swaying bamboo structure with a single-plank footpath bridged the gap, and we all had to file across. True to form, when we had settled on the far side, volunteers were called for. The cookhouse was on the side we had just left and rations for the party had to be carried over the precarious flimsy structure which was difficult enough to walk over. I was one of the suckers and the journey with a four-gallon can of hot scalding tea was one to be remembered. Fortunately, no accidents occurred. After the meal the empties had to be returned the same way, and we slept in another line of trucks on our side of the bank till morning.

The following day we reached Bangkok where, once again, the steel bridge that crossed the river was demolished, as also were all the other bridges in sight. This time, only a line of stone piers marked where they had been, the steelwork on each bank, dipping into, and disappearing beneath, the sullen grey waters of the river. This was as far as we could go. We embarked on a line of barges and went downstream, through the city and were put ashore on a quayside flanked by huge godowns. They were completely empty and, for the next two weeks or so, here we made our home. We slept on the concrete floors, watched over day and night by two morose Nip sentries. From time to time we went out by lorry into the city to do odd jobs, one of which was tidying up the Jap HQ. Here we found again some of the Koreans who had been our jailers on the railway and, much to our surprise, were greeted like long lost friends. We had never noticed much amiability on their part in our earlier meetings. It was interesting to see the city, the first civilized abode of man we had seen since Singapore. A vague memory remains of wide open spaces, a few beautiful buildings, houseboats and traders on the canals which seemed to be everywhere, the great excitement and furious wolf whistles that greeted the occasional sight of a western woman, cool and unattainable in white. Whatever nationality they may have been, they looked sufficiently like our dream girl to arouse a feeling of nostalgia in every breast.

Then we were on the move again. A train drew up on the line that ran along the dockside by the godowns. We waited while the wagons were loaded with drums of petrol, then our kit was thrown in and we climbed on top. This was the signal that everyone had been waiting for. The banshee wail of air-raid sirens filled the sultry air, the Japs disappeared like vampires at dawn light, and we were left to sweat it out. We heard the rumble of distant bombs, the roar of aircraft engines, and there we were, a tempting target, sitting on a load of petrol, outside massive godowns which only we knew were empty. At last, the all clear sounded, the guards materialized again, and we were off.

Some time later we drew into a little station, which rejoiced in the tongue twisting name of Sra Buri. We dismounted, withdrew our kit and lined up. A road ran away to the east and we marched along this for the best part of an hour, until the familiar sight of a bamboo fence came into view, and hanging round the gate, men whom we recognized as an advance party which had left Tarauan some time previously.

The camp had evidently been built on *padi* fields, a low bank still enclosing a few inches of muddy water, around which were grouped half a dozen of the usual bamboo and attap huts. On the way to the camp we had met several Thais and, now, sensation! The previous occupants told us that messages had been passed to them on their way to the camp, asking them to contain themselves in patience a little longer, the end was at hand. When the fighting broke out in the vicinity, we were all to present ourselves at the local Thai barracks where we would be armed to continue fighting in the Jap rear. 'Rubbish,' said most of us, myself among them, 'another bloody rumour' and with that dismissed it from our minds. But there were believers with implicit faith and, for them, the end was in sight.

Our work, when we had settled in was yet another indication of the coming holocaust. Some little distance from the camp was a small conical hill. Each day, in parties of twelve men with an NCO, we were checked out by the camp staff, marched alone down the path to the gate, saluted the guard, 'Kashila magee', and were met outside the camp confines by a little perky Jap engineer sergeant. We then, in company with other such parties, were marched to this hill where our task was to drive shafts into the sides. The only reason for these could have been to act as ammunition dumps in the coming struggle.

The original intention was to drive straight into the hillside, from all directions, but, at least in our position, this proved to be impracticable. The ground was so soft that each night the previous day's digging fell in, so a cut and cover operation was substituted. We used huge baulks of timber, and nails, and the greatest crime that could be committed was to bend a single nail. Amidst 'Kurras' and 'Bageros' the nail was ceremoniously straightened and used again. The most sophistcated piece of equipment was the sergeant's plumb line, a stone on the end of a piece of string.

Every day the sergeant bumbled around, generally supervising, while we dug out and erected the framework, which we covered with boards and earth. At twelve, food was brought out from camp and we broke off for a while. Two or three of the Japanese would gather nearby for their own meal of rice, veg, meat and fish, served in separate dishes, and eaten with chopsticks. I had always imagined that chopsticks were used for everything and I was amazed to see them lift up the bowls of rice to their mouths and literally shovel the stuff in, a contrast to the delicate way in which they selected a tit-bit of fish or meat. We had the usual rice and slop. Everything seemed free and easy, compared to the way we had become accustomed to being treated by the camp Koreans.

Their close proximity at mealtimes had its drawbacks. One of our party was a tough little Londoner from the East End. In his colourful speech, every other word began with the letter F.

'We goes down the effing road,' he would say, 'to meet my effing mates. "Let's pick up some effing birds and go to the effing pictures," I said.' We became aware that dead silence had fallen over the Jap party, and all were listening intently. Our gunzo got up and walked over.

'What this word effing?' he enquired, pleasantly enough. Now giving the lie to its sound, there are no swear words in the Japanese language, and they detested to hear other people swear. Many a slapping I had witnessed because of this and we had no desire for another. We smoothed the incident over as best we could, but the gunzo was not completely satisfied. He knew sufficient English to be aware that the word was cropping up more than it should.

'Be quiet you fool,' we enjoined the cockney. He managed quite well for about twenty minutes, and his effing language started again. We gave up. We were all swearing too much and, indeed, often wondered if we would be able to shed the habit if and when we returned to polite society. In the event, in a different environment, we had no difficulty in making the transition.

At six we were escorted back to the camp gates, a cheery wave of the hand, smartened up, marched past the guard, 'Kashila hidali' and back to the parade ground where we were checked against the morning figures and dismissed. After dinner, a visit to the camp library, to the canteen or a game of cards till lights out. Only one thing marred the smoothness. We had been told just before leaving Tamuan that we no longer needed to salute Koreans, only Japanese nationals. Crossing the parade ground one night with Allan we met a Korean and, revelling in our newfound freedom, passed him by. A furious 'Kurra' stopped us in our tracks. An imperious inverted wave of the hand summoned us to the presence, where I was met by a blow so hard that I lost my balance, ears ringing. I looked up to see Allan on the ground as well, the Korean kicking furiously at his crotch and stomach. Then, having given vent to his feelings, he stalked off. We saluted everything that moved after that.

The bunkers were never finished. One night, after a full day's work, we were again escorted back to camp by the gunzo, who left with the usual cheery wave. We marched in. 'Kashila hidali' but no guard. We swung on to the parade ground and I stood the squad at ease. No one to count us in, which was even more unusual. Prisoners were milling round the perimeter.

'You may as well come in,' one shouted. 'The Nips have gone. You won't get a Tenko tonight.' After a moment's hesitation, we dismissed and went into our huts. The place was a hubbub of talk and speculation. I went to the library to change a book and on the 'counter' a radio set was tuned in to Radio Delhi. I remember a record of Vera Lynn was on. We had supper.

The talk was of a giant bomb which had been dropped on Japan, laying waste an area of seven square miles. The date was 16 August 1945.

Suddenly everyone froze, and a strange hush descended on the camp. Outside came the sound of a bugle, sounding not 'Get your rice balls' or any other of the cracked, tinny Japanese calls but the familiar, yet half-forgotten, sound of 'Fall in A, Fall in B'. A ragged cheer rose from several hundred throats, and an excited mob surged out on to the parade ground, a mob of ecstatic, weeping, backslapping ragamuffins, as the implications of that call were realized. All the pent-up emotion of three and a half years of repression was released in one savage shout of pure joy.

Sergeant Majors Sewell and Christopher mounted the stage which dominated the cookhouse end of the parade ground and they held up their hands for silence. From somewhere they had produced a battered Union Jack and this they held up aloft.

'I have just returned from IJA Headquarters,' began Sergeant Major Christopher. 'They have told me that the war is over and, from this moment on, you are no longer prisoners.' The remainder of his words were drowned in a roar of sound and for a few moments all was absolute pandemonium. Gradually the hubbub subsided somewhat and he was able to continue. He told us that the Nips had withdrawn from camp and that, consequently, we were on our own until arrangements could be made to get us out and take us home. However, in the hills behind the camp, a Nip artillery regiment was encamped and it was therefore imperative that, for the time-being until the situation was clarified, we remain inside the camp area, as no one knew exactly how the Japanese might react.

By now Dutch, and Australian and US flags had been resurrected from God knows where. There were a few Dutch in camp and about three United States soldiers. It was decided that each national group should sing its own anthem. A spirited rendering of God Save the King, was followed by the Dutch anthem, but the Americans, so few in number, got only a few words out, before drying up and shambling, red-faced, away. Many were in tears, incoherent in speech, others inconsolable in their private grief, but those who were able, and they were some two hundred or more, stayed on the square till long after one o'clock, singing, talking, wondering. I felt the uncalled tears well in my own eyes and had to go back to the hut for peace for a while. Then I rejoined the throng. How long to go? We had waited three and a half years, now a few days seemed too long.

The following day we were awake long before reveille, eagerly discussing the events. News came of two Koreans who had rashly ventured out the previous night, and had come to grief on the rock of Thai revenge. One, 'Four eyes', had been stabbed and Morimoto had lost both his ears, probably to the same weapon. The Konyu Kid had been one of the camp officers, having come up with us on the draft. The strutting, pompous little turkey-cock came into camp for something the second day. Gone was all the old arrogance and bombast. He shuffled instead of strutting, shoulders bowed, eyes fixed on the ground as he walked. It must have been hard for the pride of the officer classes when the invincible Japanese legend was shattered for all time.

We began to take nominal rolls and fitness states. Further drafts came into the camp from outlying districts, not many, but a few parties of a dozen or more men who had been used by the Japanese on small projects in the district. We erected a flagstaff and a previously carefully hidden Union Jack was hoisted. This was promptly taken down again on the following day, following a visit by Colonel Sukasowa. He reminded us that a Japanese artillery unit was still entrenched in the hills behind the camp, and that from their position the flagstaff was in full view. He suggested that the unit was quite capable of dropping a round or so on our huts, and that perhaps, in the circumstances, discretion was the better part of valour. After due consideration, it was decided to strike the flag temporarily.

During the day a giant plane, bearing American markings, flew low over camp, the crew waving, and a parcel of leaflets and some PX rations were dropped. The leaflets caused great hilarity. We were warned not, in any circumstances, to overload our stomachs and, among other helpful hints to released prisoners of war, were instructions on hygiene, so that we wouldn't catch nasty dysentery.

Some kit, a leftover from a previous Red Cross issue, was found and distributed, and the Japanese also hurriedly discovered that there was mail for us in camp, which we could have 'after it had been censored'. They were politely told what the censor could do with his blue pencil, and many men were soon lost in the luxury of news again from home, fifteen months old, no matter. With the kit issue, we were all resplendent in new khaki shorts and white PT vests – for a time.

Quite a lot of the kit found its way over the wire to the Thai traders who infested the area of the 'bund'. The market had commenced almost as soon as the news of the capitulation had spread and a thriving business had built up, trading trinkets and such valuables as we had left for, in the main, a rather potent brew of Thai whisky on the other side. This hellish concoction was reputed to be about 98 per cent proof, and it certainly had some kick. One Australian who consumed the best part of a bottle, was unconscious on his bunk for over twenty-four hours. It was decided to import Thai police to patrol the 'bund' and keep the traders away. The only difference that this made was to cut in a middleman, and the police took their share of the proceeds of the trading which did not diminish in any way.

A concert had been arranged for the 19th but a heavy rainstorm rendered the auditorium uninhabitable. The venue was moved to one of the huts and, in the middle of the performance, a terrific 'flap' developed. Someone rushed in shouting that the cookhouse kualies had disappeared. True enough this proved to be the case, and there wasn't even the wherewithal to cook even one small riceball, A search revealed one errant kuali moving rather unevenly towards the camp perimeter and, on further investigation, it was found to be inhabited by one elderly and rather inebriated Thai gentleman. Twenty-four kualies had disappeared and, on being taxed with the theft, the Thai admitted the felony, and with whisky-laden bonhomie bragged of being personally responsible for the removal of six of them.

'Why worry?' he belched expansively, 'All belong Nippon, Nippon no good now.' The true ownership was explained to him and he was immediately contrite. The missing kualies were not returned, however. That night a further fourteen went AWOL from the abandoned Japanese cookhouse.

We were requested not to go into Sra Buri for a day or so but we were allowed out in the immediate vicinity of the camp in parties of half a dozen or so. On one of these excursions I made my first acquaintance with the inside of a Buddhist temple. We climbed the innumerable steps and, pausing to remove our footwear (yes, by this time we again had footwear   of a sort), we entered the dimly-lit interior. Just inside the door, a huge beaming idol squatted, his huge body reaching up into the shadows of the roof. His hands were clasped comfortably over his protuberant, golden stomach. We acknowledged him and he smiled benignly on us. We spent some half an hour admiring the other minor deities and gazing at the richly gilded wall paintings before finally helping ourselves from the bundle of josssticks provided. We presented the maître d'hotel with a couple each to join the others already smouldering before his cherubic gaze.

There were one or two men who went absent from camp, only to be found later, living in the village. Then, on 27 August, eleven days after the sudden collapse, the camp was formally handed over to the British. Two officers and a sergeant arrived to represent the Japs while Colonel Lilley, with a Dutch, an American and an Australian officer represented the Allied forces. Also in camp was a Captain Redman of the Scots Guards and we learned that, for the past nine days or so, he had been living with the Mayor of Sra Buri. The invasion of Thailand and Malaya was scheduled for the second half of August and, well aware that this was imminent, the Japanese High Command had issued orders for the liquidation of all prisoners as soon as it occurred to prevent their impeding Japanese operations. The effective date was said to be 20 August and Captain Redman had been dropped into the country to liaise with the Thai forces and prevent this happening. Similar officers had been planted by all PoW camps, and the intention was to arm all fit men and harass the Jap rear. It would have been a close thing and, on the whole, I am rather glad that, at that late date, the theory did not need to be put to the test.

That afternoon we went on an organized march, down the lane from the camp to the junction with the main road to the village. On the way we passed several places where roadblocks had been constructed and, at the junction itself, we found a Thai barracks, filled with happy smiling brown-skinned little men. We then heard the fantastic tale of how, in the jungle, not far from Kanburi, a weapon training school had been established, with American personnel, quite unbeknown to the Nips. Here, over a period of months, some thousands of Thais had been trained in the use of small arms and light automatic weapons in a series of courses, the trained returning to their villages to be replaced by a further batch. From this school we learned that several of the men who had mysteriously disappeared from prison camps over the past months returned, having been sheltered and employed there since their disappearance.

We returned to camp, past the roadblocks. Presumably, they had been erected by the Nips for their own use in the coming battle, but I rather feel that, in the event, they might have found the faces looking at them over the concrete blocks and barbed wire were brown and far from smiling and happy.

Even before the situation was sorted out we received a visit from Edwina, Lady, Mountbatten. That amazing woman swept into camp in a US jeep, as calmly as if she were out for a weekend drive through Windsor Great Park. We were much taken by the jeep, and by the steel-helmeted Negro soldier sitting impassively at the wheel, neither of which had we seen before. Lady Mountbatten mounted the stage, and gave us an impassioned pep talk.

'My husband,' she declared, 'is moving heaven and earth to get you out of this, but you will have to be patient for a few days. It is a great task to assemble the necessary planes and ships, but arrangements are well under way, and it will be only a few more days before you are all on the way home.' Her talk over, she came down from the stage, and mingled with the excited throng, chatting here, comforting there, and talking about conditions in

England as if to old friends. Soon, however, she had to push on. It was her avowed intention to visit all the camps in Thailand and talk to the men, and I have not the slightest doubt that she carried out her self-imposed task. A woman of tremendous courage and determination. True to her words, the first few men left from Bangkok on 1 September on the way home.

In the meantime, we were allowed down into Sra Buri and jumped at the opportunity to spend a few hours in a Siamese village. It was an education. Brick buildings, attap and wood erections, nestled cheek to jowl. We spent some time looking round the shops, and were surprised by the variety of merchandise still on sale after nearly four years of war in the area. Many of the items were blatant copies of western items and trademarks, and some well-known names stared at us from windows and stalls. I was quite interested in a beautiful pair of brown shoes, apparently well made, and bearing inside, the legend 'Barratts of Northampton'. We took tea with a well-to-do Chinese merchant in his house and politely declined his invitation to take his daughter, aged about sixteen, 'for a walk'. Later we strolled farther and came across the local billiards saloon. It boasted one table and we hung about, hoping to get a game. In one corner of the open-fronted saloon a curtain hung, disguising a doorway and stairs to the upper regions, and it was obvious that some ex-prisoners had lost no time in finding their way about for, as we waited, a constant stream crossed behind the table, and lost themselves behind the curtain, only to reappear half an hour or so later and pass out into the night. We eventually got on to the table but, after some ten minutes, all the lights in the township suddenly went out. This was the regular eight o'clock blackout to conserve electricity they informed us, so we had to look further.

Sounds of music issuing from a building attracted our attention and we cautiously made our way inside. It was the Wayang Glap, or local theatre. The audience was enrapt and took no heed of our entry. On stage beautiful maidens, gorgeous suitors and angry fathers bellowed and contorted, while fantastic dragons and evil spirits writhed and gesticulated from all parts of the stage. The while a crashing wailing tintinnabulation came from what was obviously supposed to be an orchestra in the pit. The noise was indescribable, the action impossible to follow. There obviously was a plot; the crowded auditorium gave out not a sound as the men and women followed every twist and turn enthralled but, to us, it seemed to have common ancestry with the pantomimes so beloved of children in the west. After about half an hour we returned to camp. We were met at the gate. Obviously word of the staircase in the corner had returned home.

'There is a blue lamp room open in the MI room,' we were informed. 'All personnel who consider they have been at risk are advised to report there before going to their quarters.'

A day or two later a column of trucks arrived and we were told to board for Bangkok. We set off in a cloud of dust. The only remarkable incident in that interminable journey across the flat coastal plain of Thailand was when we passed a cage full of native soldiers. They were Gurkhas, the race that had perhaps been treated worst of all by the Nips. In spite of all blandishments they had steadfastly refused to fight for, or co-operate with, the Japanese, and remained loyal to the Crown to the last. They crowded the wire as we passed, waving and shouting, obviously overjoyed to see their beloved British soldiery again. At Don Muan airport we debussed, were given billets and a meal, and told that we would be flying out for Rangoon the following day. My feet were blistered by the unaccustomed shoes I was wearing, so I decided to seek out the MI room. I knocked and entered. The solitary occupant, an RAF man was sitting at a table, his back to me.

'Be with you in a second,' he said, and then turned to face me. The last time I had seen him was in 1939 when we walked home together after a night at the cinema. Our houses were about thirty yards apart. Across thousands of miles and four long years, home was reaching out and whispering 'Welcome back'.

Chapter 16

Random Thoughts

In 1941 those caught up in the mad social whirl which was Singapore little realized that they were celebrating the end of an era. The lot of the private soldier in those days, was epitomized by the notice on Raffles Hotel – OUT OF BOUNDS TO ALL OTHER RANKS. His world was bounded by the Union Jack Club with its eternal egg and chips, the three 'Worlds' with their comforting taxi dancers, and the dubious delights of Lavender Street.

Japan's ambitions had never been in doubt: the question was when? America was not in the war and Britain's tenuous capabilities were stretched between the Far East, home defence, and the need to sustain Russia. She was stretched to the utmost. Could we keep a large force in the Far East to face an undefinable threat, when supplies and men were so urgently needed elsewhere? I believe the question was asked and a calculated risk was taken. A facade was kept up in Malaya and when it became obvious that the hour was, in fact, approaching, attempts were made to build up strength there, but too little and too late. When the Japanese attacked, men were thin on the ground, equipment was sketchy and, worst of all, few aircraft were available. It was lack of aircraft that was to blame for the loss of the *Prince of Wales* and *Repulse*, sent at the last minute to bolster an impossible situation. The Buffaloes were hopelessly outclassed by the Japanese fighters, and the Hurricanes which came to save Singapore never got going properly. Many were still crated up on the docks after capitulation.

The command was too often neither inspired, nor inspiring, giving rise to the bitter comment, 'They'll never bomb Fort Canning, leaving it intact is their only hope of winning'. But what could any command do with half-trained or untrained men, and a dearth of the right equipment. With all the ballyhoo, there was no real hope of saving Singapore, and most knew this, with the exception of the public at home who believed the place to be impregnable.

The troops themselves fought magnificently. They stood, they fought, they died. Whole battalions were decimated, remnants were reformed and amalgamated, and fought and were decimated again. Gallantly they held, fought, withdrew, and fought again, battle after bloody battle, bemused and bewildered against an enemy that appeared and melted again into the ground as if by magic. Many of the later arrivals could not tell the difference between Malays, Chinese, and the Japanese they were supposed to fight, but they hung on desperately. And did they ever ask themselves why? A line had to be drawn somewhere, and the Japs must be denied the rich prizes of India and Australia.

Every day the enemy could be held was an extra day in which to rally and re-organize, and how near they came to both India and Australia. When one sees what has been given in the Halcyon days of peace, it hardly seems worthwhile to have fought so disastrously to deny them similar gains in war. Still all war is futile, and this no less than any other.

We were rescued from captivity by a new and terrible weapon, spawned in the deserts of America and, though we were too grateful to question the cost at the time, I have often wished since that the weapon had never been envisaged. It was the most obscene invention known to man, and the foul manner of its dropping left a shadow over mankind that will never be completely erased. We cannot even say, as we tried to, in self-justification, that it has, or will, remove the spectre of war from our fears, for, although war has never been formally declared since 1945, we have been almost continually at war in one part of the world or another ever since. Japan never declared war, but we never questioned that we were in a fight where she was concerned.

Whatever the causes of that conflict, and they were legion, the end result as far as we were concerned was that 27,000 men found themselves herded into incredibly primitive conditions, cut off from their normal accustomed food and living on an inadequate diet, consisting almost entirely of rice. I once worked out my consumption over the three and a half years, based on the official Jap ration scale, and taking into account the time I spent in hospital. I reckoned it came to nineteen and three quarter hundredweights. Added to this was the brutal treatment, part of the Japanese military code, but totally unaccepted by the European troops, and the almost total dearth of medical supplies for the first two years. Had it not been for the superhuman efforts of the British and Australian doctors, and their unflagging staffs, how many more thousands must have died.

It was the first time that such an overwhelming defeat had been inflicted on the 'superior' white races by an eastern power, and they were overcome at first. When they recovered, they could not help taking gleeful advantage of this fortuitous boost to their ego. War had ripped the facade of politeness from a race renowned for this very virtue and they had reverted by a hundred years or so. Many of them were, at best, brutal, uneducated types and their brutality showed in their pastimes and amusements and in their treatment of the prisoners presented to their tender mercies by the tide of war.

But worse was to come. The Japanese lines of communication for capturing Burma and India were desperately overextended, and their sea lanes were increasingly harassed. They were aware that a railway line from Thailand had been surveyed and found possible. They had no sophisticated equipment, but in the prisoners and the natives in the captured Indies they had an inexhaustible supply of labour, and, except for rice, of which Thailand was a great producer, no maintenance was necessary for this human machinery. It was decided to push forward with all speed, and the building was to be completed in early-1944. Then it was found that if the armies in Burma were to be supplied at all, and any advance to be made, it would become necessary for the link to be in operation earlier, and orders were given for its completion by the autumn of 1943, at any cost. More natives from the former Indies were shipped in, more prisoners from Singapore and beyond, and the infamous 'Speedo' campaign was born.

The exhausted men worked from daylight to dusk, food got less and worse, the rains fell incessantly, and the emaciated men were never dry for weeks on end. Malaria, dysentery, beriberi and that dreaded scourge, cholera, wiped out thousands. Malnutrition and loss of the will to live accounted for many more. Their own lack of knowledge of existing in these conditions, the blatant and, at times, horrifying disregard of the elementary rules of hygiene did not help.

Every camp experienced the raids on the hospitals and sickbeds by the furious Japanese, seeking more and more victims to feed the voracious maw of 'Speedo'. No one who saw him will ever forget the bespectacled Doctor Death, who stalked the sick wards of the camps, gazing disinterestedly at the weak and the dying and saying 'This man no sick. Worku' without even a pause in his stride. Obviously all camps were not alike in this respect and looking back, it seems that C, H and F in Tonchan, with probably IV Group as a whole, fared better than most. This was due, in no small measure to the calibre of the officers, who never failed to stand up to the Nips when the welfare of their troops was in question. Men like Colonel Lilley, Major Brodie and many others. It is thanks to them that we existed as well as we did.

The railway completed, the camp broke up, and the men were scattered to the four winds. Some went to the mines in Formosa, some to Malaya, to Indo-China, to Japan. They worked in mines, factories, ammunition dumps, docks and all kinds of military installations, forbidden by the Geneva Convention which the Japanese had so conveniently forgotten to ratify.

For those of us left in Thailand, food, accommodation and treatment all improved in direct ratio to the realization that the day of atonement was fast approaching. Our cooks became adept at disguising the unpalatable rice, and Red Cross parcels were at last allowed in and distributed. We had two or three issues but, after many Nipponese fingers had been dipped in, a parcel originally intended for just one man had to be shared between anything up to a dozen.

For all of us it was the blackest time of our lives and many were so physically or mentally blighted that they have never since been capable of living a normal life.

But how bad was it? For the wrecks who survived, and for those who died, the asking of the question is superfluous. For the rest of us, we endured degradation, ill treatment, disease, lack of normal human care, and living conditions entirely beyond adequate description. All this without basic medical care or drugs, save only those British medical staff who worked in some cases until they dropped, many perishing to the diseases they were striving to treat. And yet, in retrospect, it was but one more entry on the bloodstained pages of the enlightened and civilized twentieth century in which we lived.

We must wait, I suppose, for the verdict of future historians to put the whole thing into perspective, that is if there be any future for this sadly maltreated planet of ours, and its inhabitants.

Compared with the shipping back of the Russians after the war, the atrocities of Hungary, Czechoslovakia, Korea, Vietnam, the Congo, Laos, Lebanon, and so many more, the railway incident seems to lose the vital importance with which we once invested it. Murder, rape, pillage, torture and brute force seem to have become the norm in this brave new world we fought to save. The list of horrors grows apace, and I wonder what the feelings of those we left behind might be, if they could see what a mess we have made of the world they left in trust for us.

I have no doubt someone might say, 'But it didn't happen like that' to some of my assertions. This story has not been meticulously researched. My diaries were jettisoned in early 1945 in fear, and the record is from memory, first committed to paper in rough in the early post-war years. These thoughts represent no more than personal recollections and opinions and it is just one man's story. From the thousands of prisoners of war many separate and different stories can be told, for no two experiences were completely identical.

I have often marvelled at the skill of the make-up men in films and television. With deft touches they remove the grey from the hair, erase the lines from the face, cover up warts and blemishes and end up with some Greek god or goddess from the most unpromising starting material. Perhaps the human memory is the best make-up artist of them all. In retrospect the blacks fade to a softer grey, the hurt and pain of past experience is quietly erased, and a golden glow suffuses all our yesteryears. No time was ever like those long glorious holidays from school, a riot of hot sunlit days with never a cloud in the sky for weeks on end. It never rained at all from July to September, we are prepared to swear, hand on heart.

So, with the distant view softening the memory of those terrible days of long ago, it is with the railway. As the years go by it becomes more and more difficult to recapture in mere words, the horror, the filth, the degradation and the saturated stinking misery of interminable day upon day with no end in sight, no time when one could say 'This is the last day of my sentence, and I am once again free'.

It is difficult to come to the realization that the ultimate horror of those days is now over and that the scene of our purgatory is now on the list of holiday venues, hardly more exotic than Bournemouth or Benidorm. Where we lived (if lived is the word) and, in many cases, died, under the rubber-soled heel of our Korean and Nipponese guards, giggling tourists now gaze idly on the steel bridge that replaced the original wooden structure, and vie for position to take their snapshots to show their admiring friends at home. Where we sweated under back-breaking work, they now lightly say 'Isn't it warm here?' Can it be the same place? One of these tourists told me that he was in conversation with a plantation manager in the area that was once Tarsoa. Asking about the railway incident he was told, 'That's the trouble with you Europeans. You place too much store on that kind of thing. Death is not important.' But it was to us, and even more so to those who now lie in nice even rows in Kanburi cemetery. And all in vain. The railway no longer runs from Bangkok to Rangoon. It terminates a little way above the bridge, not far from Tonchan. (Wonder what did happen to the fabulous golden spike that marked the final sleeper?)

The camps have long since returned to the jungle, but memories remain.

Reverie

Autumn leaves are falling
Back there in England too.
I hear the woodlands calling,
Would I were there to view
Those dancing leaves come falling down,
Golden, russet, turning brown
Baring every sighing bough
In England now.

We do not miss those country walks,
Till far away, in evening talks
We speak of days that used to be
Those sights and views we used to see
It's heavenly, we always vow
In England now.

Out of sight is out of mind.
That opinion's hardly kind
We are far from Albion's sight,
Yet remembrance is delight.
Oh, just to be, we care not how,
In England now.

We'll come back to you some day,
Once again to laugh and play,
Spending each sweet carefree hour
In Mother Nature's airy bower.
Country fellows make a bow
To England, now.

S. H. Young
Tamuan PoW Camp
September 1944

C Battalion (10 Bn) 1942–45

Unit	Officers	ORs	Total	Deaths
85 A/Tk Regt RA	20	167	187	42
125 A/T Regt RA	2	78	80	20
18 Recce Bn	1	40	41	10
148 Fd Regt RA	5	74	79	22
88 Fd Regt RA	1	31	32	5
135 Fd Regt RA	1	30	31	6
118 Fd Regt RA	1	19	20	3
14 Sect RAOC	3	57	60	14
5 S/Lt Regt RA		13	13	2
1 Cambs.		25	25	9
4 FMS Vol Force	1		1	
55 Inf Brigade		2	2	1
1 Leics		2	2	1
Royal Army Dental Corps		1	1	1
3 Hy AA Regt RA		18	18	1
Rifle Bde		1	1	
RAMC	1	4	5	2
Malayan Field Amb		2	2	
5 Suffolks.		2	2	1
1 Indian Hy AA Regt		1	1	
35 LAA Regt RA		6	6	3
16 MBU		1	1	
	36	574	610	143

Those Who Stayed Behind

Lt Rich, A. H.	125 A/Tk	25.2.44	Tarso	Dysentery Malnutrition
Gnr Allen, J. H. W.	148 Fd	19.8.43	Tarso	do
Pte, Adamson, G.	RAOC	15.4.43	Chungkai	Dysentery
Gnr, Armstrong, L.	85 A/Tk	18.11.42	Tonchan	do
Gpl Ashard, H. P.	RAOC	20.7.43	Tarso	do
Gnr Attrill, J. J.	135 Fd	9.4.43	Tonchan	Malaria
Gnr Bell, E. E.	85 A/Tk	8.12.44		Air raid
Pte Badman, P.	RAOC	19.4.43	Chungkai	Cardiac beriberi
Pte Barnes, F.	18 Recce	10.8.43	Kanburi	Not known
Gnr Bates, G.	88 Fd	17.7.43	Chungkai	Dysentery, malnutrition
Pte Bateson, N. H.	85 A/Tk LAD	22.10.43	Chungkai	Not known
Sgn Beck, R. G.	R Sigs, 148 Fd	11.9.43	Chungksi	Dysentery
Gnr Blyth, T. E.	85 A/Tk	1.1.43	Tonchan	Dysentery, malnutrition
Pte Boulton, R.	RAMC	22.7.45	Tamarkan	Not known
Gnr Briggs, R.	85 A/Tk	3.10.43	Chungkai	Not known
Gnr Brook, C.	125 A/Tk	1.11.43	Tarso	Dysentery, beriberi
Pte Brown, A. A.	RAMC		Chunkia	No Record
Gnr Bubb, L. T.	118 Fd	16.6.43	Ton. Sth	Cholera, malaria, dys.
Sgt Buckle, C.	85 A/Tk	28.8.43	Tamarkan	Beriberi
Gnr Garling, A.	85 A/Tk	8.6.43	Chungkai	Beriberi
L/Bdr Carney, G.	125 A/Tk	29.12.42	Tonchan	Peritonitis. Malnutrition
Gnr Gharnley, R. E.	135 Fd	22.6.43	Ton. Sth	Cholera
Gnr Clark, R.	85 A/Tk	28.11.42	Tonchan	Dysentery, shock
Pte Clarke, A.	1 Cambs	14.12.42	Tonchan	Dysentery
Gnr Clarke, F.	148 Fd	5.12.43	Chungkai	Malnutrition
Bdr Colbourn, P. V. G.	85 A/Tk	3.9.43	Chungkai	Dysentery
Sgn Coles, E. M.	5 S/Lt	8.8.43	Tarso	Malnutrition, diarrhea, vitamin deficiency
Sgt Coles, J. M.	85 A/Tk	3.7.43	Tonchan	Dysentery
SQMS Collins, R. P.	RAOC	5.1.43	Tonchan	Dysentery, malnutrition

Gnr Cook, R. W.	125 A/Tk	6.12.43	Tarso	Amoebic dysentery
Pte Cooper, J.	Suffolk	28.11.43	Tarso	Diarrhoea, malnutrition
Sgn Cotton, D.R.	125 A/Tk	27.4.43	Chungkai	General debility
Sgt Crawford, E. W.	125 A/Tk	29.11.42	Tonchan	Dysentery
Gnr Grump, B.	148 Fd	22.9.43	Chungkai	Dysentery
Gnr Cullender, W. C.	85 A/Tk	3.7.43	Chungkai	Dysentery
L/Sgt Curry, H.	118 Fd	21.7.43	Tarso	Cholera
Gnr Curtis, A. E.	148 Fd	2.11.43	Tarso	Dysentery, chronic malnutrition
L/Bdr Davis, D.	125 A/Tk	16.6.43	Ton. Sth	Cholera
Pte Davis, J. R.	RAOC	18.7.43	Ton. Sth.	Cholera
Gnr Dean, T.	85 A/Tk	1.10.43	Chung,	Paly avitaminosis
Dvr Dennigan, J.	85 A/Tk	18.12.42	Tonchan	Malnutrition
Gnr Dickens, L. C.	148 Fd	22.6.43	Ton Sth	Cholera
Gnr Eaves, G.	85 A/Tk	27.4.43	Tarso	Cholera
Gnr Eggington, H.	148 Fd	11.6.43	Ton Sth	Cholera
Sgn Fox G. H. W.	R. Sigs 135 Fd	16.3.43	Ton	Cardiac beriberi
Pte Freeman, H.	1 Cambs	13.12.42	Tarso	Cardiac beriberi
Gnr Fuller, E.	125 A/Tk	17.6.43	Ton Sth	Cholera
Pte Purey, E. J.	RAOC	30.7.43	Kanburi	Dysentery
Gnr Gazeley, A. R.	125 A/Tk	18.8.43	Tarso	Malaria, bronchial pneumonia
Pte Geary, G.	18 Recce	29.12.42	Tonchan	Dysentery, malnutrition
Dvr Glasby, W. E.	125 A/Tk	28.12.42	Tonchan	do
BQMS Green, V. L.	85 A/Tk	2.7.43	Ton. Sth	Dysentery
Gnr Greenhough, H.	85 A/Tk	26.3.43	Tonchan	Cardiac beriberi
Pte Gregory, E.	18 Recce	9.7.43	Ton Sth	Cholera
Pte Guy, J. W.	RAOC	10.4.43	Chungkai	Beriberi
Pte Hardy, W. H.	1 Cambs	23.3.43	Tarso	Chronic Dysentery, malnutrition, malaria
Pte Haynes, L.	1 Cambs	Jan 44	Chungkai	No record
Pte Heffer, A. G.	1 Cambs	14.10.43	Tarso	Dysentery
Gnr Heath, F. H.	118 Fd	21.4.43	Tarso	Cerebral malaria
L/Bdr Hendy, R.A.S	85 A/Tk	7.1.44	Tarso	Beriberi
Gnr Heward, H.	148 Fd	8.10.43	Tarso	Dysentery
Pte Hickey, W.	18 Recce	5.7.43	Ton Sth	Cholera
Gnr Hodgson, J.	85 A/Tk	15.6.43	Chungkai	Cholera
Pte Holding, E. H. T.	18 Recce	21.12.42.	Tonchan	Dysentery, malnutrition
Pte Hollick, H. T.	RAOC	17.6.43	Ton Sth.	Cholera
Pte Hollis, D. H.	RAOC	29.12.42	Tonchan	Dysentery, malnutrition, avitaminosis

Pte Holt, W.	18 Recce	25.7.43	Ton Sth	Cholera
Gnr Howarth, W.	85 A/Tk	26.9.43	Tarso	Malaria
Sgt Hudon, F. W.	125 A/Tk	15.8.43	Tamarkan	No Record
L/Bdr Hughes, H. L.	85 A/Tk	17.9.43	Tamarkan	Dysentery
Pte Hull, F.	Leics	19.11.42	Tonchan	Malaria
Gnr Hutson, T.	35 AA	18.10.43	Tarso	Tropical ulcers
Gnr Ibbotson, S.	35 AA	13.6.43	Ton Sth	Cholera
Pte Inman, S. G.	18 Recce	11.7.43	Chungkai	Dysentery
Gnr Johnston, J. I.	38 Fd	15.12.44	Tamarkan	Air raid
Gnr Johnstone, F.	88 Fd	3.9.43	Chungkai	Tropical ulcers
Pte Jones, E.	RAOC	18.6.43	Ton Sth	Cholera
Pte Jones, H. C.	RAOC	20.2.43	Tarso	Dysentery, malnutrition
Sgt Kelly, J.	R. Sigs 148 Fd	10.6.43	Ton Sth	Cholera
Pte Kerry, W.	1 Cambs	17.6.43	Chiang.	No Record
Gnr Law, J.	85 A/Tk	21.7.43	Tonchan	Cholera
Sgt Lee, S.	RAOC	8.6.43	Tonchan	Beriberi
Gnr Lee, J.W.	35 LAA	16.4.45	Tamuan	Cerebral malaria
Pte Muncaster, L. R.	18 Recce	8.12.44	No record	No record
BSM Marsh, H. C.	125 A/Tk	8.1.43	Tonchan	Dysentery, malnutrition
Gnr Marshall, E.	85 A/Tk	15.12.42	Tonchan	Dysentery
Gnr Marshall, E.	135 Fd	1.12.43	Tarso	Cholera
Gnr McDonald, H.	5 S/Lt	2.7.43	Tonchan	Dysentery
Pte Moon, W. E.	RAOC 85 A/Tk	24.5.43	Tarso	Beriberi
Gnr Osbourne, E.	85 A/Tk	29.6.43	Ton Sth.	Cholera
Gnr Parker, K.	85 A/Tk	30.11.42	Tonchan	Beriberi
L/Sgt Parker, R.	85 A/Tk	17.11.42	Tonchan	Dysentery
Gnr Pearson, W. L.	148 Fd	10.6.43	Ton Sth	Cholera
Bdr Percy, W. H.	135 Fd	25.6.43	Ton Sth	Cholera
Sgt Platt, J.	85 A/Tk	22.7.43	Chungkai	Dysentery, avitaminosis
Bdr Plummer, L.	125 A/Tk	14.3.43	Tonchan	Dysentery
Gnr Pollard, L. A.	148 Fd	5.7.43	Tarso	Dysentery
Gnr Prior, A. R.	85 A/Tk	11.9.43	Tarso	Pneumonia, avitaminosis
Bdr Quigley, G.	85 A/Tk	29.6.43	Ton Sth.	Cholera
L/Sgt Raine, W. T.	125 A/Tk	19.11.42	Tonchan	Cerebral malaria
Bdr Ratley, C.	85 A/Tk	25.10.43	Chungkai	Amoebic dysentery
L/Bdr Raynor, E. G.	148 Fd	17.11.43	Tarso	Malaria, debility
Gnr Richards, C.	85 A/Tk	29.6.43	Ton Sth	Cholera
Pte Riding, J. F.	18 Recce	21.6.43	Ton Sth	Cholera
Pte Ritchie, D. A.	1 Cambs	12.7.43	Chungkai	No Record
Sgt Roberts, E.	85 A/Tk	17.7.43	Tarso	Cerebral malaria
Gnr Robinson, A.	148 Fd	20.11.43	Chungkai	Amoebic dysentery.
Pte Ross, J. M.	RAOC 85 A/Tk	26.11.42	Tonchan	Dysentery

L/Bdr Rymill, J.	85 A/Tk	29.10.43	Chungkai	Debility
Gnr Read, F. G.	148 Fd	8.12.44		Air raid
Pte Salter, A.	18 Recce	9.3.43	Tonchan	Cardiac beriberi
Gnr Saye, A. E.	85 A/Tk	17.12.42	Tonchan	Malaria, dysentery, malnutrition
L/Sgt Shaw, F. J.	148 Fd	29.6.43	Ton Sth	Cholera
Gnr Shellard, H. D.	85 A/Tk	29.12.42	Tonchan	Dysentery, malnutrition
Gnr Sinfield, R. S.	35 AA	26.6.43	Chungkai	Dysentery, beriberi
Gnr Smith, D.	148 Fd	11.9.43	Chungkai	Amoebic dysentery
Pte Smith, F. C.	RAOC 148 Fd	30.9.43	Tarso	Dysentery, debility
Pte Smith, J.	do	13.9.43	Chungkai	No record
Gnr Smith, J.	85 A/Tk	30.11.43	Chungkai	Amoebic dysentery
Gnr Smith, R.	3 Hy AA	19.2.43	Tonchan	Dysentery
Gnr Southgate, B. P.	148 Fd	29.11.43	Tarso	Malaria, debility
Gnr Spary, A. A. M.	148 Fd	19.11.42	Tonchan	Dysentery
Gnr Stanley, G. H.	85 A/Tk	3.9.43	Chungkai	Polyavitaminos, malnutrition
Gnr Stanley, T.	85 A/Tk	19.8.43	Chungkai	Avitaminos, cardiac beriberi
Gnr Steadman, F.	85 A/Tk	28.9.43	Tonchan	Dysentery, beriberi
Gnr Sullivan, J.	125 A/Tk	2.5.43	Chungkai	Cardiac beriberi
Gnr Teasedale, W.	125 A/Tk	6.9.43	Tarso	Pneumonia
Gnr Terry, F.	125 A/Tk	23.5.43	Ton Sth	Cerebral malaria
Cpl Tolley, F.	R. Sigs 148 Fd	30.6.43	Ton Sth	Dysentery
Gnr Tonks, J.	88 Fd	3.12.42	Tonchan	Dysentery, debility
Gnr Tring, R. C.	85 A/Tk	7.7.43	Ton Sth	Cholera
Pte Tuckett, R.	1 Cambs	4.12.42	Tonchan	Dysentery
Pte Wallace, C.	1 Cambs	3.7.43	Ton Sth	Cholera
Gnr Wallis, A. J.	85 A/Tk	18.11.43	Tarso	Cholera
Cpl Waplington, H.	RAOC	19.8.43	Tarso	Dysentery, malaria
Pte Watchman, A. C.	RAOC	8.7.43	Tonchan	Dysentery
Gnr Ward, G.	125 A/Tk	26.5.43	Tonchan	Cardiac beriberi
Sgn Waterhouse, A.	R. Sigs 88 Fd	15.11.43	Tarso	Dysentery
Pte Weekes, R.	RAOC	9.7.43	Ton Sth	Cholera
L/Bdr Wells, W. H. A.	148 Fd	12.12.42	Tarso	Internal ulcer
Gnr Whittle, E.	88 Fd	30.11.43	Chungkai	Cardiac beriberi
Gnr Williams, R. A.	125 A/Tk	27.7.43	Chungkai	Dysentery
Pte Wilson, J. T.	ADC	20.1.43	Tonchan	Cerebral malaria
Gnr Wood, K. A. W.	148 Fd	7.1.43	Tonchan	Dysentery, malnutrition
Gnr Wise, A. F.	85 A/Tk	22.11.42	Tonchan	Dysentery
Gnr Withers, A.	135 Fd		Chungkai	Not known
Gnr Young, W.	125 A/Tk	11.2.43	Tonchan	Dysentery, malnutrition.

Glossary (Phonetic) for Aspiring Japanese PoWs

Arigato Geseimas	Thank you very much
Ah Soka?	Is that so?
Ah Soka!	That's right.
Bageero	You silly boy, you.
Benjo	Toilet.
Benjo skoshe	Piss.
Banjo	A number. To number off.
Beri Beri	Vitamin disease. Deficiency of Vitamin B 1.
Banzai	There's a little Nip in the air today.
Borehole	Deep latrine.
Boreholes	Rumours recounted to friends during polite conversation at above.
Bed bugs	Delightful pets kept in bed slats or mosquito net corners and fed on liquid refreshment only.
Banjo fish	Dried and gutted fish (from shape when dried).
Blackwater fever	Often fatal complication of malaria due to lack of or inadequate treatment with quinine.
Chinese radish	Chinese radish.
Chappattee	Baked rice cake (Not to be confused with Indian).
Chungkol	Native hoe, used for building railways.
Changee changee	Give me that gold watch and I'll give you this broken lighter – or else!
Cabbage Patch	Imperial Japanese H.Q. Singapore.
Clip clops	See daps.
Daps	Homemade sandals made with wooden soles with toe straps of rope, old tyres, etc.
Dami da na	Really that's not good enough old man. Try again.
Dysentery	Bacillary or amoebic, wasting killing disease born of flies and filth.
Dengue	Virulent sandfly fever.

Fuck you bird	So named from its call. One of the strangest birds in Siam, it is in fact a lizard.
Fort Canning	Japanese secret weapon in Singapore.
Gula Malacca	Native sugar. Liquid molasses in 4-gallon cans.
Gunzo	Japanese sergeant.
Godown	Warehouse.
Good Nip.	Rare breed whose sole joy in life was not beating the hell out of PoWs.
Gott Verdommer	Our Dutch allies.
Heitai	Japanese private soldier.
Hag's bush	Siamese fireweed. Growing, picked, cured and in the pipe for smoking in twenty-four hours.
Hammer and tap	Like cricket, a sport for summer afternoons pleasant yet gentle exercise.
Jap nappy	A loincloth.
Jap happy	Collaborator. One who goes to any lengths to avoid trouble with one's captors.
Jungle juice	Nourishing vegetable stew.
Jungle happy	Dirty and careless of personal hygiene.
Jungle ulcer	Putrefying sore resulting from a scratch on arm or leg.
Kampong	Council housing estate.
Kanero	I don't believe your mother and father were actually married, lad.
Kuali	Disc-shaped, slightly concave cooking utensil.
Kashila migi	Eyes right (many words of command seem to start with the 'k' sound).
Kashila hidali	Eyes left.
Kiri	Salute.
Kuchi koi	Kindly come over here (with an inverted wave of the hand that to western eyes says 'go away').
Kurra	Hey there, you with the stars in your eyes.
Kioski	Attention.
Kempetai	The friendly local bobby on the beat.
Lage	More (Malay).
Leggy queue	Would-be Oliver Twists.
Ma mi pa	Flied lice and two veg (Thai).
Mai mi	Ain't got none (Thai).

Modern girl	A flapper. Dried herring-like fish.
Maya s'mi	Quick march.
Mishi	Food. A meal.
Misu	Water.
Nanda?	What?
Nanda?	Why?
Nanda?	Where?
Nanda?	When?
Nanda?	How?
Nanda?	What is this?
Nanda?	What are you doing?
Nanda?	Where are you going?
Nanda?	What the hell?
Nai.	No.
Nan ji des ka?	What's the time?
No bridge.	Would you kindly put those playing cards away after you have picked them up from the floor.
Number one.	The ultimate, e.g. Tojo No.1 Churchill No. 100.
Nowori	Eyes front.
Nip	Citizen of the imperial Japanese Empire.
Poached egg	Flag of the Imperial Japanese Armed Forces.
Proud	Raising of a digit to indicate a wish to visit the toilet.
Pellagra	Ugly red blotches on skin from vitamin deficiency Disease leads to insanity and eventual death.
Pap	Rice porridge (Dutch).
Road	Japanese word signifying three feet of mud and water, the longest distance between two points.
Speedo	Work to exhaustion and then work some more.
Squitters	Like another five letter word – diarrhoea or dysentery.
Satang	100th of a tical.
Shoko	Japanese officer.
Sarnbal	Piquant, spiced chutney from jungle herbs.
Sikh's beard	See Hag's bush.
Syonan	Singapore whilst temporarily on loan.
Sawat di	How do (Thai).
Singapore foot	Fungoid growth between the toes.
Singapore balls	Private grief about private parts.
Toast	Layer of cooked rice burnt on to the kualis.

Tid' apa	It doesn't matter (Malay).
Tojo presento	With the compliments of the Imperial Japanese Army.
Tenko	Fall in chaps, let's have a Roll call.
Tommorrow	war finish.
Toru go home	You stay here till you rot.
Wakaru masta	I understand.
Wakaru maseng	I don't understand (Ref bagero, kanero, etc.).
Wihu	Little woman back home.
Watashi tashi nomono	My name is.
Yasumi	Arguably the most pleasant sounding word in the Japanese language: finish, rest, knock off.

Index